INTENTIONAL
BALK

INTENTIONAL BALK

BASEBALL'S THIN LINE BETWEEN INNOVATION AND CHEATING

DANIEL R. LEVITT & MARK ARMOUR

Submitted January 23, 2022

Published by Clyde Hill Publishing
Seattle, Washington and Washington, D.C.
In the United States of America

www.clydehillpublishing.com
Follow us on Twitter @ClydeHillPub

Jacket Design by Kate Thompson
Typesetting by Nord Compo, France

979-8-9852632-6-8 (Print – Clyde Hill Publishing)
979-8-9852632-7-5 (eBook – Clyde Hill Publishing)

CONTENTS

INTRODUCTION

I N THE 1949 FILM *It Happens Every Spring*, Ray Milland plays a
chemistry professor who accidentally invents a liquid substance
that repels wood.[1] A man of middle age and no known athletic
ability, the professor leaves his established life and secretly becomes
(under an assumed name) a pitcher for a fictitious St. Louis team
that was neither the Cardinals nor the Browns. Using his proprietary
formula, he wins 38 games and leads his club to the World Series.
The screenwriters were nominated for an Academy Award for their
efforts, and the film has retained a reputation among film buffs as an
unpretentious and enjoyable fantasy.

Although the movie was intended as a comedy, when baseball
Commissioner Happy Chandler learned of the plot, he prohibited the
participation of any major or minor league player.[2] Chandler might
have been overly sensitive about a story casually condoning cheating in baseball but perhaps his concern was heightened because the
cheating was wildly successful. In the film, crime does pay, and the
dishonest nonathlete dominates the honest (supposedly major league)

ballplayers. Although baseball has a long history of pitchers applying less ambitious foreign substances to the baseball, during Chandler's tenure as commissioner not a single pitcher was disciplined for such an action.

As baseball historians, we are fascinated by the issue of cheating. What is cheating, exactly? Who cheats? Is cheating common? Why is some cheating tacitly condoned and other cheating punished? How has our perception of cheating evolved over time? How and why can cheating turn into a scandal, and how has baseball dealt with that? What enforcement or punishment has proved more, or less, successful?

We are also interested in the relationship between innovation and cheating. The professor in *It Happens Every Spring* was not a "mad scientist" intending to do harm; he was an innocent who stumbled upon an unintended use for his discovery. Baseball history is filled with similar stories of new inventions (binoculars, amphetamines, petroleum jelly, high-speed video) for which someone within the world of baseball (or, more generally, sports) finds an unscrupulous use. In these cases, the innovation and cheating are employed by different people.

But there are many cases where the inventors are not so innocent. In baseball, players and management are constrained by books of rules, but those rules often struggle to keep up with new ways to circumvent them. Famous figures like John McGraw and Bill Veeck didn't just find new ways to break rules (although they did that), they also looked for loopholes, or situations that the rules did not address. They were creative and innovative people. Creativity, generally a valued trait, often shows up in the act of finding novel approaches to age-old problems. But sometimes creators cross the line. And then you have cheating.

For instance, Wall Street traders are constrained by rules regarding insider-trading, acting on information not yet available to the general public. But in a world where information can be exchanged on proprietary fiber optic cables and instantly analyzed by software on high-speed computers, a firm could profit with an advantage of just a few seconds. The rules sometimes struggle to keep up.

Baseball and Wall Street are different worlds, and the people within them have different problems to solve. But baseball teams (at least 10 of which are owned by men who made their money in trading and investing capital) are constantly looking for innovative edges in much the same way that Wall Street firms do. When smart people, in any field, are looking for an edge, or a new way to succeed within a defined set of rules, they will inevitably run into potential solutions that reach or cross ethical or legal lines.

This is a fascinating problem, as baseball teams value intelligence and creativity more than ever before.

Our research convinces us that there is little agreement in baseball circles regarding the definition of "cheating." So, let's start there. What is cheating?

Rogers Hornsby, an ornery, uncompromising Hall of Fame second baseman who later managed or coached for three decades, said in 1961, "I've been in pro baseball since 1914 and I've cheated, or watched someone on my team cheat, in practically every game."[3]

This may be true, but a lot of the cheating Hornsby enumerated was, and in some cases still is, perfectly acceptable behavior within the game. For example, Hornsby described the "neighborhood play" (when a middle infielder deliberately does not touch second base on a double play) as cheating. The rules say he has to touch the base to record an out, and in this instance the infielder is deliberately not touching the base while behaving as if he did. Hornsby was saying that everyone cheats, but he was also saying that this is how baseball is supposed to be played. Hornsby was one of the more reviled players in the game because of his often cruel bluntness, but his perspective on cheating was not unique. Cheating, or least some forms of it, were and are considered to be honorable.

As we will refer to this philosophy throughout the book, we are giving it a formal name.

The Hornsby Doctrine: Baseball players and others within the game will and should find ways to bend and break the rules. It is the job of the authorities to stop them.

In the decades since Hornsby laid down these views, baseball has endured a number of cheating scandals (performance-enhancing drugs, sign stealing, pitch doctoring, and more) because enterprising people have found ways to cheat that threatened to throw the game out of balance. Often the authorities (and in many cases the players themselves) came to believe that a particular method of cheating had gone too far, resulting in perceived unfairness and then more authority. One of the more fascinating parts of the story is examining how and why the game took these turns.

We broadly define "cheating" as an act of breaking agreed-upon rules in order to help your team win. By this reckoning, throwing a World Series or recreational drug use, which do not help your team, are not "cheating" as defined here. In addition to the *Official Baseball Rules* (a book in the pocket of every umpire), there are several other documents that define roster rules, how teams trade or exchange players, how scouts can recruit overseas, and more. Management and players are also both party to the Collective Bargaining Agreement and the Joint Drug Agreement. The arguments start when we explore the different kinds of cheating, and how they are treated by the game and its observers.

In addition to all of the written rules, we are faced with the undeniable truth that baseball also has a set of "unwritten rules" or guidelines, what we could call "consensual ethics," which govern the game just as much as the rulebook. There is a collective culture within the sport that tolerates, and even admires, certain sorts of explicit rule-breaking, and conversely treats certain behaviors as unethical even if there is not a specific rule being violated. A good way to determine if something is considered cheating within this culture is whether the perpetrator would deny it if confronted. In this book, we will describe rule-breaking that players have admitted and opponents have grudgingly admired. We also describe seemingly similar levels of rule-breaking that are criticized and abhorred.

This is not a culture unique to baseball. Just as the greater society does not want policemen ticketing pedestrians who jaywalk or motorists driving two miles per hour over the speed limit, we also don't want umpires throwing pitchers out of the game for having a little pine tar on their gloves, or hitters with pine tar too far up their bats.

"Our job," said Hall of Fame umpire Nestor Chylak, "is to keep the game moving. If we stopped play on every minor infraction, it would slow up the flow and the beauty of the game. People pay money to see the players decide the game, not us."[4]

In early June 2021, as the storm over pitchers using newfangled sticky substances on the baseball intensified, New York Yankees star Gerrit Cole was asked whether he used Spider Tack, one of the new substances being used to increase spin rate. His confusing but telling response: "I don't quite know how to answer that, to be honest."[5]

"I mean, there are customs and practices that have been passed down from older players to younger players," Cole continued, "from the last generation of players to this generation of players, and I think there are some things that are certainly out of bounds in that regard and I've stood pretty firm in terms of that, in terms of the communication between our peers and whatnot." In 2021, however, Major League Baseball decided the problem had gotten out of hand, and Cole was one of the first prominent players at the center of the allegations.

Baseball writer Tyler Kepner sympathized with Cole's predicament. "Here is what the Yankees' Gerrit Cole should have said last week," Kepner wrote, "when asked if he had ever used Spider Tack while pitching: 'I follow all the rules that baseball is willing to enforce.'"[6]

Kepner was suggesting that Cole was operating within baseball's consensual ethics. Many of baseball's most difficult cheating struggles have occurred not when the sport has changed its rules, but when it has decided to enforce the existing ones.

We consider an act of cheating to belong in one of four categories. These are in no way rigid, and the lines between them can be quite fuzzy.

- An action that does not violate any formal rule but that baseball's culture believes to be cheating. Sign stealing during much of the twentieth century (using binoculars, for example) fits this category.
- An action that clearly violates a rule, but about which baseball culture is ambivalent. Players are unlikely to admit to these infractions but would not be ostracized or meaningfully disciplined if caught. The spitball, used throughout most of the twentieth century, falls into this category.
- An action that violates a rule and that the culture agrees is cheating, but which the authorities do not or cannot meaningfully enforce. This category would include steroid use during the 1990s.
- An action that violates a widely accepted and enforced rule. Violation of the spending limits for international amateurs or steroid use under current rules would be examples.

Not surprisingly, most of the controversy that occasionally erupts around cheating in the game involves the first three categories, each of which is an inherently unstable situation. When the rulebook, the enforcement of those rules, or the consensual ethic do not align, or when rules are not enforced, problems usually arise. In some instances, when the rules or their enforcement are deemed lacking, the game relies on the culture to police itself, and the vagaries of the culture can change rapidly. These changes often take place after an innovation affects the frequency or efficacy of the cheating, such as with the introduction of Spider Tack or high-speed video. In other instances, there is not even agreement about which category an action falls into, which causes further controversy, until the commissioner's office formally rules or a consensual understanding evolves.

The efficacy of the cheating also affects how it is perceived. Illegal drugs that do not enhance performance or pitcher substances that would not improve ball movement may be illegal under baseball rules but would likely not be viewed under the consensual ethic as cheating, as they do not help the team win.

In fairness, detection and enforcement of cheating is easier said than done. Drug testing is intrusive and costly; x-raying bats for cork or other enhancements would be time consuming; and the

2020 experiment prohibiting hitters from reviewing in-game video (to minimize sign stealing) was considered detrimental to batters attempting to improve their game. Baseball must constantly evaluate the time and effort spent on preventing rules violations. The most noteworthy controversies occur when a rule is repeatedly flouted in an unanticipated way before enhanced detection and penalties can be put in place.

Today, baseball cheating is taken more seriously by baseball fans and media than it was in earlier times. Many players from the 1960s or 1970s have admitted to taking amphetamines, throwing the spitball, or stealing signs, with the confidence that their actions were an accepted, or at least tolerated, part of the game, and their reputations would therefore not be harmed. In fact, the rules—both written and unwritten—barring these actions have evolved considerably. The lack of such admissions from modern players does not mean that the behavior has stopped, only that those actions are no longer an acceptable part of the culture. Perhaps this results from the high-tech nature of some of the modern cheating—whether pharmaceutical, video-based, or sticky stuff—which seems more insidious than using saliva to influence a pitch or gallons of water to impede an opponent's running game.

Our title, *Intentional Balk,* is meant to imply some of what we've written in this introduction. A balk is an illegal move by a pitcher trying to deceive a baserunner about whether he is throwing home or to a base, and there are many creative ways of trying to do this. Of course, nobody wants to get caught, but except for the occasional occurrence of pitcher stumbling during his delivery, the intention is to get away with something. The hurler is pushing the margins of what is legal with the intention of gaining a small advantage, and sometimes a small advantage can be enough.

The coming chapters will discuss many different forms of baseball cheating, its origins, its practitioners, and how cheating has been treated within the game. Some of the stories are humorous, others are serious. Many rule-breakers are in the Hall of Fame, while others are pariahs in the sport. There seems to be much less tolerance for cheating today than ever before—are we becoming more honest, or just more judgemental?

When we first began work on this book in 2019, the game was embroiled in a sign-stealing scandal. As we were wrapping up our first draft, the focus had shifted to pitchers' use of grip-enhancing substances on the baseball. At first blush these stories may seem unrelated, involving completely different people and different parts of the game. But they had at least two things in common: Both involved smart people looking for new ways to help their team win, and both of these stories began more than a century ago.

Chapter One

DECEPTION

I N THE INTRODUCTION, we defined the Hornsby Doctrine (named after the great second baseman Rogers Hornsby), which says that baseball players will, and should, break whatever rules they can get away with. This strongly connects with the notion of gamesmanship—the leveraging of morally dubious yet legal methods to secure an advantage. "I know if I'd played strictly by the rules," said Hornsby, "I'd have been home feeding my bird dogs a long time ago instead of earning a good living in baseball for 47 years."[1]

Recent pitcher C. J. Wilson sees baseball as particularly suited to struggle with this dilemma. "It's such a technical game," he says. "There are so many opportunities for gamesmanship."[2]

Within baseball, gamesmanship often comes down to deceiving the umpire, making it harder for him to make a decision that you don't want him to make. Many of the examples presented in this chapter are clearly rule-breaking, though there is a consensus within the game that they are acceptable, even honorable. But, inevitably, not everyone agrees.

If you drive a car on a public road, you probably witness law-breaking every day. If the posted speed limit is 55 miles per hour, many people—perhaps even you—drive faster than that without risk of penalty. We all—drivers and law enforcement—are participants in a societal compact that tolerates some level of law-breaking. We agree that someone driving 80 miles per hour is taking things too far and should pay a price. But if the police started pulling over everyone who drives 57 mph, there would be chaos. In fact, our roadways would cease to move efficiently, at least for a while.

Baseball has evolved in much the same way. Many of the biggest cheating controversies start with people searching for ways to stretch the boundaries of the game's rules or the game's tolerance for rule-bending, only to find that they have taken things beyond what the sport is willing to allow. A pitcher can use a resin bag, or perhaps a little pine tar to get a better grip, but then he finds something a little better, and then a little better again, and suddenly everyone is driving 80 miles per hour.

If an infielder deliberately drops a popup to retire the faster lead runner rather than the slower batter, is this cheating? Technically, yes, because the rules forbid a fielder from deliberately dropping a ball in order to gain such an advantage. Yet most players and observers would not consider this cheating. You most likely would get away with it without penalty. This has been part of the game from its start, and likely always will be.

"Ballplayers will cheat under any circumstances if they can get away with it," said umpire Nestor Chylak in 1966. "That's why we're out there. Our job is to prevent it."[3] Umpires are a critical part of this compact, though they often resent some of the most egregious hypocrisy. "What makes me so angry," said Hall of Fame umpire Doug Harvey, "is that owners, players, and managers go through all sorts of contortions to cheat our asses off."[4] If the players and umpires do not have the same understanding of how a rule should be enforced, the compact collapses and the game requires adjustment.

Most of us learned the game of baseball on rough fields with no umpires, like the kids in *The Sandlot*. An outfielder who trapped a ball on an attempted shoestring catch might have pretended it was caught cleanly and played on as if an out had been recorded. If the opposition protested, the outfielder might fess up (perhaps after a mild protest). Assuming everyone wanted to keep playing, and play again tomorrow, they learned how far these cases could be pushed before giving in.

No one considered this to be cheating—trying to get away with such a play is simple gamesmanship. Sometimes the other team would protest, but you'd often gain an out on a catch that was not made.

Once games included an umpire (or umpires), the ethical dilemma is effectively removed from the players. Their job is to play on. If the umpire doesn't notice the trap, all the better. The other team might protest, but this is no longer the fielder's problem. Most fans and players do not consider this cheating because it is understood that the other team would do the same thing if the roles were reversed.

This conduct is not specific to baseball. In pickup basketball, if you step on the out-of-bounds line with the ball, you learn to keep playing unless the other team notices. Once a referee is involved, you are taught to play until the referee blows the whistle. Certainly, none of us expect to see a player hand the ball to the referee to self-report being out-of-bounds.

From the 1840s to the 1860s, as competitive baseball was evolving, each team supplied an umpire, and a third neutral official would step in if these two could not agree. Eventually the partisans were scrapped. The teams would handle most calls themselves, occasionally turning to the remaining umpire, who was seated between the batter and stands, to ask for a ruling. In the 1860s, as the sport developed from a gentlemanly pursuit to more heated competition, appeals increased in frequency, to the point that the umpire's role was officially expanded.[5]

Remnants of the appeal process remain in today's rulebook. Specifically, there are four rules violations that an umpire will not call unless there is an appeal by one of the players.

- A runner misses a base
- A runner advances on a caught batted ball without properly "tagging up"
- A batter bats out of order
- A batter overruns first base and doesn't immediately return

In all four cases the onus is on the opposition to notice the violation, and on the umpire to rule if an appeal is made.

Perhaps the most direct and egregious form of cheating is to bribe an umpire to fix a game. After the final series of the 1886 season, several Detroit players—needing to sweep the series for a shot at the pennant—disparaged umpire Gracie Pierce for some of his calls. Pierce later claimed that the players were particularly abusive because he had refused a $200 bribe to act on their behalf.

The Detroit players denied it. The most telling response came from Hall of Fame third baseman Deacon White, who said, "The best evidence that the $200 was not offered is that Pierce did not take it."[6] Regardless of who was telling the truth, the lack of repercussions testifies to the prevalence of this activity in the sport at the time.

Short of outright corruption, there are many ways in which players are currently encouraged, directly or indirectly, to deceive the umpire. Hornsby classified all of them as "cheating," though he very much believed that they were part of the game, and he was unrepentant about engaging in them himself.

A currently popular form of this is "pitch framing," in which the catcher receives the pitch in such a way that a strike is more likely to be called. Managers frequently describe framing as "giving the umpire the best view," while noting that a poor catcher can cost his pitcher strikes by jerking his glove out of the strike zone after catching the ball. Thus, keeping the glove steady will result in a "fairer" call. This is all well and good, but catchers can also "steal" strikes by subtly moving their glove *into* the strike zone after receiving the pitch.

Umpires are understandably sensitive about the practice. Randy Knorr, a longtime major league catcher in the 1990s, tells the story of framing a pitch for the Blue Jays only to have the umpire call it a ball. "Fifty thousand fans in the stands are booing," he said. "I knew it was a ball. I was just trying to bring it back over. And he smacked me in the back of the head and said, 'Don't ever do that to me again. You know that was a ball, and now you made everybody in the stadium think it was a strike.' "[7]

Now that we have high-speed video, there is convincing evidence that catcher framing can have an impact on ball and strike calls. In 2019 for example, the top framing catchers (Austin Hedges of the Padres and Atlanta's Tyler Flowers) received credit for providing their team 15 runs a year (about 1.5 wins) over an average framer, and twice that over a poor framer. Right or wrong, catchers are being valued for deceiving the umpire into calling more strikes.

Baseball analyst Joe Sheehan noted that the success of pitch framing reveals a flaw in the game: the inability of an umpire to correctly call the strike zone. "It demonstrates clearly that umpires are not calling balls and strikes according to the rules of the game, but rather based on the crutch of catcher actions. This isn't out of laziness, out of a character flaw, out of a desire to bend the rules, but a concession to what has been true for decades: that human eyes cannot possibly track a baseball and render a decision on its position pursuant to the letter of Rule 2.00."[8] The solution, says Sheehan, is an automated strike zone. Many agree.

Connie Mack, the taciturn manager of the Philadelphia Athletics for 50 years, began his baseball days as a catcher in the 1880s, playing 11 years in the majors. It is not known whether Mack pitch framed, but he did do something that might be considered more ethically dubious. Early in Mack's career a foul tip was treated just like any other foul ball, registering an out if a catcher caught it even if it was not a third strike. Mack developed a habit of making a clicking sound with his glove that sounded like a tip in order to get the call on missed swings. "In fact, in a majority of cases the batter himself was fooled and actually thought he had been legitimately retired," Mack later recalled. "The rule was changed [for 1889] so that a foul ball had to go at least ten feet in air or be caught ten feet away from the plate for the batter to be declared out, so this was no longer possible."[9]

Larry Brown, longtime catcher for the Memphis Red Sox of the Negro American League, hit on another form of deception. With a runner on first, a pitch scooted by him, but instead of chasing it Brown put his glove back to the umpire to ask for another baseball. The umpire, governed by routine, gave him one, and Brown threw the runner out.[10]

Another form of fooling the umpire is the phantom hit by pitch. On September 15, 2010, Yankees shortstop Derek Jeter was awarded first base after a pitch appeared to hit his hand. Replays clearly showed that the ball had actually ricocheted off the knob of his bat. Jeter sold the play, however, shaking his hand in pain, and called the trainer out to work on his "injury." After the game, Jeter admitted the ruse. "He told me to go to first base," he said. "I'm not going to tell him I'm not going to first, you know. It's part of the game. My job is to get on base." Opposing manager Joe Maddon protested so vehemently that he was ejected, but also said "If our guys did it, I would have applauded."[11]

In 2015 a similar play transpired, with higher stakes. On June 20 the Nationals' Max Scherzer lost a bid for a perfect game with two outs in the ninth when his pitch struck pinch-hitter José Tábata. Though Scherzer completed the no-hitter with the next batter, Tábata faced criticism for apparently lowering his elbow into the fateful pitch. "That's my job," he said. "I got to get on base whatever the situation."

Scherzer, who had pitched a one-hit shutout with 16 strikeouts in his previous start, was disappointed but level-headed. "It was a slider that backed up, and it hit him," he said. "I don't blame him for doing it. I mean, heck, I'd probably do the same thing."[12]

One of the more famous, and disputed, baseball cheating stories transpired during Game 4 of the 1978 World Series. The Dodgers held a 2–1 series lead over the Yankees and led this game 3–0 entering the sixth inning. During what turned out to be a two-run Yankee rally, the Dodgers' attempt at an inning-ending double play went awry when shortstop Bill Russell's throw to first struck baserunner Reggie Jackson in the hip. Replays seemed to show Jackson moving his hip into the ball, which is illegal, though the umpires (decades before the introduction of replay review) ruled that there was no intent and the play stood. The Yankees won the game 4–3 in the tenth inning.

Dodgers manager Tommy Lasorda protested long and loudly in the moment and remained upset about the play for decades afterward.[13] Jackson denied intent after the game but could not hide his laughter. "Things were happening fast and I'm a slow thinker," he said. "You know, I don't see good. I don't move too good. When I saw the throw coming, I didn't have a glove, so I just tried to tense up and take it."

First baseman Steve Garvey had the best view and expressed anger after the game. But even after losing a crucial World Series game, when asked if Reggie had cheated Garvey stopped short. "Maybe a subcategory," Garvey said. "But that's what they always say, that it's only cheating if you get caught? If I were Reggie, I wouldn't say anything either. I congratulate him."[14]

Faking getting hit with a throw, or with a pitch, is analogous to flopping in basketball and soccer, sports that have been beset with players embellishing or faking contact, often by falling down and moaning in pain, in order to draw a foul call from the referee. The NBA and FIFA will penalize a player with a technical foul or yellow card if caught, and occasionally with a fine or suspension. Jeter took some heat in the press, but MLB does not penalize such actions.

Players have been doing similar things for more than a century. The rule granting a batter first base when struck by a pitch did not come along until the 1880s, but within a few years deliberate hit-by-pitches were rampant. One player often accused was Hughie Jennings, who still holds the all-time (287) and single-season (51) records for being hit by a pitch. "That gag was working well before my time," Jennings later told a reporter.[15]

Another hit-by-pitch controversy took place in the Mets-Marlins game on April 8, 2021. The Mets scored the winning run when Michael Conforto was hit by a pitch with the bases loaded in the bottom of the ninth. Replays showed that the pitch was in the strike zone and that Conforto, seemingly on purpose, moved his elbow into the path of the ball. The ball barely nicked his thick elbow pad—in fact, the play was reviewed to determine whether he had been hit at all. According to Rule 5.05(b)(2), a batter is not entitled to first base if he's hit by a ball in the strike zone, or if he makes no attempt to avoid the pitch. In this instance, both clauses applied. But Conforto got away with it.

Plate umpire Ron Kulpa, after starting to call strike three, changed his mind as he considered the barely perceptible sound of the ball grazing Conforto. After the game, Kulpa admitted his error. "The guy was hit by the pitch in the strike zone," he said. "I should have called him out." Conforto denied purposely getting hit, but allowed that "a win's a win."[16]

Like nearly all forms of "cheating" discussed in this book, the art of fooling the umpire goes back to the very beginning of the sport.

The Baltimore Orioles of the 1890s were one of the best, most colorful, and most innovative teams in baseball history. Led by their brilliant manager Ned Hanlon, and stars like John McGraw, Wee Willie Keeler, Hughie Jennings, and Joe Kelley, the team has been credited with inventing or popularizing the hit-and-run play, the pickoff, a system of cutoff plays on defense, a pitcher covering first base on ground balls to the right side, the pitcher intercepting a catcher's throw to prevent a double steal, the Baltimore chop, the bunt, and the suicide squeeze.

They likely did not invent most of these acts, but their success legitimized them as strategies, and the team's most famous players (especially McGraw, Jennings and Wilbert Robinson) continued to preach the genius and talents of the old Orioles for many years to come. If they were not the first with these tactics, they were among the best, winning three pennants and finishing second twice between 1894 and 1898.

Balancing their undeniable skill and intelligence, the Orioles had a well-earned reputation as a team more than willing to skirt the rules. They hid balls in the outfield grass to be grabbed by an outfielder if the real ball was farther away. They tripped baserunners, or grabbed their uniforms as they ran past. Sometimes, they simply blocked a runner's advance. Orioles catchers threw their masks onto the baseline as a runner approached home. On offense, the Orioles skipped bases on their way around the diamond if the umpire was looking elsewhere. They used their spikes on opponents and umpires, making sure to do so in ways that they could claim were accidental. Less covertly, they engaged in violent arguments and full-scale brawls on a moment's notice. They got away with much of this for the simple reason that games often featured a single umpire. (Dual umpires did not become common until the twentieth century, and it took another few decades for three, and then four, to be the norm.)

John McGraw came to symbolize the Orioles. "I had trained myself... to think up little and big things that might be anticipated by the rule changers," he said. "With us, only the written rule counted... and if you could come up with something not covered by the rules, you were ahead of the slower-thinking opposition by at least a full season."[17] McGraw articulated an overriding theme of this story: Shrewd baseball professionals will innovate to improve their chances of success, and not always with much regard for the agreed-upon rules of the game.

The art of skipping bases (for example, cutting well inside of third base on the way home) has been attributed to Mike Kelly in the 1880s, but as historian Peter Morris wrote, "It was a fairly regular practice in the 1870s and almost certainly originated not long after the rules specified that runners had to touch each base."[18]

Another theme of this story is that cheating exists because it is beneficial, and it will stop only if it becomes harder to get away with or if the penalty for getting caught tips the risk-reward balance away from the cheaters. We don't condone rule-breaking on the part of players; fair and valid competition requires players' adhering to a set of rules. But with fifty or so highly competitive athletes arrayed against each other every game, it is unrealistic to believe no one will try to find an advantage if the probability of getting caught or the penalty for doing so is minimal compared with the benefit. The rules must properly balance the risk-reward.

Outside of Baltimore, the Orioles were generally despised. But the National League did little to rein in their behavior, and soon other

NL teams were similarly offensive. One of the reasons for the success of Ban Johnson's (newly major) American League in 1901 was his crackdown on hooliganism, including fines and suspensions for the most flagrant conduct. It is important to note that players did not become more ethical, they simply modified their behavior because there were consequences for their actions.

Historians have largely been kind to the old Orioles, treating their rule-skirting as a romantic extension of the times. Their behavior was recounted as colorful rather than offensive, and their manager and many of their stars were duly enshrined in the Baseball Hall of Fame, with nary an asterisk. While the Orioles' particular style of cheating ebbed during the twentieth century, players' predilection for cheating in general has not abated.

Don Hoak, a National League infielder in the 1950s, was accused by opposing manager Rogers Hornsby of playing third base just as McGraw had decades earlier, deliberately impeding baserunners and holding onto their belt loops as a runner tagged up. Hornsby responded by having a baserunner, Clint Courtney, deliberately jump into Hoak's midsection, spikes first.[19]

The claims of the old Orioles hiding extra balls in the outfield grass may sound far-fetched, but similar tactics have continued into the modern era. In Los Angeles on September 3, 2018, Dodger Alex Verdugo hit a pop foul behind third base. Mets third baseman Todd Frazier reached into the stands to make a terrific catch, holding the ball aloft as proof of his feat. He got the out call he wanted, but replays revealed that while Frazier's glove was over the fence he dropped the baseball and quickly grabbed a souvenir ball that was lying nearby. After the umpire ruled in his favor, he quickly tossed the ball back into the grandstand.[20] This seems like cheating no matter how strict your definition, but Frazier openly joked about his misdeed and received neither punishment nor public shaming.

Cubs star Ernie Banks was denied the first crack at his 500th home run by an outfielder's deception. Playing in Montreal's makeshift Jarry Park, Banks hit a line drive that went over the fence. Umpire Tony

Venzon lost track of the ball and ruled it a ground rule double. Cubs manager Leo Durocher and coach Joey Amalfitano rushed out to Venzon, complaining about the call. Expos outfielder Rusty Staub, seeing what was happening, enlarged a hole under the fence with his foot. "Maybe it went through here, Joey," Staub told Amalfitano. "When Tony sees the hole in the fence he says to Leo, 'Look, it went under the fence through that hole.'" Staub's conscience was clear. "I'm having to turn away to keep from laughing out loud," he remembered. "I mean, it's not like I misled the umpire. I didn't actually say the ball went through a hole."[21]

There is almost certainly less cheating on the field today than in the past, if only because every game is televised. With the advent of instant replay, many of the most common techniques of fooling the umpire no longer work.

For decades, first basemen would often shorten the distance of any throw by pulling off the base and toward the thrown ball. Ed Kranepool, Mets first baseman, learned this skill in the major leagues. "I had to work awful hard with Gil Hodges on the play before I got the knack of getting off the base without getting caught," he said. "If you aren't quick the movements are herky-jerky and they'll call you for cheating." In his defense, Hodges earnestly explained: "It's never done to deceive; it's done to win. Naturally you want to make the play correctly with your foot on the base, but if this is the only thing left to do, you must do what you can to help your pitcher." With all due respect to Hodges, he was very clearly acting to deceive the umpire.

Vic Power, another highly regarded first baseman, explained the umpires' role on such a play. "Sure I cheat coming off first." he said. "Everybody does. If I get warned I might not cheat for the rest of the series. Next series I start all over again. Umpires will never call a cheat play on you if it looks like an out from the stands. They don't like to get booed."

Bobby Richardson, a five-time Gold Glove–winning second baseman with the Yankees was known for turning double plays so quickly that umpires missed the fact that he never touched second base. "My job is to make the play," he said. "It is the umpire's job to call it." His manager Casey Stengel was typically terse in explaining the rationale: "Why wouldn't you cheat if it would help you win?"

The "neighborhood play," as it came to be known, occurs when a second baseman or shortstop receives a throw from another infielder, straddles or skips over the bag without touching it, before firing the ball to first. This was tolerated in part because the infielder could clear out and avoid the hard-charging baserunner. It is also an easier play to make if you don't have to worry about the precise location of the bag.

Phil Linz, an infielder who occasionally backed up Richardson, also understood the value of seniority. "When I get into a game the umpire figures I'm not as good at making double plays. They bear down real hard on guys like me." Another common cheat around second base was the sweep tag on an attempted steal. It is often difficult for an umpire to see the tag, so the infielder might be able to steal an out.[22]

Prior to the 2016 season, MLB ruled that the neighborhood play, first baseman foot pulls, and deceptive sweep tags were reviewable by instant replay, effectively ending their practice. Fooling the umpire now requires you to fool several high-speed video cameras as well.

In May 2010, Dodgers third baseman Casey Blake accused Cubs pitcher Ted Lilly of pitching from several inches in front of the rubber. "I know he doesn't have an overpowering fastball," Blake said after the game. "I know he's trying to get as much of an edge as he can. But he moved in." First base umpire John Hirshbeck told Blake that he could not see any issues from where he was standing and declined to move closer.[23]

Lilly was far from the first pitcher to do this: Hall of Famers Nolan Ryan and Whitey Ford each confessed to doing as much, at least on occasion. Longtime manager Bobby Valentine similarly accused star hurler Kevin Brown, "He balks every time, and no one calls it."[24] And here again, older players have more license to cheat. "Warren Spahn got away with that pitch," said manager Gene Mauch, "because he's been around and it's expected of him. Young kids like Bill Wakefield of the Mets get called on it."[25] Most pitchers known to do this cheat only in key spots, understanding that they can get away with it just once or twice in a game. But that could be enough.

In the early days of baseball, the rules governing how a pitcher should throw the ball continually evolved, and the pitchers frequently bumped up against the strictures. Beyond prohibiting overhand throws, the original rules covering the pitching delivery were not specific. Most sporting clubs interpreted this regulation to mean that the pitching motion should be full underhand, delivered with a straight arm. Not surprisingly, pitchers began skirting these requirements almost immediately.[26]

In early 1872 the National Association (the first fully professional baseball organization) partly capitulated. Sidearm deliveries up to hip level were legalized as was bending the arm. Given the huge advantage of throwing with a more overhand delivery, pitchers were soon inching up over the hip. In fact, pitchers took to hiking up their pants to redefine their waistlines.

In 1883 the allowable (though still sidearm) release point was moved up to the shoulder. Over the next two years both major leagues, the National League and the American Association, resigned themselves to their lack of will for enforcing the rules and legalized full overhand deliveries. When rule-breaking gets out of hand, either additional enforcement is needed, or the rules must be changed to meet reality. It took three decades of experimentation and cheating, but baseball's owners arrived at a solution that has held ever since.

Prior to the introduction of the pitching rubber in 1893, pitchers were required to throw from within a boxed area. With only one umpire, it was very difficult to police whether the pitcher stepped over the front line. In the mid-1880s, the American Association came up with an ingenious, if somewhat dangerous, solution, installing a marble or glass slab on the front edge of the pitcher's box. If a pitcher's spike landed on the slab, he was liable to hurt his groin or hamstring or knee as his metal cleats skidded forward. It didn't really work; pitchers either wore rubber-soled shoes or altered their delivery to step clear over the slab.[27]

Pitchers also sought advantages against baserunners. From the beginning of codified rules in the 1840s, a balk—the act of faking a pitch to catch the runner off guard—was prohibited. The penalty for a balk was, and still is, that all runners advance one base. Unlike other deceptions described in this chapter, the actions that came to be defined as a balk were not done primarily to deceive the umpire, but another player—the baserunner. While deceiving the opposition is frequently a legal and consistently necessary means of competing in baseball, the rules-makers felt that the balk unduly hampered the running game.

The balk has never been well understood by fans, and despite occasional attempts to describe it better, pitchers push the boundaries of what remains an imprecise rule. With the introduction of overhand pitching, in 1887 the rules specified that the pitcher "shall hold the ball before delivery, fairly in front of his body." This essentially codified the pause that pitchers are still required to make before delivering a pitch.[28]

As of 2021 the baseball rulebook lists 13 ways for the pitcher to balk. These range from faking a pitch, to faking a throw to first or third, to throwing a "quick pitch" before the batter is ready, to delaying the game. Over the years specific guidelines have been introduced to remove ambiguity, but the precise rule remains imperfectly understood and enforced, and a balk call almost always leads to an argument with the pitcher.

After the elimination of the pitcher's box and installation of the rubber, pitchers' deceptive movements intensified. Prior to the 1899 season, baseball cracked down, further identifying actions that constituted a balk. Pitchers were formally banned from faking a throw to the plate or a base, not initially stepping toward the plate or base when making a throw, and not keeping a foot on the rubber when throwing to the plate.

As with many of the unfair advantages discussed in this book, the balk rule evolved to keep up with the creative methods pitchers devised to hold runners. Some of these may not have been technically illegal at the time, so the rule had to change to close a loophole; other times, the method may have been illegal, but the rule needed to be clarified to make this clear.

The pitching motion is so complicated and swift, however, that any interpretation is subject to nuance and judgement. The league, umpires, and teams hope to minimize balks as they are controversial and controversy slows the game. This sometimes results in lax enforcement, at which point the league may issue a memorandum to teams and umpires to call balks closer to the letter of the rulebook. It is a pendulum constantly in motion.

Kansas City Monarchs pitcher Bill Drake talked about his "half-balk" move in the 1924 Negro World Series against Hilldale (Philadelphia). "Everybody used to cheat back then," Drake recalled. "I'd get on the mound and just bend my knee a little, like I was going to throw home, then wheel and throw to first. Sure, it's a balk but I used to pick off a whole lot of runners that way. Anyway, the first base umpire says to me, 'You have to do away with that move.' … The other umpire, Buck Freeman, says, 'Hell, he's been playing like that all season." So they let me keep it."[29]

Thirteen years later in May 1937, the day before a much-anticipated pitching duel between the St. Louis Cardinals' Dizzy Dean and the New York Giants' Carl Hubbell, NL president Ford Frick sent a memo to teams and umpires saying he wanted the balk rule better enforced. Dean was notorious for pushing its boundaries. Opposing teams, in particular, believed he didn't stop his motion as required, and they often complained loudly to the umpires. "One major league manager went so far as to say that his club could beat Dean," wrote a St. Louis sportswriter, "whenever it could persuade the umpire to enforce that hesitation or pause rule whenever runners were on base."[30]

With the Cardinals up by one in the visitor's half of the sixth, the Giants had a runner on second and one out. Dick Bartell flied out to left field, and St. Louis appeared close to getting out of the inning. But umpire George Barr ruled that Dean had not paused in his delivery.

The runner was awarded third, and Bartell was sent back to bat. With new life, Bartell flied to right where Pepper Martin muffed the ball while preparing to make a throw to home. The Cardinals unraveled, and New York scored three runs in the inning, taking a 3–1 lead.

Over the rest of the game, a seething Dean threw at the heads of a parade of Giants batters. Finally, with one out in the ninth, Jimmy Ripple bunted toward first, hoping to run into Dean covering the base. When the two met at the base they immediately started fighting, sparking a full-scale brawl. Only the two catchers, Gus Mancuso of the Giants and Mickey Owen of the Cardinals, were ejected, for fighting with each other. New York won the game 4–1; Dean and Ripple were fined $50 each, a meaningful statement for the time.

Days later, Dean was still raging at a church banquet in Belleville, Illinois, that Frick and umpire Barr were "the two biggest crooks" in baseball.[31] The wire services picked up the story, and Dean found himself in the middle of a firestorm. Impugning the integrity of the league always brought swift retribution, and Frick suspended him indefinitely. Shortly thereafter, Frick crafted an abject letter of apology for Dean to sign. Instead, Dean threatened to sue, and Frick backed down. Frick held a hearing where he allowed Dean to deny the comments attributed to him, and then reinstated him. This chaos was not atypical of the many occasions when baseball has abruptly and aggressively tried to enforce the balk rule.[32]

Branch Rickey once claimed that Yankees pitchers gained an advantage over the Dodgers in the 1952 World Series by ignoring the pause requirement. According to Rickey, New York's Game 6 starter Vic Raschi balked 26 times, none of them called by the umpire, which allowed the Yankees to control the Dodgers' running game. Rickey went so far as to attribute the decline in stolen bases during the 1930s and 1940s to lax enforcement of the balk rule. As with the Dean debacle, Rickey's claims illustrate that players act in accord with however they believe umpires will call a game. Future attempts at balk enforcement met with similar results—heavy enforcement for a short period of time, a strong counter-reaction from pitchers and managers, and retreat to something like the status quo.[33]

To reach the pinnacle of their profession, baseball players must be highly competitive. So it has long been accepted that players can and should do whatever they can to win, particularly as it relates to the game on the field, even if such play is technically a rule violation. The introduction of the umpire as a neutral arbiter in the 1860s seems to have removed much of the moral stigma around such deceptions.

Only when the cheating becomes too blatant or begins fundamentally to change the game—as with recent pitch doctoring—does it become a crisis that must be faced. But the fundamental culture, winning at nearly all costs, is 150 years old.

Chapter Two

BINOCULARS AND TELESCOPES

O N JANUARY 13, 2020, Major League Baseball issued a long-awaited nine-page report on its investigation of the Houston Astros' sign-stealing operation, which the team had employed during their 2017 championship season. The report detailed a sophisticated, multiple-person scheme, and concluded that the program was player-led, specifically naming veteran Carlos Beltran and bench coach Alex Cora. General manager Jeff Luhnow and manager A. J. Hinch were suspended by MLB for the 2020 season for what happened on their watch, and the Astros soon fired both.

But sign stealing is nearly as old as signs themselves. For 120 years, teams have been using mechanical or electronic means to intercept and decipher their opposition's signals. What has changed is the underlying technology and the traditionally feeble attempts to deter this practice.

High-quality prism binoculars were first sold in 1894 by Zeiss, a German optical company. These binoculars represented a significant upgrade from previous designs, and it did not take long for someone in baseball to find a way to use them to their advantage. In 1899 that someone was Morgan Murphy, a backup catcher for the Philadelphia Phillies … and sign stealer extraordinaire.

Murphy's story presents intriguing parallels to the modern Astros. Houston's scheme was formally exposed in a November 2019 article in *The Athletic*. The only player willing to go on the record was Mike Fiers, who'd pitched for the Astros in 2017, and had since moved on to the Athletics. Many details of the Phillies' 1899 scheme were also revealed by a pitcher who had left the club: Bill Magee, who had joined Philadelphia in midseason 1899, and then went public in October after he had been released.[1]

Also like the Astros, the 1899 scheme involved several participants. Murphy stationed himself in manager Billy Shettsline's suite in center field with a $75 pair of binoculars. (This new technology was not cheap—the average annual salary for a manufacturing employee was roughly $500, and starting ballplayers earned perhaps four times that amount. In fact, team owner Colonel John Rogers refused to reimburse Murphy for the field glasses until he demonstrated his scheme's success.) After deciphering the catcher's signals, Murphy pulled an awning on the left side of the suite's window to indicate a breaking ball and the right side for a fastball or other straight pitch.

Such a program was frowned on but not illegal, and players and executives soon struggled with how to respond. As one Philadelphia player observed, "Morgan Murphy has earned every dollar of his salary this season. Had it not been for the signal service department we would have been in the second division, as every game we have won has been won with the bat, and in many games where Morgan was not working we could not hit a balloon, and were easily beaten."[2] In fact, the Phillies improved from 78–71 to 94–58 that season. Murphy's contributions were so highly valued that the Phillies carried him through the season even though he never appeared in a game.

The next year Murphy and the Phillies' scheme became more complicated yet. They buried a telegraphic sounder—a buzzer-like piece of equipment used in telegraph transmission—under the third base coaching box. Rather than pulling an awning, Murphy activated the buzzer, which could be detected by Pearce Chiles, a 33-year-old hard-case reserve outfielder who often coached third base. Chiles relayed the pitch to the batter using prearranged code words.

The system was exposed in mid-September 1900 by the visiting Reds. Manager Bob Allen, who had been tipped off, paid a visit to Shettsline's office and noticed wires running through an upper window. He had shortstop Tommy Corcoran dig around the coaches' box, little by little throughout the ballgame. The Phillies tried to protest, but too late; Corcoran pulled up the board, buzzer, wires, and battery.[3]

The *Philadelphia Inquirer* amusingly linked these shenanigans with the recent electrification of American cities: "What the public was curious about, however, was that 'buzzer' snap ... the introduction of electricity as an adjunct to the presentation of the noble national sport, opened up such possibilities that the public not unnaturally wanted to learn all that was possible about the new scheme."[4]

Philadelphia owner John Rogers dismissed the complaints against his squad, while also feeling the need to disclaim any knowledge of the buzzer: "I knew that glasses had been used by Catcher Murphy, who endeavored to discover the signals of the catchers of the opposing teams. As far as I know it never worked successfully, and I poo-hooed the idea. It is a ridiculous one, but as far as being fair and legitimate I can find no fault with it. It is a game that both sides may play, and surely a club may take advantage of whatever brains it may possess."[5] This attitude—claiming innocence and downplaying efficacy—played out repeatedly for more than a century. The other owners disagreed and tried to censure Rogers and the Phillies at the NL meeting in December. One owner, in what has become an oft-repeated refrain, proposed that the Phillies' records be struck from the league's official statistics.

Fortunately for the Phillies, more serious matters intervened. The American League was launching that winter as a major league, and the contentious NL owners did not want to become any more divided than they already were. Rogers agreed to shut down the sign stealing, the other owners did not penalize him, and no formal rule was adopted.

Baseball's reaction to Murphy and the Phillies raises a dilemma the sport has faced for decades. On the one hand, there was no formal rule against their system. On the other, everyone acknowledged it was inappropriate—including the perpetrators—by concealing their actions. As we will show throughout this book, when there are no rules and penalties to prevent unwanted behavior, chaos usually follows.

Signaling from the catcher to the pitcher became commonplace in the late 1870s and 1880s, and closely followed the popularization of the curveball. As a matter of protection, the catcher must know when a breaking pitch is coming. Competitive sportsmen being who they are, teams soon began trying to steal the opposing catcher's signs. Catchers became adept at hiding their signals, which developed into what we see today: a sequence of fingers flashed in front of the catcher's crotch, requiring the pitcher and catcher to agree on the meaning of the intricate pattern. Intercepting these signs could be most readily accomplished by an observant runner on second, who would then use his own movements to alert the batter. Occasionally, canny base coaches or others stationed around the field or on the bases would do the deciphering.[6]

During the late nineteenth century, managers and base coaches also began using complicated signals to give instructions to the batter and runners. These signs were easily observable, as coaches made no attempt to hide them, but deciphering and determining their patterns and meaning became a specialized and valued art. The catcher's signs, on the other hand, can usually only be seen by a runner on second base; relaying these signs to the batter—without any mechanical or artificial aid—was perfectly legal. Opponents attempted to discourage such behavior with retaliatory brushback pitches or in-game sign switching.

John McGraw was always eager to find any advantage he could, and his perspective carried weight. He was baseball's biggest celebrity from the 1890s until Babe Ruth came along, and McGraw won nearly everywhere he played or managed with a wide array of innovative approaches on and off the field. When the Irish playwright and opinion-setter George Bernard Shaw met McGraw, he announced he had "at last discovered the real and authentic most remarkable man in America."[7] McGraw not only changed the way baseball was played but also helped to popularize the sport through his modern, almost pro-wrestling-like, us-versus-them approach.

McGraw seemed to find as much enjoyment in stealing his opponents' signs as he did when one of his speedsters stole four bases, or star hurler Christy Mathewson threw a shutout. Nevertheless, McGraw saw an ethical difference between mechanical and nonmechanical methods. "According to all the best ethics of baseball," he wrote in 1913, "any signal which can be grabbed through a quick eye and smooth intelligence may be fairly used to the advantage of the grabber. But the unfair method of getting signs is to employ artificial means, such as field glasses and buzzers and other devices that have broken into baseball from time to time."[8]

A consensus quickly formed around this **McGraw Doctrine**, surprisingly without the adoption of a formal rule until quite recently. On occasion, after a heated sign-stealing uproar or negative stories in the press, baseball officials threatened penalties should anyone be caught, but these pronouncements were not backed up prior to the twenty-first century.

The criticism heaped on the 1900 Phillies deterred teams from mechanical sign stealing schemes, at least for a few years. In 1909, however, as memories began to fade, New York Highlanders manager George Stallings devised his own system. New York's American League Park was well suited, as it featured a shielded, semi-enclosed structure in center field, slightly elevated and hidden behind an advertising sign for Young's Hats.

Stallings stationed part-time scout Gene McCann in this structure with a pair of binoculars, upping his pay to $75 per week. McCann punched a couple of holes in the fence to provide a line of sight to the catcher. He signaled the batter when a fastball was coming by moving a paddle attached to wires that slid it across the horizontal line of the

"H" in "Hats." The line was relatively short, and apparently the contraption was rigged so that the line could exhibit two different colors.

Precisely when the 1909 Highlanders began the operation is not known, but by late in the season many opposing players and managers suspected something strange was afoot. In late September, Washington manager Joe Cantillon voiced his suspicions to some sportswriters, who explored the outfield and found nothing improper. Cantillon next confided in Detroit manager Hugh Jennings, a man who occasionally engaged in a little illegal sign stealing himself.[9]

Before a Tigers game in New York on September 25, Jennings deputized pitcher Bill Donovan and trainer Harry Tuthill to investigate. Tuthill first noticed the changing color of the line of the "H," then spotted the hidden structure after reconnoitering behind the outfield wall. He struggled over the fence enclosing it to make his case.

When McCann realized he'd been discovered he abandoned his post, leaving all the sign stealing apparatus behind. Tuthill gathered up the binoculars and wires and paddles and brought them back to Jennings, who now had nearly unimpeachable evidence of the Highlanders' perfidy. The players happily passed along their stories to the press, and others felt vindicated, too. "It is no surprise to me," said White Sox manager Billy Sullivan. "I felt certain that the New York club was getting our battery signs, because they were hitting our pitchers in a way that would indicate it."[10]

Jennings and Tuthill quickly clammed up. The powers of the American League, primarily President Ban Johnson (the most important man in baseball at the time), likely feared damaging the league's New York club, which Johnson considered crucial in his long-running battle with New York Giants owner John Brush and manager McGraw. Though he usually backed his umpires and was a stickler for law and order, in this instance Johnson's concern for his New York franchise seems to have gotten the better of him.

In the end, the AL's board of directors exonerated the Highlanders without explicitly denying the sign stealing: "The New York club is free from all complicity in such a tipping affair." To discourage future mechanical stealing and to demonstrate sincerity, the board added, "Be it further resolved that it is the sense of the board that any manager or official proved guilty of operating a sign-tipping bureau should be barred from baseball for all time."[11]

Note the similarity of this sentiment to Commissioner Rob Manfred's more than one hundred years later when ruling on the Astros' affair in 2017. (We discuss this at greater length in a later chapter.) The threat of punishment was not directed at the players, but toward management. Also highly revealing is that the "sense of the board" is not binding in the way a formal rule is. And no formal rule was forthcoming.

Unsurprisingly, by the middle of the 1910 season, Stallings was happily ignoring the "sense of the board." During a July game at Hilltop Park, White Sox third baseman Lee Tannehill noticed movement beyond the outfield and headed out to centerfield to examine the signage. Once he realized what Tannehill was doing, Highlander pitcher Tom Hughes sprinted out, telling his hidden accomplice to skedaddle and take any accessories with him. When Tannehill arrived on Hughes's heels, there was no evidence in sight. The unruffled Highlanders trotted out their apparatus the very next day and were spotted by White Sox pitcher Ed Walsh, who had brought his own binoculars.

Once again, the baseball powers were uninterested in meting out punishment. Johnson would have preferred to dismiss the episode altogether, but prominent Chicago sportswriter Hugh Fullerton—later at the forefront of exposing the 1919 World Series fix—challenged baseball to address the charges. When asked if he'd received any formal complaint, Johnson replied in a manner clearly discouraging any future protest, "No, I haven't, and furthermore, I don't expect to receive any. The yarn ... originated in the fertile brain of a baseball writer with the Chicago team."[12] He reiterated how seriously he would take the matter, were it true, and added that the league would pay $500 for proof of such activity.

Fullerton accepted the challenge by pursuing substantiation from players. "I have the affidavits of players of the Chicago, New York, Boston, and Washington clubs to back up the assertion," he wrote, noting that Johnson was unlikely to find proof as long as he refused to hold hearings.[13] Johnson finally called White Sox manager Hugh Duffy to his Chicago office, but showed little interest in finding out what the manager knew. Instead, stories appeared asserting that Johnson might fine White Sox players for complaining to the press. Players had little interest in pressing further charges to an unsympathetic league president. The upshot? Baseball had placed itself in an awkward position vis-à-vis mechanical sign stealing: Though it was declared unfair, there was no rule against it, no penalty for engaging in it, and now discouraging testimony of its very existence.

Despite a pretty good year in 1910, Stallings was bounced near the end of the season, apparently because he lost a power struggle with star first baseman Hal Chase, one of baseball's most disliked and crooked players (though it would be many years before baseball's authorities unofficially declared him persona non grata). The headache caused by Stallings's sign stealing, however, likely caused Johnson to push the Highlanders to find a new manager.

For the next few years accusations of mechanical sign stealing died down, which could lead one to believe that teams and their managers had seen the light. More likely, the halfhearted response from the league office provided a tacit incentive to continue the practice. Opponents certainly saw no benefit to complaining publicly.

One way to show that the dishonesty continued is the existence of countermeasures. Before the 1923 World Series, Giants manager McGraw created a ruse to thwart the Yankees from picking up signs he was giving from the dugout. Assuming that the Yankees would focus their binoculars on him, McGraw had a young infielder named Freddie Maguire relay signals to the players and coaches. He also searched the visitors' dressing room for Dictaphone outlets that could be used for audio spying. Very little got by John McGraw.[14]

Still, the cheating continued. The Phillies stole signs in the mid-1920s by having someone wave a white towel in the clubhouse window, located in centerfield. A stretched-out towel indicated a fastball, a rolled-up towel announced a changeup, and no towel signified a curve. The Cardinals detected the towel movement in one game, and by confronting the Phillies thought they had ended the practice. In fact, the Phillies simply switched to using different colored towels to signal different pitch types.[15]

Of course, there were other purposes for binoculars in the outfield stands. "There's quite a bit of it [sign stealing] going on," said longtime baseball man Birdie Tebbetts. "But I've always felt most binoculars in the outfield were used for looking at girls in the stands. And, as far as I know, there's no rule against that."[16] There was no rule against sign stealing, either.

One of Tebbetts's most prominent teammates, slugger Hank Greenberg, later fessed up to an operation that helped their 1940 Tigers win the AL pennant. One day in early September, hurler Tommy Bridges was sitting in the left field pavilion with third baseman and hunting partner Pinky Higgins. Bridges had brought along his new rifle and was looking around the ballpark through its long-range gauge. (We hope that Bridges was using only the scope, rather than pointing a rifle around the ballpark, though sensitivities around firearms were not nearly as sharp in those days.) Bridges soon realized that he could make out the catcher's signals from the stands. Detroit's batters didn't even need the signal to be relayed through a coach; they could make out a gesture from Bridges.

Bridges later moved closer, taking up his station in the Tigers bullpen, where a second man would put his right hand down for a breaking ball and leave it up for a fastball. As Greenberg remembered, only Yankees manager Joe McCarthy suspected something inappropriate and directed some of his players to investigate. Realizing discovery was inevitable, the Tigers relocated their sign stealing to the upper deck in center field.

Coincidence or not, the Tigers had an extraordinary 22 game homestand in September, going 17–5 and averaging 7.4 runs per game. The team jumped from third place, four games back, to first place and a two-game lead at the close. The team's two power hitters, Greenberg and Rudy York, crushed the ball during the homestand: Greenberg hit .418 with 15 home runs, while York hit .409 with 8 home runs. Greenberg had no qualms: "Hitters always felt that pitchers had a big advantage and anything we did, legal or otherwise, was fair game in trying to defeat the opposing team."[17] Greenberg was simply restating the Hornsby Doctrine.

Beginning in the 1930s, many clubs expanded or built large center field scoreboards. While primarily designed to help fans follow the game, scoreboards also provided many hiding places for spies and signaling—another innovation coopted for a more controversial use. "Every team with a scoreboard in center field—and that includes most all teams today—has a spy hidden inside at one time or another," Rogers Hornsby wrote in 1962.[18] As always, if a team is presented with a better means to steal signs, it will soon steal signs.

The Cleveland Indians, owned by the ever-creative Bill Veeck, joined the party after falling back to third place in September 1948. Instead of binoculars, Cleveland's players purchased a powerful spotting scope, like those used in target shooting, to get a clear view of the catcher. The team planted Marshall Bossard, the son of groundskeeper Emil Bossard, in the scoreboard. Marshall would relay the pitch type to the batter by placing either a dark or light card into one of the holes designed to hold the count of runs for that half inning.[19]

Although Veeck left the Indians a year later, the Bossards remained, and sign stealing at Cleveland Stadium lived on. In 1950, Red Sox manager Steve O'Neill protested to umpire Charlie Berry, who made Indians manager Lou Boudreau close openings in the scoreboard. Again, the umpire's action clearly indicates that baseball believed the operation to be illegal, but not illegal enough to warrant a rule.[20]

In 1955, Boudreau found himself on the other side of the Indians' scheme as manager of the Kansas City Athletics. Suspicious after Indians catcher Jim Hegan smoked a curveball, Boudreau dispatched some coaches to investigate. They soon discovered one of the Indians relief pitchers standing near an army telescope. (The army had inadvertently left behind some equipment after a recent event.) The pitcher had been relaying information to the bullpen, where Hal Newhouser could signal batters by spreading his legs for a fastball or crossing them for a curve. According to A's second baseman Spook Jacobs, the telescope was so powerful "you could see the white on the fingernails of the catcher."[21]

In July 1951 the struggling New York Giants created baseball's most notorious sign stealing program prior to the recent Astros. On June 30 the Giants had acquired reserve infielder Hank Schenz from the Pirates. Schenz had experience stealing signs from a previous stop with the Cubs. After a team meeting in mid-July, Giants manager Leo Durocher began his club's program. He planted Schenz in the Giants' clubhouse in straightaway centerfield, with his telescope focused on the catcher. Durocher also had an electrician hook up a buzzer system from the clubhouse to the dugout and the bullpen.

Initially, the system functioned with Schenz buzzing the dugout and another player yelling a code word to the batter. Unfortunately, Schenz proved a poor signal decipherer and the shouting from the dugout risked exposure. Durocher instead installed coach Herman Franks, an ex-catcher, in the clubhouse with the telescope and had the signal go to the bullpen instead of the dugout. One of the players in the bullpen would then signal the batter, with the specific indicator changing often enough to prevent suspicion.

With the system in place, the Giants engineered one of baseball's most famous comebacks, going 40–14 during August and September and overcoming a 13-game deficit to finish in a tie with the favored Brooklyn Dodgers. In the three-game playoff series, the Giants won the first game, 3–1 at Brooklyn's Ebbets Field, then dropped the second 10–0 in their home park. This set up a winner-take-all match between these two historic rivals at the Polo Grounds.

For seven innings, the game was a pitching duel between the Giants' Sal Maglie and the Dodgers' Don Newcombe. The Dodgers broke through with three runs in the top of the eighth, giving the visitors a 4–1 lead that held into the bottom of the ninth. The Giants promptly rallied for three hits off Don Newcombe, making the score 4–2 with one out and two on. Brooklyn manager Charlie Dressen summoned Ralph Branca to face Bobby Thomson. The Giant third baseman promptly lined a home run to left field, perhaps the most famous home run in baseball history, forever known as "The Shot Heard 'Round the World." Thomson and Branca would be defined by this home run for the remainder of their lives, and the game's strategic decisions were debated by baseball fans, writers, and historians for decades.

Years later, bullpen catcher Sal Yvars disclosed that he had signaled Branca's fateful pitch to Thomson from the centerfield clubhouse. When pressed fifty years later as to whether he had relied on the signal, Thomson hesitated before saying, "My answer is no. I was always proud of that swing."[22]

Branca later revealed that he had been told by an ex-Giant three years after the home run that they had been stealing his signs. "I made a decision not to speak about it," he said. "I didn't want to look like I was crying over spilled milk."[23] In 1962 as other sign stealing accusations were popping up, Associated Press sportswriter Joe Reichler reported that a member of the 1951 Giants (whom he did not name) told him about the buzzer system. Dan Daniel wrote at the time, "The charge that the Giants, in 1951, were aided by a spotter who rushed the dope to the batter via a dugout buzzer is not new. From what I've heard about it, I would be inclined to regard the story as true. ... However, I am not ready to accept it in connection with Bobby Thomson's pennant winning homer off Ralph Branca."[24]

Durocher denied and mocked the accusation, "The story is ridiculous and not fair to Thomson.... There was no buzzer. There was no information to go on. He used his own judgement." Second baseman Eddie Stanky cannily deflected the allegation by detailing how the Giants stole signs legitimately, by getting them from baserunners. The full story of Durocher's sign stealing caper remained buried until 2001, when *Wall Street Journal* writer Joshua Prager published an article based on interviews with many of the players from the Giants.[25]

Stanky always maintained that the Giants won because of pitching and fielding. In fact, the evidence backs this up. The Giants offense over the last couple of months of the season did not improve, averaging 5.5 runs per game in the Polo Grounds before July 20, 4.9 runs per game after. It was on the defensive side where the team excelled over the final two months.

A primary reason that many of these programs stayed secret for so many years is that they were so common. If every team is cheating, the countermeasure is not to rat out the opponent, but to cheat better. Furthermore, with players frequently changing teams, none of these schemes could remain proprietary for long. When George Kell was playing for the Red Sox in 1952, he was introduced to Boston's operation: a pitcher unlikely to be needed that day, such as the previous day's starter, would hide inside Fenway Park's renowned left field scoreboard. The spotter would signal the batter through one of several predetermined signals. When Kell was traded to Chicago in 1954, he brought the tactic with him. The White Sox placed a player or employee in their electronic scoreboard, installed just a few years earlier, armed with binoculars to steal the catcher's signs. Once deciphered, the pitch type would be passed along to the compliant scoreboard operator who would flash a light—red or green—to indicate what was coming. And there were dozens of players switching teams every year.[26]

For the most part, managers merely grumbled when they believed an opponent was mechanically stealing their signs; given the lack of a formal prohibition, they had no recourse beyond hoping that exposure would shame a team into desisting. In 1956 Baltimore manager Paul Richards suspected the White Sox were up to something, and he spoke up: "They did it last year," Richards said. "And they're doing it now with a high-power telescope through a little hole in the scoreboard."[27]

According to Richards, AL president Will Harridge had told him that there was nothing the league could do to stop it.

Harridge denied that Richards formally notified the league office, and essentially threw up his hands: "If we definitely saw somebody out in centerfield with some big machine, our umpires would make an honest effort to stop it, but if the person running the machine refused to move, I don't know what the umpire could do."[28] Not surprisingly, this did little to discourage the practice.

The Giants moved to San Francisco after the 1957 season and unveiled a new operation at Seals Stadium during the 1959 pennant race. They placed an employee in the scoreboard who signaled to the batter using two predetermined slats. After a 13–6 victory over Milwaukee Braves star pitcher Warren Spahn, the Giants were two games ahead with eight to go. Their advance may have been foiled by an honest ballplayer.

Thirty-year-old pitcher Al Worthington, who had been with the Giants since 1953, learned of the scheme and refused to tolerate it. Worthington, who hailed from Birmingham, Alabama, had always been religious, but a trip to a Billy Graham crusade the previous year had deepened his faith. He went to manager Bill Rigney and told him that he considered spying from centerfield to be cheating, and that he would quit if Rigney didn't put a stop to it.

Surprisingly, Rigney was sympathetic, and the Giants terminated their spying after the ultimatum. Worthington was a useful pitcher but not essential to the squad, and one can only wonder at the commitment of the regulars to the program in the first place if they were willing to give it up so easily. Years later Worthington said that Rigney was a friend, and that many players did not support the sign stealing. In their subsequent series against the Dodgers, San Francisco lost all three games and eventually the pennant.[29]

Fate would soon bring together two prominent opposing voices on this matter. Late in the 1960 season, Worthington joined the White Sox, who, as luck would have it, were owned by Bill Veeck. Not surprisingly, Veeck had seen to it that the White Sox had their own sign-stealing operation at Comiskey Park, utilizing lights in their scoreboard. Perhaps the news of Worthington's anti-cheating stance had not made its way to Chicago, but it would not take long to resurface.

After appearing in four September games for Chicago and not pitching particularly well, Worthington learned of the spy system. When he approached manager Al Lopez, he got none of the support he'd previously received from Rigney. "As a player it was none of his business what we were doing," Lopez recalled. "But I did say, 'Show me in the rule books where it is wrong.' I told him I respected his religious beliefs. I said I hoped he would respect mine, and that my religious beliefs would not permit me to do anything I thought wrong."

Having failed with Lopez, Worthington took the matter to his boss, vice president Hank Greenberg. As we have seen, Greenberg had been an enthusiastic sign stealer as a player, and his opinion hadn't changed much since 1940. "Baseball," Greenberg responded, "is a game where you get away with anything you can. You cut corners when you run the bases. If you trap a ball in the outfield, you swear you caught it. Everybody tries to cheat a little." Worthington answered: "How can I be a follower of Christ and go along with something that's dishonest?"[30]

With two strikes on him, Worthington went to the head boss, Veeck. You can imagine how that went. When Worthington informed Veeck that someone on the club was stealing signs from the scoreboard, Veeck responded: "Of course, who do you think bought him the binoculars?"

Veeck was unapologetic. "I tried to reason with him. I said, 'Look, you cheat when you throw a curve ball, in a sense.' Then I thought about his curve ball and I realized he didn't." Worthington didn't buy the logic (or perhaps the humor). He acted on his convictions and went home to Alabama.[31]

Hornsby, in the role of an interested observer, was similarly unsympathetic: "Worthington's ethics are wonderful for a game between the Humane Society and the Salvation Army, but they're just plain stupid in the majors."[32]

Many in baseball felt Worthington "was a bit odd," and Greenberg had trouble unloading his contract after the season.[33] He spent 1961 and 1962 in the minors before resurfacing with Cincinnati in 1963.

Worthington's teammates, however, seemed to accept him—with some gentle ribbing; one year the Reds gifted him a pair of binoculars at a season-ending party. There were no continuing issues over sign stealing, which strongly suggests that the Reds and Twins were clean, in this matter at least. Worthington never expressed any regret for his stance on the issue. And he played until 1969, retiring at 40, with several solid seasons.

Worthington's teams were far from unique, and the increasing public accusations of sign stealing, especially in the NL, began to concern the league's owners, particularly since there was no reliable way to combat it. Moreover, a few of the previously guilty managers were having second thoughts. Birdie Tebbetts, who'd claimed credit for his own role in the Indians' earlier signaling scheme, was now a reformed spy, believing the use of devices to steal sign was wrong.[34]

Boudreau, who had now been on the receiving end a few times, also proclaimed a change of heart: "Every team has done it at one time or another, but I'm never going to resort to it again. I have a son (Lou Jr., 13) I'm trying to teach good sportsmanship, fairness, and honesty. Anything you can learn on the field I believe is legitimate. The other way is just plain thievery."[35]

Braves hurler Lew Burdette, a notorious spit-baller, expressed yet another criticism against sign stealing, claiming that it lengthened games. "I was talking with [Dodgers pitcher] Don Drysdale. He thought all the business we have to go through to conceal signs adds as much as thirty minutes to every ball game. I agree with him."[36] A half-hour was likely an exaggeration, but there can be little doubt the signaling cat-and-mouse contest added to game times.

In March 1962, Dick Young reported in the *Daily News* that Commissioner Ford Frick had made the Cincinnati Reds remove sign-stealing apparatuses during the 1961 World Series, and that Frick had put all teams on notice: "Should a team be proven to have employed mechanical means to steal signs during a ball game, the game shall be declared forfeit."[37] It is unknown why this policy was never announced—though Frick told the Associated Press in March when rumors of the Giants' 1951 sign stealing came to light: "I am definitely opposed to such practices. If such a charge were substantiated, I would forfeit the game, but I would have to have evidence."[38] In any event, sign stealing did not abate, and Frick's threat was never applied.

In July 1962, Frick disclosed that he had engaged private detectives to find evidence of sign stealing and said that more formal rules would be introduced at the 1962 league meetings. None, in fact, were forthcoming. Sixty years after the National League had failed to discipline the Phillies for their scheme, little had changed.[39]

In June 1971, White Sox manager Chuck Tanner accused the Indians (perennial perpetrators) of stealing signs from their center-field scoreboard. "I'm going to ask the commissioner to have that scoreboard controlled. I complained to the umpire that I wanted to play the game under protest. He said he couldn't do anything about it. Our pitcher breaks a curve ball that falls off the table and their guy waits for it and hits a frozen rope. Our guys in the bullpen say they saw guys with binoculars out there."[40]

Ken Harrelson, who played with the Indians in the early 1970s, later described their adaptation of the scheme: A man stationed in center field with binoculars would signal with his legs. When a breaking ball was called, he would bare his leg showing a white sanitary sock.[41]

Of course, you don't need binoculars if you have extraordinary eyesight. Angels catcher Buck Rodgers claimed that pitcher Don Lee was such a person. "He could stand in the bullpen in Cleveland and steal signs," Rogers recalled. "He'd put a hand on the fence if it was one pitch and take it off if it was another. Sounds impossible but I was there. I was the beneficiary."[42]

To what lengths would a team go? In 1973 Milwaukee introduced Bernie Brewer at County Stadium. Stationed in a faux chalet beyond centerfield, Bernie would speed down a 40-foot slide into a giant imitation beer stein to celebrate Brewers home runs, while an accomplice would release balloons. During a July series in Milwaukee, Texas manager Whitey Herzog reported malfeasance. "They haven't taken a bad cut all weekend, and those guys aren't that good a hitting team."[43] Herzog discovered that the balloon man had a pair of binoculars and was decoding the Rangers' signals. Bernie Brewer, who was wearing a pair of easy-to-spot white gloves, clapped twice for a curve ball.

Umpire Bill Haller investigated and told the balloon man to leave and made Bernie Brewer take off his gloves. The Brewers denied the allegations. "No one gave me no signs," first baseman George Scott said. Given the inability to prove any wrongdoing, Herzog said he wasn't going to file a complaint with the league office. "The way to stop that stuff is give the curve ball sign and then throw a fastball at the batter's head. But heck they'd probably beat us anyway if we played again."[44] It's notable that Haller was willing to act despite the lack of a rule. The league offices, however, continued to ignore the issue.

A few years later Herzog, managing the Royals, was the victim again. On the morning of September 21, 1976, the Royals led the second place A's by six games, as the two clubs began a three-game series in Kansas City. Oakland had won the AL West five years in a row and were not ready to go quietly. In the first inning A's pitcher Stan Bahnsen hit Royals centerfielder Amos Otis in the back of the head, and Otis was carried from the field on a stretcher. Bahnsen then brushed back Hal McRae. These teams did not like each other.[45]

Later in the game, two teenage members of the Royals grounds crew stationed in the visitors' bullpen noticed an A's reliever using binoculars and looking towards home plate. The kids mentioned it to Royals pitcher Paul Splittorff, who passed the message along to Herzog.

Second base umpire Joe Brinkman trotted out to the bullpen to check on the accusation, with Herzog trailing along. When the men arrived, they saw A's relief pitcher Rollie Fingers putting binoculars

into their case and covering them up. Herzog accused the A's of signaling the bench via walkie-talkie. He filed a protest with the league
office, only to be told that there was no rule against stealing signs. "I
don't know where they [the binoculars] came from," said A's manager
Tanner. "I didn't know they were out there. Anyway, you can't get
signs from the left field bullpen."[46] And so it went.

The introduction of television into baseball, beginning in the 1950s,
changed cheating considerably. With many, and eventually all, games
televised, fans at home could easily see that balls being "caught" in the
outfield were, in fact, trapped; that fielders did not always touch their
bases; and that pitchers sometimes had foreign substances on their
hats. Umpires do not like being shown up, so they naturally became
more vigilant. When instant replay review entered the game in 2009,
players could no longer get away with deceptions that had been part
of the game for more than a century.

On the other hand, teams inevitably found ways to use television
signals to their advantage. In July 1959 NBC introduced more powerful cameras with an 80-inch lens for its broadcasts, and the center-field
cameras could show the catcher's signals. With this advance, fans at
home could see catcher's signs, could anticipate the coming pitch,
could even second-guess the selections made by the pitcher and
catcher. It soon dawned on everyone that if a person at home could
do this, the opposing team could as well. Why not just put a TV in the
dugout? After the new camera had been in use for a couple of weeks,
Commissioner Ford Frick became concerned about how it could be
abused and ordered the removal of the center-field camera.

Though NBC complied, their sports director, clearly not a student
of baseball, said he did not believe any team would actually use the
signal to cheat. Yankees catcher Yogi Berra agreed: "I don't think
it would have much value. The catcher can change his signals, his
series, or system of signals all the time."[47] It is to Frick's credit that he
anticipated the potential abuse, though his solution was overkill. Just
when baseball was getting its first real challenge from professional

football, the commissioner banned a popular and useful view of the game, rather than simply prohibiting televisions in the dugout.

The first known attempt of a team using the television feed to steal signs did not come until 1976. During the that year's ALCS matchup with the Royals, Yankees manager Billy Martin stationed a couple of scouts, Bobby Cox and Jerry Walker, in the WPIX television booth to communicate with coach Gene Michael on the bench. There was no rule against having personnel in the dugout with walkie-talkies speaking with people outside the dugout. The Royals found out about the plan when a switchboard operator at a Kansas City business mistakenly plugged into a call between Yankees executive Cedric Tallis and an unidentified man. The switchboard operator listened for a couple minutes and told the Royals front office that he had overheard Tallis discussing the walkie-talkie shenanigans. Tallis denied such a conversation ever took place, bizarrely suggesting that someone else might have used his name.

Once confronted, Yankees owner George Steinbrenner preemptively informed league president Lee MacPhail of the operation. MacPhail—yes, using the same old excuse—acknowledged there was no rule against what the Yankees had done. Martin innocently claimed that the scouts were merely advising Michael on the positioning of the Yankee fielders. The Royals concern, of course, was that the men in the booth were detecting the catcher's signals from the center-field feed and communicating with Michael in the dugout. MacPhail assured the Royals that there would be no center-field feed to the television booth as long as the Yankees scouts were there.

Herzog was unappeased. "It's a joke," he said. "The league president shouldn't allow binoculars in the bullpen, and he shouldn't allow the use of walkie-talkies on the bench. Lee says there's no rule against the walkie-talkies. That's the same thing I was told when we found Oakland using binoculars in the bullpen. If there's no rule, then make one."[48] Sounds logical, but no dice.

Once the Yankees advanced to the World Series against the Reds, they hoped to use a similar setup. They received permission from

Commissioner Bowie Kuhn to station one scout in the upper deck with a two-way radio to help position the fielders. Instead, Martin posted three of his senior team—Birdie Tebbetts (an experienced sign stealer), Clyde King, and Karl Kuehl—in the CBS Radio booth on the fifth-floor press level, giving them access to television monitors, including the center-field camera feed. Cincinnati GM Bob Howsam protested this violation of the agreement, but Kuhn was surprisingly forgiving; rather than revoking permission altogether, he allowed the Yankees to resume the original agreement, even permitting a second man in the upper deck.[49]

Kuehl proclaimed his innocence, suggesting that if the Yankees wanted to cheat they could just watch the television in the clubhouse. This is true, though the TV feed would not show the center-field angle consistently, whereas the Yankee officials had all angles the entire game. The real issue, which Kuehl's sentiment highlights, is that baseball should have simply banned all electronic devices, including walkie-talkies, in the dugouts. Such a prohibition might have saved a lot of headaches in coming decades.[50]

Martin still was not satisfied, calling into further question why he'd wanted the walkie-talkies in the first place. He accused the commissioner of lying, claiming there was never any agreement limiting the Yankee officials to the upper deck. When asked if he feared being fined, Martin responded, "I'm telling the truth. Is someone not telling the truth going to fine someone who is?"[51] Kuhn later fined Martin $1,000, not so much for his actions but for this unnecessary confrontation.

For the next decade television and communications technology continued to evolve. Coaches started wearing earpieces, making their use of radio transmission less obvious. And though the "eye-in-the-sky" was still permitted, it was restricted to the press box area for defensive positioning purposes.

Teams also began using television game footage to decode their opponent's signals for later use, an entirely legal tactic that changed the nature of sign stealing. Prior to the 1980s, teams only telecast a subset of their games. With the advent of superstations and the pro-liferation of cable, teams now had a library of games with which to analyze the behavior of their competitors. When a team got a player to second base, he would no longer have to decipher signs on the fly; he potentially already knew how to decipher the catcher's signals and could quickly communicate to the batter.

The division-winning 1984 Chicago Cubs were early adopters of this approach. The club designated someone in the clubhouse to watch the center-field feed. Once the sequence was cracked, a runner on second could relay what pitch was coming. "We knew the other teams' signs better than our own," coach Johnny Oates later said.[52]

Advances in communications, video, and computing technology had altered the balance between the security of signs and the tools to decode them. The pressure to disguise signals grew commensurately, adding time and complexity, and new rules—long delayed—became even more necessary. Moreover, these new technologies affected other areas of baseball innovation, offering new temptations to cheat.

Chapter Three

ESPIONAGE

WHILE MOST OF THE CHEATING we cover in this book revolves around recognizable baseball activity, occasionally we've seen more brazen forms of rule-breaking. Like thievery.

"Competitive edge is fleeting," Oakland general manager Billy Beane said in 2013. "As soon as you think you've got it, it's probably already passed you by. That keeps us on our toes. We know someone out there is doing something better, wiser and smarter. So there's always a certain amount of intellectual insecurity that we have."[1]

Beane had been the primary subject of *Moneyball*, Michael Lewis's ground-breaking 2003 book about Oakland's innovative use of analytics, and Beane's insecurity largely centered on ideas. In an industry where operations staff frequently move from team to team, it is inevitable that successful franchises will see their best ideas replicated by other organizations. What Beane might not have anticipated was that teams could steal not merely ideas in people's heads, but computerized intellectual property.

Until the twenty-first century few would have suggested that baseball teams had trade secrets worth stealing. Clubs maintained detailed scouting reports on amateur and professional players, but these would have been stored in paper files. The value of these reports would not justify the Watergate-style operation required to steal them.

Things began to change when a significant number of teams began using computerized databases and first-generation sabermetrics to evaluate players and strategies, roughly a generation ago. Most organizations kept their modernization secret, but this was primarily because of potential controversy over using the newfangled metrics, not because they feared that their work would be pilfered.

The story advanced considerably in the spring of 2000, three years before the release of *Moneyball*. Under the direction of general manager John Hart and Assistant GM Mark Shapiro, the Cleveland Indians created a database dubbed DiamondView. Rudimentary by today's standards, the database stored scouting information and grades along with proprietary statistical rankings. The ability to quickly access detailed information about players in every organization conferred an advantage when considering recalls or trades.

Cleveland's cutting-edge program reflected the confluence of two ripening innovations: (1) new sabermetric insights into how to value players and (2) affordable increased computing power. Over the next decade nearly every MLB team would come to see the need for an organizational database.

As proprietary information became increasingly computerized, teams became much more cautious. "A veil of secrecy has descended over sports unlike anything the industry has ever seen," Matthew Futterman wrote. "All research is proprietary. General managers will barely mention which statistics they focus on, much less which companies they use to gather data, or how many people they employ to analyze it. A scout could tell a rival over a beer, 'that kid really has some pop in his bat.' But when numbers and formulas get into the picture, all of a sudden lips clamp shut."[2]

By 2009, Cleveland's DiamondView had expanded dramatically, containing, for every player, a scouting report back to high school, newspaper stories, blog articles, psychological test results, and detailed notes from every conversation with him and his agent. Other teams were aware of what the Indians were doing. However facetiously, the Arizona Diamondbacks once offered outfielder Carlos Quentin to Cleveland in exchange for DiamondView.[3]

Now there was something worth stealing. The desire to know everything that other teams knew proved to be a powerful temptation.

In 2003, the St. Louis Cardinals hired Jeff Luhnow as vice president for baseball development. Luhnow had degrees in engineering and economics from the University of Pennsylvania, held an MBA from Northwestern University, and had served as a management consultant for McKinsey—but he had never worked in baseball. Nevertheless, Luhnow soon revamped the Cardinals' player procurement and development operations, opening a baseball academy in the Dominican Republic and expanding the team's activities in Venezuela. Three years later, he was put in charge of both scouting and the farm system. The stellar 2009 draft, when the Cardinals landed Shelby Miller, Joe Kelly, Matt Carpenter, Trevor Rosenthal, and Matt Adams, testified to the Cardinals' success in blending traditional scouting and analytics.

As part of an analytical makeover, Luhnow oversaw the creation of a proprietary database, at one point called "Redbird Dog." To help with the sophisticated algorithms and valuation metrics, in 2005 Luhnow hired decision scientist Sig Mejdal, a baseball outsider with analytics credentials. In 2009, the Cardinals added Chris Correa, who had a bachelor's degree in cognitive science, a master's in psychology, and had nearly completed a doctoral program that combined psychology and education to better understand how people learn. This was part of the growing trend in baseball to hire people for their analytical skills rather than their baseball experience.[4]

In November 2011 Jim Crane, who primarily made his fortune in freight, logistics, and supply chain management, bought the Houston Astros. One month later, Crane hired Luhnow as general manager, to bring cutting-edge analytics and team-building strategies to the

Astros. The Astros had just lost 106 games and a considerable rebuild was in order. Luhnow hired Mejdal as Director of Decision Sciences.

As part of his own hiring process, Luhnow prepared a 25-page dossier on how he planned to turn the Astros around, which included a database and analytical program. Luhnow began development of the Astros' new platform almost immediately. The system, dubbed Ground Control, was up-and-running roughly a year later.

"What's happening in the baseball industry is not too different than what's happening in other industries," said Mejdal. "The amount of data available to make your decision is growing ... exponentially. The importance of assisting the human decision-maker with decision aid is important in any field."

By 2014 Ground Control included player video and statistical projections that were revised immediately after every game (including in winter and foreign leagues). The program also generated emails to all appropriate staff, noting every single player transaction throughout baseball.

Luhnow's first priority was getting the people who worked for him to collect and value information above all else. "I don't want to go back to a world where I'm making decisions without the information," he said. "That's a scary world."[5] By 2013 Luhnow likely had more information at his disposal than any general manager in history.

But the Cardinals soon caught up.

In March 2013 (and possibly earlier), Chris Correa, still with the Cardinals, hacked into the Astros' Ground Control program, in the first-known case of team versus team industrial espionage. According to the US government's later investigation, Correa's access totaled at least 50 intrusions over at least 15 months. Moreover, Correa had unfettered access to Sig Migdal's email account for roughly two and a half years (January 2012 to June 2014), giving him a matchless lens into the Astros' thinking.[6]

The government's report provided specific details on what Correa stole and when. On March 24, Correa spent more than an hour and half reviewing Astros' scouting and draft information: how the Astros ranked draft-eligible players, their proposed bonuses, and medical and scouting information. In early April Correa studied the Astros' data on Gonzaga pitcher Marco Gonzales, and many other players. On June 6, St. Louis made Gonzales their first-round draft pick (19th overall).[7]

In the leadup to the July 31 trade deadline, Correa reviewed logs of internal trade conversations. Late in the year Correa reviewed trade negotiation logs before the winter meetings.

In March 2014 Correa accessed Houston's rankings and bonus recommendations for the upcoming draft; scouting reports on targeted players; overviews of highly regarded college athletes based on Houston's sophisticated analytics; ongoing projects being pursued by the analytics team; and notes of Astros trade talks and minor league reports, including evaluations of players in the Astros system.[8]

In March 2014 Houston finally became aware of a security breach, and both MLB security and the FBI joined the hunt for the offenders. No one knew where the intrusions were coming from or had any idea of the motive.[9]

On June 30, the website Deadspin published excerpts from 10 months of Astros trade talks that had been leaked to Anonbin, a document-sharing website that allowed anonymous uploading. Someone had sent an anonymous email to Deadspin to tip them off on the upload. The publication humiliated Luhnow and the Astros, who now had to soothe the egos of the players mentioned in their trade discussions. Luhnow also had to apologize to his front office rivals for the exposure of their private conversations. Moreover, the breach provided ammunition for people who believed that Houston's front office had been over-praised.[10]

In January 2016, Correa pleaded guilty to illegally accessing the Astros' computer system. The stolen information was valued at $1.7 million. Correa was ordered to pay $279,038.65 in restitution and sentenced to 46 months in prison.

After the sentencing, Major League Baseball performed its own investigation. Commissioner Manfred found that Correa had acted alone but awarded the Cardinals' two highest picks in the 2017 draft, selections 56 and 75, to the Astros. He also fined the team $2,000,000, relatively paltry for a major league baseball franchise, but the maximum allowed under the Major League Constitution. Manfred placed Correa on the permanently ineligible list, joining Shoeless Joe Jackson and Pete Rose.

There have been no subsequent reports of team-versus-team encroachments. Given these punishments, it's not surprising.

But how was Correa able to break into the Astros system in the first place? The initial intrusion came because Correa apparently figured out Mejdal's password, starting with what it had been with the Cardinals and eventually deducing how it had been changed.

Correa took care to mask his hacking. He used the anonymizing platform Tor to disguise his identity and location and utilized a feature on Onion Browser to "spoof" or mislead the host computer as to the access source. Nonetheless, the FBI was eventually able to trace the hack to the Florida computer. According to the government's summary: "Tracking down a crime over the internet—particularly someone who is actively masking their identity and location—is not easy. It takes a lot of time and detective work to reconstruct what happened and who did it. It also requires technological skills, a scarce commodity even among FBI agents."[11]

The government conjectured that when Correa realized that his window for breaching Ground Control had shut, he uploaded the collection of trade discussions he had stolen earlier, largely to embarrass Luhnow and the Astros, but perhaps also to materially weaken the Houston organization.[12]

After he was caught, Correa claimed that he had first infiltrated Ground Control because he believed Luhnow and Mejdal had appropriated intellectual property from the Cardinals system. When he pleaded guilty in court, he offered this same excuse to the judge. Correa's attorney asked the court to subpoena materials from the Astros' computer system that might demonstrate they had come from the Cardinals' system. The request was denied.

A year later, Correa maintained this position, that the Astros had stolen from the Cardinals first, and that Correa had hacked into their system to confirm his suspicions.

Ground Control may have had elements from the Cardinals database system, but it's hard to sympathize with Correa's claim. In roughly fifty breaches of Houston's network he had reviewed proprietary information on draft-eligible players, trade conversations, and internal analysis that could not have come from Luhnow's time in St. Louis. It is perfectly natural that Luhnow's team would create a system like the one in St. Louis that Luhnow had overseen with such success. But the key element in the database is the data, which was being updated literally every day. By the time Correa hacked the Astros system, Luhnow and Mejdal had been away from the Cardinals for 18 months.

Also, per the court transcript, Correa did not do any of the things one might expect of a wronged party. He didn't report his suspicions to any of his superiors in the organization, he didn't write up a memo for his own files—despite downloading heaps of other information—and he didn't notify law enforcement. He did mention that he told "colleagues," but none were ever named, and the commissioner's report concluded that Correa had acted alone.[13]

Moreover, before law enforcement caught up with him, Correa seemed much more equivocal about Ground Control. "Nothing is the same as it was three or four years ago when Jeff left or Sig left," Correa said in January 2015. "I'm sure they're making improvements, too, to the point that they want to be, you know, better than all the other teams. But I don't really think it's all that productive for me to be worrying about what other teams are doing."[14]

The Astros denied any culpability. "I'm very aware of intellectual property and the agreements I signed," Luhnow said. "I didn't take anything, any proprietary information. Nor have we ever received any inquiries from anybody that even suggested that we had." He also concurred with Correa's pre-detection sentiment: scouting reports became outdated quickly and metrics were constantly being enhanced.[15]

In the wake of Correa's crimes and his accusations against Luhnow and Mejdal, Commissioner Manfred encouraged baseball's general managers to review their employment contracts, particularly since baseball's rules didn't explicitly address the issue of intellectual property.

Executives in most industries are free to move from a company to a competitor, and often they bring knowledge with them. Baseball is no different. "If someone leaves, they're allowed to take what's called the residual intellectual property with them, which is anything they remember in their head," Luhnow said. "They're not allowed to take anything beyond that.... Also, information gets dated pretty quickly."[16]

To date there have been no other instances of a team accusing an ex-employee of taking proprietary information to another job. Teams are prohibited under the league constitution from suing each other—lawsuits being a reliable means of wrongdoing becoming public—and are required to adjudicate their disputes in front of the commissioner. If baseball has held any such disciplinary hearings, they have not been publicly revealed.

Many other talented executives, Theo Epstein for example, have been able move between teams without any taint. We hope, especially given increased awareness and precaution, that Correa's acts were an unfortunate aberration.

The Correa story illustrates how diligently a team needs to protect its intellectual property. This has never been truer than it is today, when many teams are processing and analyzing an ever-growing amount of data gathered on the field of play.

A comparatively humorous dustup popped up toward the end of the 2021 season. During a game on September 20, the Rays' Kevin Kiermaier was tagged out at home plate by Blue Jays catcher Alejandro Kirk, the third out of the inning. Unnoticed by Kirk, a card with information on how the Rays pitchers should pitch to the Jays hitters fell out of his wristband. As Kirk headed off the field, Kiermaier scooped up the card and carried it back to the Rays' dugout. Once the Blue

Jays realized what had happened, they reportedly sent a bat boy to the Rays dugout to get the card back. Tampa refused.

Given baseball's recent controversies, many media outlets framed this story as another stealing scandal. Over the next couple of days, they weighed in on the propriety of Tampa Bay's handling of the data card. Both managers discounted the incident, though Kiermaier was plunked by a pitch two days later.

In many ways this squabble reflects the growing impact of technology and analytics in the game. Players carry cards with them because they need written cues to keep track of how to contest the pitcher or batter, or where to play on defense. But if the game is going to allow players to carry cheat sheets onto the field, the responsibility to protect them should fall on the players. If baseball allows teams to detect signs using their eyes and brains, it should allow Kevin Kiermaier to pick up a dropped note card.

New technology is driving the mountains of data that players have to act on in real time, so there will likely be more controversies. Clubs are employing scores of analysts who try to uncover exclusive insights from Statcast, a high-resolution, camera-based tracking system deployed throughout all big-league ballparks. Statcast output consists of gigabytes of data per game that track the ball, the fielders, and the batter simultaneously, offering a comprehensive look at everything that occurs on the field, including a detailed breakdown of batter-pitcher confrontation.

Adding a new wrinkle, the use of wearable devices has exploded over the past few years. Teams are actively processing and integrating an avalanche of biometric data to better understand athletic capabilities, improve training, and minimize injuries. There is an opportunity for a significant tactical advantage in being first or developing better algorithms to tease useful, actionable information from the newly available data.

And that's not all. KinaTrax uses an array of synchronized high-speed cameras to minutely map a pitcher's motion or a batter's swing. Edgertronic developed a high-speed camera to identify pitch release and grip. Rapsodo also introduced a camera and radar system to analyze velocity, spin rate, and additional metrics for batters and pitchers.

Baseball's Collective Bargaining Agreement, as of 2021, says that the use of wearable devices is voluntary. It broadly defines wearables as "activity trackers, electronic bat sensors, biomechanics compression attire, GPS/tracking compression attire and any device, sensor, equipment, attire or dashboard technology which is designed to measure a Player's health, performance and/or readiness."[17]

Four devices are currently approved for in-game use in MLB. In 2016 baseball sanctioned the Motus Baseball Sleeve with a built-in sensor to measure elbow stresses, and the Zephyr Bioharness which monitors vital signs and athletic output. The next year MLB authorized WHOOP, a wrist strap that collects physiological data (roughly 100 megabytes per day), including sleep information, and Catapult, a vest with sensors to measure swing or pitch intensity. Bat sensors from Blast Motion and Diamond Kinetics have also been approved but are not yet permitted for in-game use, though specific Blast Motion sensors may be used in minor league games and in the complex leagues.[18]

Under most circumstances, biometric data is not considered medical information under the Health Insurance Portability and Accountability Act of 1996 (HIPAA), a federal law that regulates the release of individuals' medical information. Only three states (Illinois, Texas, and Washington) have enacted their own laws to strengthen HIPAA privacy. In the meantime, each sports league and its union have negotiated how this player-specific data can be used. In baseball, the basic agreement specifically defines the personnel who are allowed access to this data, including the GM, manager and medical personnel.[19]

"I think this stuff is really useful," said Mariners outfielder Mitch Haniger, "but at the same time, you don't know who's taking this information and where it's going to."[20] How this data is used and who can use it are much more substantial issues, at the moment, than the opportunity for one team to gain an unfair advantage over another on the field. Some of the player concerns have been settled, but with the explosion of data available, there are likely to be disputes down the road. Are teams allowed to use any of the data when negotiating contracts with players? Which data can be used for injury-prevention research? These and other concerns could lead to contentious exchanges.

Biometric data also leads to several moral conundrums surrounding injury prevention. Imagine a scenario where the New York Yankees, via its own proprietary research, discover a way to reduce the frequency of ulnar collateral ligament or rotator cuff injuries in pitchers or hamstring or knee injuries for position players. Do they have an obligation to share this knowledge? Or imagine a player who benefits from this research being traded to a different team. Wouldn't he wish to continue with his theoretically proprietary treatment? Injury prevention is the current Holy Grail for baseball analytics, and you can be sure that teams are on the cusp of technological breakthroughs in this area. Moral quandaries are sure to follow.

But the potential for cheating is not negligible, as the analytics derived from this data are viewed as trade secrets by each team. Beyond its proprietary nature, the biometric data and its interpretations are not currently part of the player's medical record. So, while the CBA gives teams the explicit right to share medical information when a player's contract is being assigned to another team, biometric data cannot be shared. When a player is being considered for a trade, this has the potential to create unequal information between the teams.[21]

In September 2016, MLB suspended San Diego general manager A. J. Preller for 30 days for his misuse of medical records and fined the Padres an undisclosed amount. According to an ESPN.com story, Padres officials instructed trainers to keep two sets of medical records for their players: one to be potentially shared with other teams and the other for internal use only. The distinction was made to help the team make trades. For example, on July 14 Preller traded hurler Drew Pomeranz to the Red Sox for pitching prospect Anderson Espinosa. Pomeranz's elbow was receiving treatment, a detail reportedly not disclosed to Boston. In another reported instance, the Miami Marlins were not informed of San Diego pitcher Colin Rea's elbow discomfort before acquiring him on July 29. Miami baseball operations chief Michael Hill chose not to air his concerns publicly, but after Rea had one injury-abbreviated start, the Marlins traded him back to San Diego on August 1.[22]

"I accept full responsibility for issues related to the oversight of our medical administration and record keeping," Preller said after he returned from his suspension. "I want to emphasize that there was no malicious intent on the part of me, or anyone on my staff, to conceal information or disregard MLB's recommended guidelines."[23] One competing baseball operations executive expressed his bitterness at the relatively light penalty, "He [Preller] won. He doctored medical records and got one of the best pitching prospects [Espinosa] in baseball while doing it."[24]

Will teams try to steal or hide information in the future? The prison term given to Correa makes it less likely that we will see front office executives directly hacking into their competitors, but that doesn't mean that executives won't try to gain advantages via proprietary data. How hard will teams pressure new employees to reveal their former teams' secrets? Short of actual hacking, are there ways to procure proprietary information? Can data be manipulated to present an inaccurate picture of a player's medical or biometric records?

One can imagine future opportunities to take unfair advantage of evolving technologies. Could a team somehow release a flawed algorithm to be picked up by another team and used to its detriment? When it is finally operational, will teams attempt to illicitly interfere with the electronic ball and strike evaluator? As technology increasingly becomes part of the game, the amount of intellectual property data grows, and the rewards for stealing it grow commensurately.

As Mark Twain cleverly noted, "[While] History doesn't repeat itself, … it often rhymes." As if to underscore the point, the Houston Astros, who created the state-of-the-art database that Correa hacked in 2014, were caught three years later in their own technology-aided cheating scandal.

Chapter Four

SMART WATCHES AND TRASH CANS

S WE DISCUSSED IN CHAPTER 2, baseball players and other on-field personnel began using signs as early as the 1870s, and almost simultaneously began trying to detect their opponents' signals. Managers and coaches use signs to tell the batter whether to swing or take, the runner whether to steal or stay, and fielders when to execute a pickoff play. These signals are made in plain view of opponents and fans, and canny players have been known to successfully detect the information being transferred.

The most common baseball signals are from the catcher to the pitcher to communicate what pitch to throw. The art of pitching is based on fooling the batter with location, speed, and movement, but the catcher needs to know what is coming. Most simply, a catcher will simply flash a certain number of fingers, with "1" representing a fastball, "2" a curveball, etc., depending on what pitches a particular pitcher throws. The catcher also moves his fingers to tell where he wants the pitch thrown. The simplicity is because opponents—the batter, manager, coaches—generally cannot see the signs, concealed between the catcher's thighs. If a batter attempts to sneak a look, the next pitch might get thrown at his head.

But is there is a runner on second base? That changes everything; suddenly the catcher's signs are exposed.

Baseball history is riddled with stories of teams trying to steal a catcher's signs. Until very recently there were no rules against the practice, nor had any player or team ever been disciplined for it. That said, the people within the game have long differentiated between different methods of sign stealing. In Chapter 2, we introduced the McGraw Doctrine: any sign stealing performed with the eyes and brain is OK, but the use of binoculars or other devices is cheating.

A sign-stealing operation often involves two steps. First, a team must learn the opponent's pattern. A catcher could flash a series of signs but it might be the third sign that signifies the pitch. Or it might be the second sign after he flashes four fingers. A catcher might use the same signs for several games, or switch every game, so a team would have to steal several signs in order to break the code. The second step is to use the discerned pattern and current signal to determine what the upcoming pitch is going to be.

In the early 1990s teams began stationing their own cameras around the ballpark to capture video of their players for training and coaching purposes. Inevitably, teams realized that these cameras could also be used to steal signs. Red Sox general manager Dan Duquette complained to the league in both 1995 and 1999 that Cleveland was stealing Boston's signs via a center-field camera. The umpires ordered the Indians to put a towel over the camera, but otherwise the league took no corrective or investigative action.[1]

Most notoriously, in 1997 the Mets, managed by Bobby Valentine, had three cameras, purportedly for filming their hitters, but allegedly for stealing signs: one pointed at the third-base coach, one at the dugout, and one at the pitcher. For the pitcher, the Mets supposedly hoped to capture "tells," differentiating movements that could tip off the batter to the type of pitch that was coming. The team was apparently not using the camera feeds in real time, but to determine the sign pattern for later use. This was not a common practice; only one other team, the White Sox, had been suspected of using video to record and decode third-base coaches' signs.

The Phillies complained to the NL office. They had discovered that the Mets cameras were pointing to their coaches and dugout. The complaint reached the MLB, which said they'd checked it out but were assured by the Mets that the cameras were only to study their own hitters.

Opposing managers offered different perspectives. "We can't do anything about the cameras," Texas manager Johnny Oates said. "We're all sitting in the clubhouse watching other catchers on the clubhouse screen." In contrast, Colorado manager Don Baylor said, "It's part of cheating. It shouldn't be allowed at all. It's easy to do in today's world with cameras and things." Baylor went on to add that the Orioles in the 1980s had a similar arrangement, "They had a video that went directly into the clubhouse where someone was deciphering the signs."[2]

These reactions over the ethics of video-enhanced sign-stealing mirror the decades-long debate over binoculars. Despite umpires occasionally stepping in, and occasional threats of discipline from the league offices, no one had ever been kicked out of a game, suspended, or fined for mechanical or electronic sign-stealing. But there was always some stigma and a fear of repercussions associated with the act.

In 2001 MLB clarified the rules, telling clubs: "Please be reminded that the use of electronic equipment during a game is restricted. No club shall use electronic equipment, including walkie-talkies and cellular telephones, to communicate to, or with, any on-field personnel, including those in the dugout, bullpen, field and—during the game—the clubhouse."[3] After roughly a century, baseball was finally formalizing the McGraw Doctrine.

Nonetheless, it took just two years for the next video controversy. In 2003 the Red Sox had a television in their bullpen, installed with permission from MLB, so that their relievers could better follow the game. Before long, some of their opponents believed that Boston was using the TV for less innocent reasons. After being swept in a late August series at Boston's Fenway Park, Seattle Mariners GM Pat Gillick implied that something fishy was going on. But when asked directly if he thought Boston was cheating, Gillick only allowed, "I can't say. That's up to the commissioner's office to decide." MLB (sort of) resolved the situation, ruling that Boston had to remove the televisions from their bullpen.[4]

Allegations continued. In 2005, White Sox pitcher Mark Buehrle accused the Rangers of stealing his signs using what was described as a "high tech light system in centerfield." According to Buehrle, "I've heard rumors, so it's not just me saying this. Something's going on because they hit so good at home. Certain pitchers you throw, they lay off them like they know what's coming." At the time the Rangers were hitting .285 with 125 home runs at home and .256 with 86 home runs on the road. Texas first baseman Mark Teixeira ridiculed Buehrle, saying, "It's an outrageous accusation."[5]

In 2007, the Mets charged the Phillies with stealing their signs using a center-field camera. Someone in their video room, the allegation claimed, would decode the signal and buzz a coach in the dugout. The coach would then yell a code word to signal the batter. According to reports, MLB did not pursue this further because the camera did not send a live feed directly to the dugout, an incongruous response given the specifics of the accusation. Phillies manager Charlie Manuel dismissed the charge, saying, "I think it's just a matter of guys talking and running their mouth. You can check us all you want to."[6] The next year the Red Sox also complained about the Phillies.[7]

In 2010 the Rockies claimed that Phillies coach Mick Billmeyer was using binoculars—an old-school technology—in the Coors Field bullpen to spy on catcher Miguel Olivo. As evidence, the Rockies submitted the FSN Rocky Mountain game video, which showed outfielder Shane Victorino in the Phillies dugout using the bullpen phone. The Phillies became one of the first modern teams to be formally warned about sign stealing. MLB claimed to have found nothing conclusive but warned GM Ruben Amaro Jr. and asked umpires to be extra vigilant. Interestingly, the 2001 communication regarding electronic sign stealing apparently did not address binoculars, so there was still no rule prohibiting their use.[8]

Despite the warning, Commissioner Bud Selig was laissez-faire and somewhat nostalgic about the episode and sign stealing in general. "I have to tell you now, you could get me started on history—stealing signs has been around for 100 years," Selig said. "In my days as a Braves fan way back when, Bob Buhl was caught in the bleachers in Wrigley Field giving signs to [Joe] Adcock, [Eddie] Mathews and [Hank] Aaron."[9] After all these years, nobody in management really seemed to care.

Video had not yet fully displaced binoculars as the preferred stealing tool. In 2011, sources told ESPN that they had watched a man dressed in all white stationed in the blue center-field seats at Toronto's Rogers Centre raising his hands above his head for any off-speed pitch and keeping his arms down for a fastball. An analysis accompanying the investigation noted that the Blue Jays were hitting much better in their home park.[10]

For years thereafter there would be occasional, mostly unsubstantiated, sightings of the "man in white." But teams would soon move on to more advanced techniques.

The rapid advances in sign stealing in the twenty-first century have occurred largely because of new technologies and savvy front offices. In January 2014 when MLB expanded its video review program, they added live-feed television monitors near the dugouts to assist managers in their challenges of umpire decisions. After decades spent finding ways to hide spies in the bleachers or coaches in the press box, teams now had a full range of live video just a few steps from the manager.

Baseball's rules governing video cameras had apparently not been materially updated since 2001. They stated that "no equipment may be used for the purpose of stealing signs or conveying information designed to give a Club an advantage," which left a wide gray area around potential sign-stealing.[11] The use of video to steal signs that could be immediately communicated to the batter was clearly banned. But prohibitions on other actions were not so clear. For example, if a team used video monitors to learn the oppositions' sign sequences but the runner on second still had to detect the current sign in real time, some players and teams might not regard this as cheating.[12]

A new wrinkle popped up a year later. In April 2015, Apple introduced its Apple Watch, a wearable computer that could communicate with Internet-based devices. Within a couple years it had taken its place in baseball's long sign-stealing story. In a game against the Yankees in August 2017, a Red Sox assistant trainer was seen using an Apple Watch in the dugout in violation of the rules against using on-line electronics during a game. In response, the Yankees lodged a complaint with MLB that included several videos of the Red Sox dugout.

Boston's sign-stealing process started with a video replay operator in the video-replay room decoding the pitch selection and forwarding the information to the assistant trainer in the dugout via his Apple Watch. The information was then communicated to one or two players. Unlike many of the other systems described in this chapter, Boston's approach was designed such that the player in the dugout then relayed the pitch type to a runner on second base, who would signal the batter. This long chain, requiring a runner on second and a meaningful amount of time even with the electronic communication, obviously had limited efficacy.[13]

An investigation by the commissioner's office confirmed wrongdoing by the Red Sox. Like all commissioners before him, Rob Manfred was still reluctant to come down hard: "The investigation established three relevant points. First, the violation in question occurred without the knowledge of ownership or front office personnel. Second, when the Red Sox learned of the Yankees' complaint, they immediately halted the conduct in question and then cooperated completely in my investigation.... Third, our investigation revealed that Clubs have employed various strategies to decode signs that do not violate our rules. The Red Sox' strategy violated our rules because of the use of an electronic device. Taking all of these factors as well as past precedent into account, I have decided to fine the Red Sox an undisclosed amount which in turn will be donated by my office to hurricane relief efforts in Florida." The fine was for the electronic transmission of texts to the Apple Watch, not for using the video-replay room feed to decode catcher signals in real time. The commissioner found insufficient evidence to support the counterclaim by Boston that the Yankees were unfairly using the YES Network feed to decode the Red Sox signs.[14]

The prohibition of electronic equipment was complicated by several new (honest) technologies. For example, the BATS video system, used by players to examine their swing after each plate appearance, includes the center-field camera angle that provides a view of the catcher's signs. Many hitters have come to rely on this information for legitimate reasons.[15]

In reponse to the Apple Watch incident, Manfred drew a line in the sand. On September 15 he sent out a bulletin putting all clubs on notice that future violations would be taken very seriously and stating that the general manager and manager would be held responsible.[16]

During the 2017 NL Wild Card game, Diamondbacks coach and interpreter Ariel Prieto was caught wearing an Apple Watch in the dugout, in violation of major league rules. MLB investigators "forensically examined" the watch and found no inappropriate use. Because the violation occurred after Manfred's Red Sox ruling, however, MLB fined both Prieto and the Diamondbacks for the mere act of possessing the watch in the dugout.[17]

Baseball writer Jeff Passan balanced the Apple Watch controversy with the access to the video feed: "Almost every team in baseball blurs the line of cheating on a daily basis.... Devices like cell phones and Apple Watches are not allowed in dugouts ... and iPads are, because MLB partnered with Apple to allow them as a replacement for managers' information-stuffed binders. Meanwhile, teams position replay monitors mere feet outside of the dugout—legally—and can gain every bit the advantage Boston sought."[18] In fact, iPads were legal as a sort of high-tech, three-ring binder. They could be preloaded with analytical and video information but could not be connected through the Internet or any other link.

After the Arizona slipup, Manfred kept up his firm new stance, expanding the sign-stealing directive. In March 2018, Joe Torre, MLB's Chief Baseball Officer, issued a memo to teams, reminding them that connected electronic devices *of any kind*—phones, smart-watches, walkie-talkies, tablets, laptops—were prohibited in or near the dugout, bullpens, or field. Furthermore, using electronic equipment anywhere in the ballpark to steal signs during a game was forbidden. *"To be clear,"* Torre wrote," *The use of any equipment in the clubhouse or in a Club's replay or video rooms to decode an opposing Club's signs during the game violates this Regulation.* [Emphasis in original]"[19]

With the previous year's September memo reinforced by this directive, in-game electronic sign-stealing and decoding had finally, unambiguously, become cheating—including the ambiguity around in-game sign stealing transmitted through a runner on second. No longer simply frowned on by the game's consensual ethic or the unen-forced 2001 clarification, in-game electronic sign-stealing was now unquestionably illegal.

In a further sign that Manfred was unwilling simply to trust that teams would comply, in 2018 MLB stationed an employee in the replay booth. During the regular season a single person was assigned to watch both the home and visitors' rooms. For the playoffs, MLB stationed a monitor in each of the replay booths, a practice carried through the 2019 season.[20]

When Jim Crane bought the Houston Astros after the 2011 season, he assumed control of a depressed asset. After 40 years of existence, the team had never won a World Series, and had just concluded its worst season (56–106) in franchise history. As we learned in Chapter 3, Crane hired Jeff Luhnow—the farm and scouting director of the world champion Cardinals—as his general manager and gave him the authority to remake the organization. Luhnow got to work.

The club had terrible seasons in 2012 and 2013, which Luhnow considered unimportant in his rebuild. In 2014, *Sports Illustrated*'s Ben Reiter spent a few weeks with the Astros, partly because no other team would give him access, and came to believe that their innovative organizational philosophies would redefine how baseball teams should be run. After three last-place finishes, Reiter's cover story boldly predicted that the Astros would win the 2017 World Series. Remarkably, the team took a big step forward in 2015 to make the playoffs, and then won 101 games and the World Series in 2017, just as Reiter had forecast. The next year he wrote an entire book on the club—*Astroball: The New Way to Win It All*—further praising the geniuses in the Astros front office.[21]

Since the 2003 publication of Michael Lewis's *Moneyball*, front offices have come under the microscope as never before. By 2018, no front office was receiving as much attention and praise as the Astros.

But then the story began to change.

During the 2018 AL playoff games against the Indians and Red Sox, a Houston employee was ejected from the area next to the dugout, a spot limited by policy to specifically credentialed personnel, including TV reporters and photographers. The employee was accused of videotaping the opposing dugouts in order to record signs and other possibly proprietary information. Astros GM Jeff Luhnow claimed that the Astros were trying to protect themselves. "We were playing defense," he said. "We were not playing offense."

Because it was not obvious whether the Astros intended to use their recording to track signs, it was not a clear violation of Torre's directive. MLB exonerated the Astros, echoing Luhnow's position: "A thorough investigation concluded that the Astros employee was monitoring the field to ensure that the opposing club was not violating any rule." But MLB also prohibited such actions going forward: "All Clubs remaining in the playoffs have been notified to refrain from these types of efforts and to direct complaints about any in-stadium rules violations to MLB staff for investigation and resolution."[22]

In the NL playoffs, teams were similarly vigilant. Colorado pitching coach Steve Foster reportedly felt that in the NLDS the Brewers were anticipating pitches, particularly sliders, better than they should have been.[23] On the other hand, in the NLCS some Brewers were concerned the Dodgers were stealing their signs with the help of video. "You've seen a couple times where something looks a little bit off," pitcher Zach Davies said. "That's something that's part of the game. When you start using technology and when you start using guys outside of the baseball team to try and figure out what set of signs a pitcher is using, that's a little ... that kind of crosses the line." Follow up by *The Athletic*, however, found that baseball's security staff posted in the video areas observed no irregularities, nor was there any indication that what the Dodgers might have been up to would have been illegal. In fact, the Dodgers counter-claimed that the Brewers were stealing signs using an in-game feed. The league apparently investigated without uncovering any evidence.[24]

In light of the increasing paranoia, baseball initiated a number of restrictions before the start of the 2019 season. These included limiting cameras between the foul poles only to those used for the broadcast, putting the broadcast feeds into areas of the park on an eight-second delay, and adding a room monitor to make sure nothing illegal was occurring. According to the same *Sports Illustrated* report, MLB also required that each team's head of baseball operations and manager had to sign a document stating that the team complied with all sign-stealing rules. Baseball had moved beyond the McGraw Doctrine, advising the teams that alerting batters to the pitch type by audio signals was prohibited even if the signs were detected fairly.[25]

Nevertheless, by the fall of 2019 rumors and accusations of sign stealing were rampant. Cubs pitcher Yu Darvish mentioned a September game in which he stepped off the mound multiple times because batter Christian Yelich, the 2018 NL MVP, appeared to be looking out to left field in the neighborhood of the Brewers' bullpen, as if trying to see a signal. He stopped short of outright accusing Yelich of anything. But Yelich fired back anyway: "Be better than this. Nobody needs help facing you."[26]

In stories about the Astros filming opposing dugouts in the 2018 playoffs, other allegations surfaced of the team's malfeasance during the season. "A's players noticed Astros players clapping in the dugout before pitches and believed they were relaying stolen signs to hitters in the batter's box," wrote Jeff Passan in Yahoo! Sports. "The A's called the league, which said it would investigate the matter…. Two major league players said they have witnessed the Astros hitting a trashcan in the dugout in recent years and believe it is a way to relay signals to hitters."[27] But without players willing to go on the record, and in the absence of other actionable evidence, little came from Passan's story.

On November 12, 2019, Ken Rosenthal and Evan Drellich finally broke the story. Their reporting in *The Athletic* featured statements from several people associated with the 2017 world champion Astros, including pitcher Mike Fiers (now with the A's). He was the first player to speak on-record. Shortly thereafter, popular Twitter user Jimmy O'Brien, known by his handle of Jomboy, unearthed and published video evidence of the trashcan-banging scheme.[28]

Publication of this exposé forced the league to investigate. Manfred had drawn his line in the sand two years earlier, and here was a team that had apparently crossed the line—repeatedly and brazenly. To induce the players to talk, MLB cut a deal with the players union granting them immunity. After interviewing 68 witnesses, including 23 current or former Astros, the league issued its findings.[29]

According to the commissioner's report, Houston launched their scheme at the start of the 2017 season (before his September 2017 directive that put teams on notice). The Astros were aided in their decoding by a spreadsheet algorithm dubbed "Codebreaker" that could unravel the complex sequence of signs used by the battery. For every pitch, an employee would enter the catcher's finger sequence (example: "one finger, three fingers, fist, one finger") and the pitch that was thrown. The spreadsheet software would decipher the pattern to accurately predict the next pitch.[30]

At first the Astros were not relaying signs directly to the batter from the bench; they were detecting the current pattern so that a runner on second could use it to decode the sign in real time. Staffers in the video-replay room would decipher the catcher's hand/finger signals using the center-field video feed, and the pattern would be relayed to the bench. If the Astros got a runner to second, he could better read the catcher's signals and alert the batter.

This was clearly against the rules, because the video detective work was being used in the current game. Pitcher Clayton Kershaw, whose Dodgers had been victimized in the 2017 World Series, did not hide his disgust. "The only thing that bothers me is the real-time stuff," Kershaw told *Sports Illustrated*. "I'm sure a lot of teams were going up to that line, but once [Houston] started doing it in real time and using technology in real time, that's what separates it. I'm sick of people saying that everybody was the same, that everybody was doing it. No. We weren't all doing that. That was separated from everybody else."[31]

Two months into the 2017 season the cheating grew more egregious, as the Astros began using the video to determine the actual sign, and relay it immediately. Some of the players, including veteran Carlos Beltran (the only player identified in the commissioner's report), worked with team employees to install a monitor near the dugout that was hooked up to the center-field video feed. An assigned player would watch the monitor and, if he could determine the pitch (informed by the pattern that Codebreaker had deciphered), someone might bang a plastic trashcan located next to the dugout. Interviewees also noted that they tested other methods, including clapping, as noted in Passan's 2018 story. Perhaps most significantly, the Astros continued flouting the rules even after Manfred issued his September 2017 memo clarifying and emphasizing the prohibition and penalty.[32]

It may sound dubious that the complex series of catcher signs could be synthesized into an act as simplistic as hitting a trashcan. After all, the catcher is signaling for one of several possible pitch types, as well as its precise location. Indeed, Astros hitters weren't getting complete pitch information from listening to the smack of a plastic trashcan cover. But they got enough.

The best pitchers tend to throw different pitches while striving for a pitching motion that looks the same, to keep the hitter in the dark until the pitch is well on its way to the plate. A great slider, for example, might look just like a fastball halfway to home and then suddenly dive away from the batter into the dirt. Nothing is more frustrating to a fan in the stands, or on the couch, than watching one of their heroes swing wildly at pitch that is a foot off the plate and on the ground. "How can he swing at that pitch!" the fan will scream. Plate discipline—an important and valued hitting skill—often comes down to the ability to recognize whether the pitch on its way is going to maintain its path, or veer outside the strike zone. A hitter does not intentionally swing at bad pitches.

The Astros system—and most sign-stealing schemes—simplify all this information down to one question: Is this pitch going to break? The ability of a hitter to lay off sliders or curveballs in the dirt is a game-changing skill. If an Astros hitter heard a trashcan lid being struck, he knew that this pitch was likely to move, and he might not swing at it, even if the pitch looked like it was headed straight to the middle of the plate. Conversely, he might stay with a curveball, knowing it was likely to move into the strike zone.

In 2016, the year before their system was put in a place, the Astros struck out 1,452 times, the second-highest total in the American League. The next year, with the trashcan banging, their strike out total dropped by a whopping 25 percent, to the lowest total (1,087) in the league. This improvement, along with big gains in power and batting average, elevated the 2017 Astros to one of the best offenses in baseball history. Their 123 OPS+ (a normalized ballpark-adjusted measure of a team's offense) was the best in the AL since the 1931 Yankees. Perhaps one reason the Astros scandal has remained so persistently in fans' minds is that it was so effective. The 2017 Astros cheated, and their historic hitting won the World Series.

Before the 2018 season, the Astros apparently decommissioned their dugout monitor (perhaps because of Manfred's strengthened directives). But they continued using the replay booth to decipher the catcher's signals to use when a runner was on second, and had a player physically deliver this intelligence to the bench, where it was flashed to the runner. The program, still in direct violation of baseball's rules, was eventually dropped during the season.

Although manager A. J. Hinch was apparently uninvolved in creating or running the sign-stealing operation, his actions when he learned of it were surprisingly weak. According to the commissioner's report and his own later statements, Hinch smashed the monitor with a bat on two occasions. This did nothing but inspire the players to get a new monitor. Many told the league's investigators that they would have stopped the operation if Hinch had told them to. This naturally raises questions: Why would Hinch smash the monitor but fail to take the additional step of saying "please stop doing this"? And how could the players see the monitor getting smashed, without understanding this as evidence that their manager disapproved?

The commissioner's report generated much backlash from the public—mainly because while accusing players of driving the scheme, it named no one other than Carlos Beltran (who had already retired as a player). Named to manage the Mets after the 2019 season, Beltran resigned from that post after the release of the report. The players could reasonably contend that the commissioner's 2017 memo was issued to the clubs but not to the players or the MLBPA. In response, the MLB and players union finally agreed to stricter controls on the use of video and electronic devices in July 2020, and they enumerated specific discipline for any player who violated sign–stealing rules.[33]

Despite the report's contention that no violations were found post-2018, social media continued to buzz with innuendo that the cheating scandal had continued. It was difficult, for instance, to ignore the way second baseman José Altuve had refused to allow his jersey to be ripped off during the on-field celebration of his Game 6 walk-off home run, which won the 2019 ALCS against the Yankees. Accusers alleged that Altuve was wearing a buzzer attached to his chest that could signal the pitch type. A photo purporting to show a bulge in his jersey, and a tweet supposedly from Beltran's niece convinced some online sleuths. Altuve denied the charges, and the Beltran family denied the Twitter account belonged to a relative.

After all was said and done, the only people punished by the commissioner were Luhnow, Hinch, and bench coach Alex Cora, all of
whom were suspended for 2020. The Astros organization was also fined
and lost draft picks. But even then, the MLB soft-pedaled its findings: "The investigation revealed no evidence to suggest that Luhnow
was aware of the banging scheme," its report said. "The investigation
also revealed that Luhnow neither devised nor actively directed the
efforts of the replay review room staff to decode signs in 2017 or 2018.
Although Luhnow denies having any awareness that his replay review
room staff were decoding and transmitting signs, there is both documentary and testimonial evidence that indicates Luhnow had some
knowledge of those efforts, but he did not give it much attention."[34]

After the punishment was handed down, Luhnow continued to
proclaim his innocence. "It's pretty clear who was involved in the
video-decoding scheme, when it started, how often it happened and
basically when it ended. And it's also pretty clear who was not involved,"
he said. "I don't know why that information, that evidence, wasn't discussed in the ruling, wasn't used. The people who were involved that
didn't leave naturally to go to other teams are all still employed by the
Astros. In fact, one of the people who was intimately involved, I had
demoted from a position in the clubhouse to a position somewhere
else, and after I was fired, he was promoted back into the clubhouse. So
none of those people faced any repercussions. They weren't discussed
in the report, but the evidence is all there that they were involved."

In response, Manfred defended his findings. "The 22,000 electronic
messages that Jeff talked about over and over again were a fraction
of the evidence in the case," Manfred said. "There was a lot of other
evidence—electronic, testimonial—which indicated Jeff's culpability
in this matter. Secondly, whether he exactly knew what was going on
or not is really beside the point. After the Apple Watch incident [when
the Red Sox used the devices to steal signs against the Yankees], I
wrote to all the GMs. I put them on notice that it was their obligation
to make sure that their organizations were not violating any of the
sign stealing rules."[35]

Team owner Jim Crane also emerged mostly unscathed. Crane had hired Luhnow and by all accounts remained a strong backer as the GM rebuilt the club. Not only did Manfred not punish Crane, however, he went out of his way to absolve him: "At the outset, I also can say our investigation revealed absolutely no evidence that Jim Crane, the owner of the Astros, was aware of any of the conduct described in this report. Crane is extraordinarily troubled and upset by the conduct of members of his organization, fully supported my investigation, and provided unfettered access to any and all information requested."[36]

A common theme in most baseball cheating stories, especially in recent years, is that the person ultimately responsible for investigation and discipline, the commissioner, is an employee of the owners. The players are often well-protected by their union, which undoubtedly benefited them in the Astros scandal. But owners are protected by their position as the ultimate bosses of the sport. The people in the middle—in this case the general manager, the manager, and the bench coach—are the ones who had to walk the plank. It is perhaps telling that after all the cheating in baseball over the past 50 years, the two people who have received the harshest punishments for it are John Coppolella, a GM (discussed in Chapter 7), and Chris Correa, a scouting director.

The Astros fired Luhnow and Hinch, and Cora, who had moved on to manage the Red Sox, served his suspension. After the close of the 2020 season, Luhnow again denied any knowledge of the scheme and filed suit against the Astros to honor the remainder of his contract. Manfred stood by the conclusions in his report. In February 2021 Luhnow and the team jointly filed to dismiss the suit, and it was reported that the two sides had "resolved their differences."[37] In 2020, both Hinch and Cora were back to managing. Luhnow remains out of baseball.

Writers Rosenthal and Drellich published another sign-stealing exposé in January 2020, less than a week before the release of the commissioner's report on the Astros. During the 2018 and 2019 seasons—after the Red Sox had been fined and in the wake of the

Apple Watch controversy—they reportedly continued with their sign-stealing system, now minus the watch. Having resolved the Astros matter, Manfred launched a second investigation, again interviewing more than 60 witnesses, including many players, who were again granted immunity from punishment for participating. Manfred's investigation found that J. T. Watkins, a video replay room staffer, decoded signals during a game by the use of live feeds, but he had not relayed the information through electronic communications.[38]

Complicating the investigation was the fact that Watkins was also the advance scout responsible for providing to the players the signs of the opposing catcher. He studied video extensively between games to provide the correct patterns for players to use when they reached second base. Watkins denied using the in-game feed in real time; any feedback he provided came from his previous research or live feedback from players who reached second base. Nonetheless, several players told investigators that "Watkins's in-game communication … indicated to them that Watkins had at times acquired the sign sequence information from the replay room during the game." As somewhat mitigating factors, Manfred noted that the scheme only worked with a runner on second, and concluded that the Red Sox used the in-game feed "in only a small percentage of those occurrences." As a result, Watkins was suspended for 2020, and the team was docked a second-round draft pick.

Unlike the Houston case, Manfred did not discipline the Red Sox manager or general manager because he felt Watkins led a rogue operation that was not reasonably discoverable: "I do not find that anyone was aware of or should have been aware of Watkins's conduct," the commissioner wrote. "The Club's front office took more than reasonable steps to ensure that its employees, including Watkins, adhered to the rules."[39]

The prevalence of electronic sign-stealing during 2017 and 2018, beyond Houston and Boston, was subsequently reported by *Sports Illustrated*'s Tom Verducci. "Two sources familiar with the investigation," wrote Verducci, "which lasted three months and included more than 70,000 e-mails and 60 interviews, said various Astros personnel told MLB investigators about eight other teams who used technology to steal signs in 2017 or 2018—such was the culture of the time."[40] Precisely what they were doing, how often they were doing it, and how successful they were is unknown. In any case, MLB did not commence additional investigations (at least not publicly).

Earlier, we mentioned the Astros' incredible drop in strikeouts in 2017. This is true, but also true is that they remained a very low strike-out team through 2021, finishing best or next-best in fewest strikeouts every year from 2017 onward. The 101 wins in their breakthrough 2017 title year were surpassed in both 2018 and 2019, and they remain an excellent team, with or without cheating.

The debate over the usefulness of sign stealing has lasted almost as long as the debate over its legitimacy. No matter how good the sign stealing, there is always the possibility of being crossed up. Yankees legend Joe DiMaggio famously confronted coach Charlie Dressen, known as a master sign-stealer, for giving what turned out to be an incorrect sign that nearly caused DiMaggio to be hit in the head. Two others greats who didn't want to be given signs were Cal Ripken and Tony Gwynn. "What if they're wrong?" Gwynn once said. Cubs Hall of Famer and player-manager Frank Chance remembered being right about the pitch type, but still getting crossed up when the pitcher missed the sign and threw the "wrong" pitch.[41]

Moreover, hitting with knowledge of the pitch requires a different approach at the plate. Any time a player alters a rhythm he has per-fected over years of practice, he could be at less than peak efficiency. The benefits of pitch intelligence, in such cases, might be more than offset by deficits stemming from this change in approach.

Longtime manager Fred Hutchinson thought the value of sign stealing was exaggerated. "Most hitters don't know how to use 'em or don't want 'em," he said. "[Stan] Musial didn't or Joe DiMaggio, but I understand Ted Williams liked to know what was coming." Validating Greenberg's memory, Hutchinson recalled, "Two who were really terrors when they could be tipped off were Hank Greenberg and Rudy York."[42]

All that said, the energy and effort spent trying to crack codes, both legally and illegally, suggests that players and managers believe in the payoff. Former Marlins president David Samson testified to the importance his club placed on sign stealing. "Just know that the year we won the World Series in 2003," Samson said, "the bench players, their entire role every game of the World Series, they had one job to do; that was to steal signs of the New York Yankees."[43]

There have been few scholarly studies on the efficacy of sign stealing, partly because there is no certainty as to which signs have been stolen. Despite years of interviews and investigation, there is still doubt about Bobby Thomson's famous 1951 home run. (Did he get the sign? Did the sign help him?) In their research, Jayson Stark and Eno Sarris highlight this difficulty even for the Astros, who have been extensively examined. "Do we know if all those bangs on that trash can were completely and accurately recorded and detected? We don't," they point out. "Can we truly be sure exactly when that scheme began, or when it ended? There's still so much we don't know."[44]

But whiff rates are a pretty good measure. Backing up what we wrote earlier, Tom Verducci found that the Astros had a phenomenally low whiff rate on changeups outside the strike zone in 2017, which suggests that getting the signs is a benefit. During the 2017 postseason the Astros whiffed on only 5.6 percent (4 of 74) versus 21.4 percent for their opponents. During the 2019 postseason when there were MLB monitors in the video-replay booth, the ratios were much closer (18.4 percent for the Astros, 16.7 percent for their opponents).[45]

Since then, there have been several in-depth articles, many based on Tony Adams's video analysis of every game in which he could hear a trashcan bang. One investigator posted his research to Reddit: "Overall, Astros batters largely benefitted from the trashcan banging signal when it was more accurate (later in the season, as the scheme was honed) by laying off pitches that rarely ended up being called strikes.... However, they were negatively impacted by making contact on [off-speed] pitches at a lower clip when not receiving the bang signal in the latter part of the season."[46]

When factoring in the error rate in deciphering the pitch correctly, Rob Arthur concluded, "The net effect of the banging comes astonishingly close to being zero. Nothing. Statistically, for all the work and effort that went into the cheating scheme, the grand result of it, at least as measured in this way, turned out to be no runs at all."[47] At The Ringer, Ben Lindbergh concluded, "Knowing the next pitch just has to help, right? But no matter how we slice and dice the data, the statistical case is less compelling than it would be if sign stealing made hitting as simple as it seems like it should."[48]

Perhaps it simply takes time to learn to hit when knowing the signs. "You've got to know how to hit with signs as well as know how to get them," longtime player and manager Buck Rodgers once said. "And a lot of young players just aren't interested."[49]

Whether, or how much, the Astros benefited from their sign-stealing system is a relevant question for those who seek to understand how baseball works and what goes into making a hitter successful. But it does not change the fact that the Astros cheated, a charge not even the Astros have denied. Nor that the people who led their operation, the players, got away with it.

Going forward, we can assume that advances in technology will provide new opportunities for sign stealing: coded messages on the scoreboard, a specified advertisement or innocuous fan message. There are now many wearable technologies that could be used to inform players on what pitch is coming. Video, too, is widespread throughout ballparks: commercial feeds for television, league-sponsored video for analytical purposes such as Statcast, video used for replay challenges, and video installed by the teams for their own scouting and player development purposes. Everything that occurs on the field is now recorded in high resolution in real time.

With all of these temptations, baseball, 120 years into its story, finally appears committed to stamping out mechanical or electronic sign-stealing. Apart from the ethical questions, an indisputable benefit is faster games. Commissioner Manfred and the MLB have embraced this, echoing what Don Drysdale noted many years ago: the effort to continually camouflage and modify signs slows the game significantly.

But technology operates at warp speed, and baseball had begun experimenting with technological solutions to aid the catcher and pitcher, even before *The Athletic*'s exposé of the Astros. Pitcher Jeremy Hellickson and catcher Spencer Kieboom tested a specialized wrist device to transfer signals during spring training in 2019, but were not enthusiastic. "It's not practical at all," Hellickson said. Kieboom was more circumspect, saying, "Very rarely the first time you ever try something is it gold."[50]

Since then, the technology has advanced. In the summer of 2021, MLB tested a new electronic-signaling system, named PitchCom, in the Low-A West minor league. A transmitter with multiple buttons worn on the catcher's wrist connects with a receiver in both the pitcher's cap and catcher's helmet. After some initial skepticism, at least one league hurler felt like the device could be useful. "You're always hesitant to try new things," said Stockton Ports pitcher Jake Walkinshaw, "and now you're thinking it's kind of going to mess with your routine…. Honestly, I have no complaints with it and I think using it with a guy on 2nd base instead of throwing down 4 or 5 signs and figuring out a sequence, I think it's going to speed up the game for us."[51] MLB also allowed the device to be used in the Arizona Fall League in 2021.

Other options under consideration include earpieces for communication between pitcher and catcher, lights embedded in the mound that can be activated by the catcher, and a wearable random number generator used to indicate the correct sequence.[52]

But perhaps the simplest and best solution would simply be to turn off all transmitting and receiving technology to the dugout during the game, including the video replay booth. The initial purpose of the challenge replay system was to allow managers to protest calls that were obviously wrong as seen by the naked eye. It was not to hold up the game while team staffers look at a call from multiple angles to see if a runner's hand came off the bag for one-tenth of a second while the fielder held his tag. If that is the level of scrutiny baseball wants, then someone can review these plays in a national booth in real time and call down to the umpires to reverse the call. In any case, it should not be the responsibility of the team, and removing that responsibility would allow baseball to remove the monitors. As for the old-fashioned binoculars and signaling operations, it has never been difficult to spot—the problem has always been baseball's unwillingness to investigate and punish.

Policing sign stealing should also be aided by its nature as a group activity. Nearly all the players on a team will be aware of any shenanigans because of the scheme's inherent complexity. One of the most-surprising aspects of the Astros' arrangement—and all the ones that came before it—is that it stayed secret as long as it did despite so many people knowing or being involved.

As we will see, exposing a violation often depends on the trade-off between how easy it is to detect and how much baseball's culture is committed to eliminating it.

Chapter Five

PENNY NAILS AND CORK

I
N A 1966 TELEVISION EPISODE OF "Bewitched," Samantha, a witch living a normal life in contemporary society, attends a Halloween party with her husband, Darrin. Also in attendance is Willie Mays, who greets Samantha as one would an old friend. When Darrin expresses surprise at the presence of the superstar, he asks his wife if Mays is also a witch. "The way he hits home runs," says Samantha, "what else?" Mays tells his companions that it's about time he headed to the ballpark and … promptly disappears.[1]

A couple of years later, the show returned to baseball. In a dream sequence for Darrin, Samantha receives a phone call from Mickey Mantle (who does not appear onscreen). "Oh, Mr. Mantle, I'm surprised at you," she says into the phone. "But that wouldn't be fair. If I worked it out so that you could hit .600, I'd have to let all the other players bat .600…. And besides, I'm a Mets fan."[2]

While no baseball player is known to have practiced actual witchcraft, history has no shortage of batters concocting all manner of methods for breaking the rules.

The most famous incident of a baseball player using an "illegal bat" goes back to 1983, in what has become known as "The Pine Tar Game." On July 24, a Sunday afternoon, the Royals and Yankees played at Yankee Stadium. The clubs were both in contention, though trailing in their division races. Having played four league championship series in the past seven years, the teams took these games seriously, whether in July or October. "There was no love lost between the teams. We didn't like each other," remembered Lou Piniella.

On this day, 34,000 fans in the stadium watched their Yankees enter the ninth inning clinging to a 4–3 lead, and the first two Royals went down easily. When U. L. Washington lined a clean single to center field, Yankees manager Billy Martin summoned relief ace Rich Gossage to face George Brett. Brett was the Royals star and leader, and entered the game hitting .352. It was a classic matchup. "I hated George Brett," remembered Gossage.

Gossage threw a high fastball and Brett hit it into the right field seats, giving the Royals a 5–4 lead. Or so most everyone thought.

By the time Brett had circled the bases, Martin had grabbed his bat and was conferring with home plate umpire Tim McLelland. Martin claimed that Brett had used an illegal bat, with pine tar extending above the lower 18 inches. The facts of the case were not in dispute, nor was Rule 1.10(b), which set the 18-inch maximum. After the four umpires conferred, McLelland called Brett out, and the game over. Brett went berserk and stormed home plate, aggressively confronting McLelland. It took several minutes to clear the field.

Martin had been alerted to Brett's bat a few weeks earlier by Graig Nettles, his third baseman. Because he was Billy Martin, he kept this information to himself until the absolute perfect moment. Which, give the man his due, he found.

So why did Brett have so much pine tar on his bat? "I applied [pine tar] before every at-bat. I was one of the few players that never wore batting gloves. On July 24 it's pretty hot in New York and a little muggy, so your hands sweat, so there was a lot of rosin, there was a lot of pine tar on my bat, and I used that bat for probably three or four weeks. As a result of using a bat for that length of time and putting pine tar on four, five times a day, it's going to get pretty ugly, and the bat was pretty ugly, but it was still working."[3]

No one believed, then or now, that Brett was trying to gain an advantage. Slobbering pine tar on the bat does not make the ball go farther. The Royals protested the game, not because Brett's bat wasn't illegal, but because they felt that the punishment did not fit the crime.

A few days later, American League president Lee MacPhail agreed, and in his first ever upholding of a protest, reversed the umpires and restored the home run. Yankees owner George Steinbrenner, at the height of his George-ness, said, "If the Yankees should lose the Eastern Division Race on the ruling of MacPhail, I would not want to be Lee living in New York City."[4] This comment led to a $300,000 fine for the Boss.

On August 18, 25 days after the home run, the game was resumed with the Royals now leading 5–4 and still batting with two outs in the ninth. Martin would not go quietly—he started the proceedings by appealing that Brett had missed second or third base, either one. The umpires on hand for the end of the game were not the same crew who had been on the field three weeks earlier, when the home run was hit, but realizing that they were dealing with Martin and his legendary intelligence and temper, they came prepared. They presented sworn affidavits from the previous crew that both Washington and Brett had touched all the bases. With that settled, the third Royals out and the Yankees three outs in the bottom of the ninth went very quickly.

This was not the first time baseball had to deal with the pine tar issue. Prior to the 1975 season baseball fine-tuned the rule concerning illegal bats. A batter would be out if he "hits a fair ball with a filled, doctored or flat surfaced bat, in which case he should be immediately ejected from the game and suspended by the league president for three days." Opposing players and managers treated this like an appeal play, keeping the violation to themselves until it would most benefit their team. If they saw an opposing player with too much pine tar on his bat, they would wait until he got a hit and then inform the umpire.

Sometimes the umpire would declare the batter out; sometimes he would disregard the complaint (or simply not acknowledge that excessive pine tar was in fact "doctoring")—it was all highly arbitrary.

In July 1975 with two out in the first inning of a game at Minnesota, Yankees star Thurman Munson seemingly singled home Roy White from second with the first run of the game. Twins catcher Glenn Borgmann and manager Frank Quilici appealed the hit to umpire Art Frantz. The two claimed Munson had pine tar beyond the regulation 18 inches. The umpires bought out a tape measure and verified the Twins' claim. They ruled Munson out, and the Twins escaped the inning. After a game in August in which Cubs' pitcher Steve Stone was similarly declared out, umpire Andy Olsen opined that roughly a half-dozen players had lost hits that way. In neither the Munson case nor the Stone case did the hitter's manager appeal the decision.[5]

Adding to the confusion, the league presidents ignored the dictum that they were supposed to suspend the player. NL front office executive Fred Fleig said, "That part of the rule is too severe.... I happen to think doctoring a ball is much worse an offense than using an illegal bat. Yet a pitcher, for throwing a spitball, only gets a warning on a first offense."[6] In another novel take, umpire Tom Gorman refused Mets manager Roy McMillan's request to take a hit away from San Diego's Dave Roberts on the grounds that the league had guided him to use the bat's trademark as the upper bound, not a measured 18 inches. Many other "appeals" were denied as well.[7]

At least one ruling led to a protested game. The California Angels believed the Royals' John Mayberry had pine tar too far up his bat, and after he homered they appealed to umpire Bill Kunkel. Kunkel allowed the home run to stand, and the Angels protested the game. MacPhail, league president in 1975, rejected the protest. He noted the spirit of the rule mattered, and in any case, he was not going to order the game replayed over such a minor issue. It is certainly easier to support the umpires and turn down a protest than to order a game replayed—as MacPhail did in 1983—but his sentiment was clear: too much pine tar was not an at bat altering offense.

The owners recognized the confusion and changed the wording of the rule, making it more specific. But they didn't explicitly address the penalty for too much pine tar, other than mandating that the bat be removed from the game. They did, however, issue a regulation that "the use of pine tar shall not be considered doctoring the bat."[8] This seemingly terminated the numerous "appeals" over too much pine tar. At least until the Brett affair in 1983.

The rules governing the physical structure of the bat are clear. The bat must be made from one piece of solid wood. It must be no more than 42 inches in length, and no more than 2.61 inches in diameter at its thickest part, dimensions not much different from 150 years ago. A batter can use pine tar or other sticky substance on the handle, but no more than 18 inches from the end. Bats today are typically made of ash or maple, but players have experimented with many other varieties of wood, hoping to uncover some advantage, however small.[9]

Hall of Fame baseball pioneer George Wright told stories of players experimenting with doctored bats as early as 1860. Some would drill a hole into the end of the bat and stuff it with various materials to see which might be most effective. Among the substances Wright reported was the use of lignum vitae (an extremely dense and heavy wood), and later "small rubber balls." The batter was trying to get more weight, or alternatively, more "spring."[10]

Bat doctoring expanded with advent of baseball's first professional association in 1871. "There were many suspicious circumstances and shady incidents," wrote John H. Gruber in 1915. "The bats had, no doubt, suffered desecration by having holes bored into them, in which metal, particularly lead, was poured." This led to the National League, when it was formed in 1876, modifying the rule to require that the bat be *wholly* made of wood.[11]

For several decades most bat doctoring was designed to add weight to the bat, especially once Babe Ruth brought the power game to the sport. Ruth, and contemporaneous writers, claimed he used a bat that weighed as much as 52 ounces, though the records of his orders with the Louisville Slugger company, as well as the many Ruth bats that have survived, indicate that his bats weighed 38–42 ounces in mid-career, and about 35 ounces by the end. That is still a very big bat by today's standards. Hitters in the 1920s held the view that they should wield the largest bat they could effectively swing.

George "Specs" Toporcer recalled George Sisler, the great St. Louis Brown of the 1920s, loading his bat with nails and having it confiscated. Ted Kluszewski, Cincinnati slugger of the 1950s, hammered 10-penny nails into his bat. The idea was more weight, specifically more weight in the barrel.[12]

The problem, of course, is that a heavier bat is harder to swing. "There are two things which drive a baseball hard," Rogers Hornsby said almost a century ago, "the weight of the bat and the speed with which it moves. The two are direct opposites. No matter how much strength a batter has, he cannot handle a heavy bat with as much speed as a lighter one." Along the same lines, Harry Heilmann thought Ruth would be an even better hitter if he used a lighter bat.[13] In fact, Ruth did begin to lighten up soon after.

In the past few decades, players have generally used light bats, more in the 31–33 ounce range, with thin handles, swinging them at maximum speed. Cheating has transformed accordingly, with the focus shifting to making bats lighter. Instead of filling the hole with lead, how about cork?

A modern bat corker will drill a hole, about one inch in diameter and 10 inches in length, into the end of the regulation bat. He then fills the resulting hole with cork (or Styrofoam, or rubber balls), glues a wooden plug on the top of the hole, and finally sands and finishes the top so the alteration is hidden. The bat will now weigh about 1.5 fewer ounces.

There are other illegal ways of doctoring a bat. In 1975, Ted Simmons had a home run disallowed and was called out for having a grooved bat. "I took a knife and put some grooves in the grain of the bat so it wouldn't fray on me.... All they do is keep the bat from splitting." Longtime manager Dave Bristol had another take: "All those old guys used to burn their bats and groove them and put pine tar in there. Makes a harder surface than wood." Precisely how the grooves helped was not entirely clear. Hall of Famer Pee Wee Reese believed the reason for grooving a bat "is to get the ball airborne." On the other hand, umpire Paul Pryor said, "You're less likely to pop up a ball" with grooves. Chuck Tanner, who spent nearly all his adult life in baseball, including stints as a player and manager, remembered a unique way St. Louis Browns third baseman Bob Dillinger doctored his bat. "[He] used to take a plane and just barely plane off one side of his bat," Tanner recalled.[14]

One of the first famous bat-doctoring incidents involved Yankees third baseman Graig Nettles in a 1974 game at Detroit's Tiger Stadium. Facing Woody Fryman in the second game of a September 7 double header, Nettles blooped a single to left field, and the end of his bat fell to the ground in front of home plate. Tiger catcher Bill Freehan handed the bat in pieces to umpire Lou DiMuro.

As the story is often told, Nettles's bat was filled with Super Balls, and after his bat broke, players ran around picking them up. Made of highly resilient synthetic rubber, Super Balls were first introduced by Wham-O in 1965. Nettles had apparently taken advantage of the innovative new substance, though the concept wasn't far removed from the small rubber balls of the 1860s. A couple of weeks after the incident, Peter Gammons wrote in the *Boston Globe* that Nettles had admitted that he had used Super Balls.[15]

This makes a great story, but it might not be true. All contemporaneous sources said that when DiMuro examined the bat he found it corked, and that Freehan simply picked up the bat. There were no stories of players running around picking up balls. (Catfish Hunter later identified reserve catcher Ed Herrmann as the person who loaded the Super Balls into Nettles's bat. Unfortunately, neither Hunter nor Hermann were in the ballpark—they did not join the Yankees until the following year.) Despite all evidence, the Super Ball version of the story eventually won out.[16]

After the incident, Nettles was declared out but remained in the game. The Tigers were not amused, especially when the game ended in a 1–0 Yankee victory, with the only run scoring on a Nettles home run in the second inning, presumably hit with the illegal bat.

Nettles, employing a strategy that would become familiar in the years ahead, claimed to be just as shocked as the rest of us. "Some Yankee fan in Chicago gave it to me and said it would bring me good luck…. I just picked it up by mistake. As soon as the end came off, I knew something was wrong."[17]

Tiger catcher Freehan had an interesting reaction. "I know a lot of guys put cork in the ends of their bats to make them lighter," he said. "I used to see Norm Cash do it a lot…. But Nettles did it differently than I've ever seen it done before. It looked like he had sawed the end off, drilled a hole and put cork in, then glued the two pieces back together again. It came apart because he hit the ball on the end." This seems like an awful lot of effort for a "Yankee fan in Chicago" to go through.

Cash had been a longtime teammate of Freehan and was then enjoying his first year of retirement. When apprised of Nettles's claims of innocence, Cash did not hold back. "Why that lying sonofagun," he said. "I ought to know. I used a hollow bat my whole career. In fact, I owe my success to expansion pitching, a short rightfield fence and my hollow bats." Cash said he could alter a 36-ounce bat so that it had the weight and feel of a 34-ounce bat.[18]

As Cash described it, the important thing was hollowing out the bat, making it lighter. The cork (or superballs) were of secondary importance—just something to fill space and keep the bat from breaking.

The Nettles incident fit right in with all the spitball controversies of the era and was taken about as seriously. "I don't begrudge the pitchers," said Nettles. "But until the umpires have the guts to stop them from marking the ball, I see nothing wrong with using a corked bat."[19] Other than losing the single, Nettles was not disciplined—he played every game the rest of the year.

Like Cash, Amos Otis waited until his career was over before fessing up to his deceit. In fact, he claimed, likely with some hyperbole, that he used a corked bat his entire 14 years with the Royals. "Back then a lot of people did it, and very seldom did anybody get caught," he said in 1992. "The only people I know who got caught were Graig Nettles and Toby Harrah."[20]

At least one player who did see something wrong was Andre Thornton, who also has the distinction of coming clean while he was still playing. After the 1978 season, he admitted that he had tried a corked bat for two weeks but hit poorly because he felt so guilty about it. "I felt so much joy when I discarded that bat, you can't imagine. My flesh told me to go ahead and use it. And the Lord asked are you gonna stand for me or stand for the flesh and the world. All men face such decisions, in any walk of life. Do you cheat? Or do you rise above it?"[21]

While Al Worthington would likely agree with Thornton, many others would not "rise above it."

The first player to be suspended for using a corked bat was Angels outfielder Dan Ford in 1981. Playing in Cleveland on September 4, Ford broke his bat on a weak ground ball to second base. "I remember Don Baylor yelling, 'Get the bat, get the bat!'" Ford said. "I didn't know whether to run to first or grab the bat and run into the dugout."[22]

"I just got caught. There's nothing I can say or do. When I used the bat in Cleveland, I was going bad and the team was going bad. I was trying to do something to help the team win." Like Nettles's 1974 bat, Ford's had the end sawed off, cork inserted, and then the pieces glued (and, in Ford's case, nailed) back together. "The cork gives a little acceleration to the ball. It makes the bat lighter and the inside a little more flexible. It doesn't make a good hitter out of you. It just gives you an advantage."[23] One wonders about the nails, but it seems they did not materially affect the bat's weight or aerodynamics.

MacPhail suspended Ford for three games. When Orioles manager Earl Weaver was informed of the suspension, he was outraged by the light penalty, saying, "That's unbelievable. Hell, you are better off cheating."[24]

On September 1, 1987, Astros outfielder Billy Hatcher broke his bat on a routine popup to the catcher. "The bat was hollowed out at the barrel and had three or four inches of cork inside it," umpire crew chief John McSherry said. "When he hit the ball, the bat broke. [Chicago Cubs third baseman] Moreland picked it up and brought it to me. After that, it was easy. The cork was obvious to see." Hatcher was immediately ejected.

Yet he claimed innocence. "I was out of bats, so I grabbed one of the pitchers' bats. I don't even know whose bat it was," Hatcher said. "I ran down to first and they told me that bat was corked and I was out. I had no idea it was corked. You could have checked any of my bats." Subsequently, pitcher Dave Smith said it was indeed his bat, but that he had no idea where it came from. Astros manager Hal Lanier defended his player, saying it was a bat Astros' pitchers used for friendly batting practice competitions.

Cubs manager Gene Michael was having none of it. "There is more cheating going on now and we've got to do something about it," Michael said. "You've got to have tough penalties. Three months. Suspend him three months."[25] Ultimately he got 10 games—the same penalty pitcher Joe Niekro got a few weeks earlier for doctoring the baseball.

One of the more comical stories about bat corking took place in Chicago's Comiskey Park on July 15, 1994. By this time teams could challenge one player's bat per game, and the White Sox chose to challenge Indians slugger Albert Belle, one of the game's best hitters, when he came to bat in the first inning. Umpire Dave Phillips took Belle's bat, locked it in the umpire's dressing room, and the game resumed.

Belle's teammates, knowing the bat was corked, devised a plan to rescue it. Pitcher Jason Grimsley entered the umpires' room via a crawl space above the ceiling and replaced Belle's bat with a legal one belonging to Paul Sorrento. After the game the umpires unlocked the door and found pieces of ceiling tile on the floor, twisted metal brackets in the ceiling, and a bat that looked nothing like the one they had confiscated. MLB security treated this breaking and entering as a serious offense. The Chicago police and the FBI investigated, and the Indians finally handed over Belle's bat. When it was sawed in half, lo and behold, everyone discovered that it was indeed filled with cork. Belle was initially suspended for 10 days, later reduced to seven.

The culprit responsible for the break-in, however, was not revealed until 1999, when Grimsley confessed. Asked why he'd replaced Belle's bat with Sorrento's, a decision that proved to be the crucial flaw in the plan, Grimsley said he'd no choice—because all of Belle's bats were corked.

The Belle case was noteworthy not only because of the rescue caper, but because Belle's irascible personality had already made him an unpopular player outside of Cleveland. Fans didn't need an additional reason to dislike Albert Belle. A great hitter, having a great season, but now people could wonder whether his power was legitimate. This was before rampant speculation about steroid use spread such suspicion to scads of players.

If Belle was a controversial figure, the Sammy Sosa of 2003 was not. Credited with Mark McGwire for helping to reinvigorate baseball with their 1998 home run chase, Sosa had hit 292 homers over a five-year period, and his upbeat personality made him a beloved figure in Chicago and popular just about everywhere else. In April 2003 he hit his 500th career home run.

Sosa's unraveling took place two months later, on June 3. Facing Tampa Bay at Wrigley Field, Sosa hit a first-inning ground ball to second base and his black bat broke in half. The umpires examined the bat, found it full of cork, and ejected Sosa from the game. Afterward, Sosa said it was a batting practice bat that he would normally use to put on a show for fans.

"I just want to say that I first want to apologize to my teammates, the fans, and the commissioner of Major League Baseball," he said. "What happened today was something that wasn't meant to have happened. I took the wrong bat and I went up there and it happened. It's a bat I used for batting practice. It's a mistake."

Dusty Baker, his manager, backed his player. "Deep down in my heart I believe Sammy didn't know what was down in there, Baker said. "I just hope this event doesn't tarnish his career and all that Sammy Sosa has done for baseball and Chicago."

But Yankees skipper Joe Torre predicted that this was precisely what would happen. "Even if he never used the cork before that, you're not going to convince people of it," Torre said. "It's really unfortunate for the game. The most important part of the game is respect for the people before you. It's embarrassing; he's too good of a player. It's too bad. That's one of those things you don't enjoy, even if you're on the other team."[26]

Of course, after Sosa was accused of steroid use, the corked bat incident took a back seat as a reason for his tarnished legacy.

In more recent revelations, Pete Rose has been accused of corking bats in his final seasons. In 2001 *Vanity Fair* published a Rose exposé based on interviews with his longtime pal Tommy Gioiosa that included first-hand accounts of corked bats. "When Gioiosa asked Rose what would happen if it broke," author Buzz Bissinger wrote, "The response was 'There'd be fucking cork all over the place.' Then he told Gioiosa that it wouldn't break because he would lay off the kind of pitches that cause a bat to break. Gioiosa also says that Rose, as a precaution against detection by umpires, would hit the bat on the concrete floor so it would look scuffed."[27] Rose later denied the allegation, saying he never used an illegal bat in a game. Of course, Rose, like Sosa, faced other issues—in Rose's case, betting on baseball while a manager of the Reds—so whether he did or did not cork his bats is not a major factor in the way his career is remembered.[28]

In 2020 Montreal sportswriter Danny Gallagher reported that Rose had been corking his bats during his season [1984] in that city. The *Palm Beach Post* followed up on the story, interviewing Bryan Greenberg, the man who reportedly corked them. Greenberg said he corked bats for "a couple of" unnamed Expos players, including Rose.[29]

"He called me 'Corky,'" Greenberg recalled. "He'd call me up and say, 'Corky, I need four.' Rose told me he was using them for batting practice. I don't know what he did with the bats. Maybe he did only use them in BP. I don't know if he used them on the field."

The story detailed Greenberg's method: "Rose shipped two cases of his Mizuno bats—12 per case—to Greenberg's house.... After drilling 12 inches deep, he inserted about 8 inches of cork; he used a hand punch tool to cut out 40 to 50 discs, roughly the diameter of a penny, from a sheet of cork. He glued them together five at a time to form a cork stack, which he shoved into the bat under pressure with a wooden dowel sheathed in glue. After it dried overnight, he sawed off the end of the dowel. Finally, he sanded over the end of the barrel and touched up the wood with paint or a colored pencil to make the grains appear untampered. 'It took me 10 minutes to do a bat,' Greenberg said."[30]

There are a couple of big differences between a pitcher doctoring a ball and a batter doctoring a bat. For one thing, the hurler is out there on the mound with everyone watching, and he has only a few seconds to alter the ball to his advantage. A deceitful batter is operating out of sight, perhaps over the course of hours or days, and while on the field can focus complete attention on his at-bat. They are both violating the rulebook, but one does not have to feel the same way about the two infractions.

Keith Hernandez wrote about this difference in his book *Pure Baseball*: "Now, hitting with a corked bat, that is cheating because there's no way to catch this trick on the field. But if you can stand on the mound and somehow scuff the baseball in full view of the umpires and everyone else and not get caught, more power to you."[31]

Hernandez Doctrine: An illegal action done in front of the umpires and opponents is acceptable behavior, while one done outside of the field or ballpark is not.

Secondly, it is not clear that the batter's efforts are doing him much good. While it is true that a lighter bat increases bat speed, it is just as true that the lighter bat strikes the ball with less force. Scientists have examined this issue for years.

One of the more definitive studies was conducted in 2010 at the Sports Science Laboratory at Washington State University. In the experiment, a ball was shot out of a high-speed cannon at a bat. The study concluded that the higher swing speed does not compensate for the "less effective collision" with the ball, and most likely a well-struck ball will travel slightly farther with the heavier bat. The study also examined the "trampoline effect," the idea that a corked bat with a narrower wall of wood might compress differently when in contact with the ball, increasing the elasticity of the collision. Again, no beneficial effect was detected. The authors of the study were not ready to completely discount the benefits of a corked bat. A lighter bat and increased bat speed might make it more likely that the hitter can control the bat and thus strike the ball with largest part of the barrel.[32]

It seems that baseball has found the right balance between crime and punishment for doctored bats. The benefit from using one is likely small, though it still affords an unfair advantage. The seven- to ten-day suspensions that baseball has handed down for these violations seem to have been sufficient to mostly eradicate the practice without being too draconian.

But bats represent just one part of a player's physical tools and environment. And for many decades, whether with other equipment or with the playing field itself, teams and players have tinkered with it all, legally and illegally, clandestinely and openly, to try to eke out an advantage.

Chapter Six

RAKES AND HOSES

I N HIS WONDERFULLY CANDID MEMOIR *VEECK AS IN WRECK,* Bill Veeck defended his relationship with baseball regulations. "I don't advocate breaking the rules," he wrote, "but I do advocate testing their elasticity."[1]

Veeck tested their elasticity throughout a colorful life in and out of baseball, aggravating commissioners, league presidents, and his fellow owners, while generally delighting fans. He maintained his popularity because he seemed open and honest, appeared more interested in having fun than making money, obviously loved baseball, and won pennants in both Cleveland and Chicago.

His most famous stunt in baseball took place on August 19, 1951, when he owned the hapless St. Louis Browns. To begin the bottom of the first inning in the second game of a Sunday double-header, Browns manager Zack Taylor, on instruction from Veeck, inserted pinch-hitter Eddie Gaedel, a 3'7" little person. Gaedel walked on four pitches and was removed for a pinch-runner.

Veeck had signed Gaedel to a standard player contract and notified the league office as required. He did so the day before (Saturday) and hoped Gaedel's diminutive stature would escape scrutiny. But American League president Will Harridge got word and tried to contact Veeck, who avoided the phone and ignored all messages. Taylor presented to the umpires Gaedel's contract and a program with Gaedel (number "1/8") listed. Although the Browns went on to lose the game 6–2, Veeck and Gaedel had reason to believe that his appearance had been a success. Unfortunately, the next day Harridge voided Gaedel's contract, effectively banning him "in the best interests of baseball."

Veeck was angry, pointing out that there were no rules prescribing a player's size or any other physical characteristics. "I want to protest right now that visiting clubs that play such men as Larry Doby and Ted Williams present an unfair advantage over us.... Gaedel drew a base on balls, good for one base, while fellows like Doby and Williams hit homers against us."[2] Veeck lost this argument, and Gaedel never played in the major leagues again, nor has any other little person.

League presidents rarely made the news in those days, and many fans likely had no idea who Harridge was when he made the ruling. "Has anyone ever proved that Will Harridge was in the best interest of the game?" sneered the *Boston Globe*.[3] Harridge kept his job for another seven years but managed to stay out of the headlines.

As concerns the theme of this book, it is worth noting that the one time authorities acted decisively to stop Bill Veeck, it was over something that did not break any regulation. Nonetheless, the AL soon created a rule requiring that contracts be approved by the league president, rather than merely requiring that he be informed. Harridge made clear that he would never have approved the contract, and that the problem with Gaedel was not only his height. For one thing, he was obviously not a baseball player, though he had succeeded in getting on base. Veeck remained unrepentant, "We're paying a lot of guys ... good money to get on base and even though they don't do it, nobody sympathizes with us."[4]

If Veeck's actions were technically aboveboard in the Gaedel case, he freely admitted to lots of deliberate rule-breaking in other matters. Much of his cheating involved the groundskeepers, whom he once claimed could win 10 games a season. This claim is dubious. But in his first opportunity running a big league club in Cleveland, Veeck inherited Emil Bossard, whom he referred to as the "Michelangelo of grounds keepers."[5] There was no part of the playing field that escaped Veeck's or Bossard's attention.

Start with the pitcher's mound. Rules of the 1940s stated that the mound could be no more than 15 inches above the playing surface (as of 1969 it was fixed at 10 inches), and also dictated how the mound should slope. No matter. At Cleveland Stadium, the mound could be contoured overnight, depending on the next day's starters. Indians ace Bob Feller liked the mound high so he could take a long stride downhill before unleashing his blazing fastball. Other Indians pitchers might prefer a legal mound. Veeck also learned the desires of the opposing team's pitchers and had Bossard work against them. Yankee Ed Lopat liked the mound flat. So, according to Veeck, when he pitched against the Indians "we'd make it so high that if he had fallen off he'd have broken a leg."[6]

Let's call this **the Veeck Doctrine, in which the grounds and the equipment of the game can be manipulated to help your team win.**

Why didn't the Yankees complain? Likely because they were tampering with the mound on their own home turf. Ryne Duren, a Yankee relief pitcher, recalled: "Bob Turley wanted the mound at Yankee Stadium to be flat and since he was the top gun of the staff in 1958, the groundskeeper kept it that way."[7]

Arthur Daley, longtime *New York Times* columnist, considered this to be a long-standing art. "As a means of utilizing to the full the blinding side-arm speed of Walter Johnson," Daley wrote, "Washington leveled off the 'mound' so completely that it almost was a depression instead of an elevation. Usually it was so scuffed that finding the rubber was not easy. Hence Senator pitchers acquired the understandable habit of edging up a few inches before each pitch."[8]

There are many other ways to doctor a field to benefit the home nine, and Veeck's Cleveland club was at the forefront of these machinations. The Indians had fine infielders in the late 1940s, including Ken Keltner at third, Lou Boudreau at shortstop, and Joe Gordon at second. Veeck got Bossard to tailor the infield to their specific needs: Boudreau was slow but had good hands, so the grass in front of him was long and the dirt soft. Gordon was quick and acrobatic, so he got very short grass and hard dirt. Keltner needed soggy dirt for his knees.[9]

The Indians also contoured their foul lines so that they sloped imperceptibly toward the mound in order to help his team's bunters, "not only so that fair bunts won't roll foul, but that foul bunts can roll fair."[10] For similar reasons, the dirt in front of home plate would be soggy enough to keep balls from rolling too quickly. Needless to say, if the Indians did not have much bunting in their repertoire, Bossard would modify the field in the reverse manner.[11]

"It's all part of the business," Bossard told Kansas City sportswriter Ernie Mehl. "We do a lot of things here in Cleveland calculated to help our club and make it a little tougher for the visitors. We work over the field every day according to who is pitching, what sort of speed the other team has and what kind of hitters they are."[12]

In Veeck's era, there was no formal rule against manipulating the infield. Though doing so was not explicitly banned, the practice was considered unfair by many of those within the game. Bossard was unique in talking about his exploits; most others doing the same thing avoided exposure. The same article that discussed his manipulations noted, "We would not be surprised if Emil since has been spoken to by his employers."

In 1950, the rulebook was revised to formalize some of these details, and the wording has expanded several times since. The 2021 Official Baseball Rules state: "The infield shall be graded so that the base lines and home plate are level. The pitcher's plate shall be 10 inches above the level of home plate. The degree of slope from a point 6 inches in front of the pitcher's plate to a point 6 feet toward home plate shall be 1 inch to 1 foot, and such degree of slope shall be uniform."

Veeck also stretched the rules with his outfield fences. Cleveland Stadium was an enormous field, with its center field fence standing 470 feet from home plate. "There was so much pastureland in the outfield when I arrived," said Veeck, "that I suspected warfare between the sheepmen and the cattlemen to be renewed momentarily." To address this situation, Veeck installed a wire fence with more manageable distances from foul line to foul line. All perfectly legal.

The fence poles were inserted into metal sleeves driven into the ground. What few people knew was that the field had several sets of sleeves, so that the fence could be moved overnight depending on the Indians' opponent. If the Yankees were coming to town, the field distances would be set at their maximum, while with the Browns they could be moved in to help the Indians' hitters. According to Veeck, when he owned the minor league Milwaukee team, he had a fence that could be moved *between innings*. Baseball put a stop to all this when Frank Lane threatened to install his own between-innings operation with the White Sox in the early 1950s.

The 1948 Indians became one of the better stories in baseball history, setting all-time attendance records, winning their first American League pennant since 1920 (after winning a one-game playoff) and then also winning the World Series. They did all of this, Veeck wrote, "by resorting to gamesmanship—the art of winning without really cheating—as never before in the long and sometimes devious history of baseball."[13]

But while Veeck and Bossard excelled at field manipulation, they can't be credited as originators of these tactics. The 1890s Baltimore Orioles, had a groundskeeper named Tom Murphy, who became a coconspirator with John McGraw and his teammates.

"We got Murphy to mix the soil of the infield with a form of clay," McGraw remembered, "which, when wet and rolled, was almost as hard as concrete and gave us a fast track to work on."[14] (The field undoubtedly helped with their famed Baltimore chop, in which a batter drove the pitched ball into the ground and reached first during its high bounce.) Murphy did much more, including tapering the foul lines to help with bunts, soaping the soil in front of the mound to cause opposing pitchers who used the dirt for grip to stand up with slippery hands, building a slope in right field that Willie Keeler learned to play, keeping the grass long in the outfield so an extra ball could be hidden there, and building up the pitcher's mound.[15]

Murphy raised his art to a higher level in a game against the Giants. As McGraw told the (possibly apocryphal) story many years later, the Orioles were at bat, an overthrow to first base rolled into the Orioles clubhouse. Murphy, who usually sat by the open door, quickly got up, closed the door ... and locked it, allowing the batter to run all the way around the bases. Whether factual or an enhanced remembrance, this story offers perspective on the extent to which groundskeepers considered themselves contributing members of the team.[16]

Groundskeeping shenanigans were not confined to the white major leagues. Chicago American Giants owner and manager Rube Foster, who preferred the Deadball Era–style of strategy and speed, engaged in similar mischief in the 1920s Negro National League. "He would wet down the infield so much that it seemed like the middle of a rainstorm," St. Louis Stars center fielder James "Cool Papa" Bell remembered. "Bunts would roll dead about 10 feet from home plate. He also built little ridges along the baselines. You could hardly see them, but they kept bunts from going foul."[17]

One of the more famous grounds-related controversies took place at San Francisco's Candlestick Park in 1962. The Giants spent the summer in a battle for the National League pennant with their archrivals, the Los Angeles Dodgers. The Dodgers big star that season, and the most talked about player in the game, was shortstop and speedster Maury Wills, who would go on to set the all-time record for stolen bases in a season (104, since broken) and be named the league's Most Valuable Player.

In early August the Dodgers had built up a 5 ½ game lead over the Giants and came to San Francisco for a three-game series. Just two weeks earlier the Dodgers had swept a three-game set in Los Angeles, with the Dodgers stealing six bases, including three by Willie Davis and two by Wills. With the Giants' chance at a pennant beginning to slip away, manager Alvin Dark paid a visit to head groundskeeper Matty Schwab and asked if he had any thoughts on how to slow down the Dodgers running game. Schwab did.

As far as Schwab was concerned, this was part of his job. After all, the Dodgers had already utilized a 1,000-pound roller on the basepaths (to make it easier to run) and in the outfield (to help balls scoot past outfielders). The 1962 Dodgers stole 198 bases, double the second-highest total in baseball, and also led the major leagues in triples. If the Dodgers could make their stadium's basepaths faster, couldn't the Giants make theirs slower?

Before dawn on the morning of the series opener, Schwab and his son Jerry dug up the soil in the area where Wills would take his lead, and replaced it with a concoction of sand, peat moss, and water. They then camouflaged this quagmire with some normal soil, making it look like one continuous basepath.

Well before game time, the Dodger coaches and players discovered the misdeed and brought it to the umpires' attention. Tom Gorman found Schwab and told him the Giants would forfeit the game if he couldn't fix it before the start. The old swamp was carried away in wheelbarrows, replaced with what appeared to be new dirt.

"It was the same stuff," Schwab's son Jerry recalled. "We mixed it with some dirt and brought it right back. When we put it down a second time it was even looser." Nevertheless, the umpires seemed satisfied by the (purportedly) good faith effort and remained so even after the Schwabs watered the infield liberally before the game began.

After an 11–2 Giants victory and before the next day's game, the Schwabs decided to cover their tracks by removing all of the swamp and putting real soil down. They then watered the basepaths, so much so that the umpires demanded that sand be put down as a drying agent. This made things worse, and the frustrated Dodgers dropped the next two games as well. They attempted just one stolen base all weekend.[18]

Los Angeles general manager Buzzy Bavasi called the series a "fiasco" and threatened to lodge a protest with Commissioner Ford

Frick. Specifically, Bavasi charged that the Giants had acted with "vileness of purpose"—actions meeting this designation were banned by the NL—for the additional risk of injury to the players. The Los Angeles writers used all of this as an opportunity to pen some memorable prose. Melvin Durslag said, "There was enough water there to run a hydro-electric plant." Jim Murray claimed, "They found two abalone under second base" and "when the wind came up it made waves and Maury Wills wasn't sure his canoe would make it to shortstop."[19]

Despite all the protests and wisecracks, the Giants received no punishment, and went on to catch the Dodgers on the last day of the season (both teams finishing 101–61), forcing a three-game playoff for the pennant.

Game 1 of the playoff series was in Candlestick Park, the Dodgers' first visit since the August shenanigans. This time the league was on alert. But by the time the umpires showed up the field had again been drenched with water from the grounds crew's hoses. Still, it would be difficult to blame the field for the Dodgers 8–0 defeat; Billy Pierce's 3-hit shutout was the more obvious culprit.

The final two games were at Dodger Stadium: an 8–7 Dodger win, and a 6–4 win by the Giants to clinch the series and the pennant. Los Angeles stole five bases in their two home games, but this was not enough to defeat the Giants' bats. After the season, the players awarded Schwab a full share of their World Series loot, amounting to $7,290.

This Dodgers-Giants chicanery did not end with the playoff series. Umpire Tom Gorman later recalled Giants manager Herman Franks poking his head out of the dugout before a game when he thought no umpires were looking. He quickly signaled to the grounds crew to roll out the fire hose and soak the basepaths. Despite Gorman catching him, Franks tried the same stunt again the next day. Gorman also complained that Dodger manager Walter Alston was trying to gain the opposite edge by speeding up the basepaths. Before a game in Los Angeles, Alston had the grounds crew drive a tractor around the basepaths to harden them.[20]

Meanwhile, Veeck had bought the Chicago White Sox in 1959 and, as fate would have it, now had a new secret weapon. The head groundskeeper at Comiskey Park was none other than Gene Bossard, Emil's son. Gene became a legendary craftsman in his own right, holding the job for more than 40 years (at which point he passed the job down to his son Roger). The Bossard family talents continued to weaponize the ballpark to assist the home team.

The Go-Go White Sox were famous for running, bunting, and small ball, and Gene Bossard optimized the infield and basepaths for their small ball practitioners like Nellie Fox and Luis Aparicio. "We could have an eight-month drought in Chicago," recalled third baseman Pete Ward, who arrived a few years later." There'd be a swamp in front of home plate. During batting practice, with the writers all around the batting cage, guys would hit down on the ball and try to splatter the writers with mud—thinking there'd be a mention of it in the papers. And there'd never be any."[21]

"[Tommy] John, [Joel] Horlen and [Gary] Peters were all low-ball pitchers, and Dad had the front of home plate watered down," son Roger Bossard recalled. "The union wasn't that strong back then, and you could get away with it. So there was like mud in [the batter's box] in front of home plate. They called it 'Bossard's swamp.' And the infield grass was 3 inches high."[22]

Brewers manager Tom Trebelhorn caught the Tigers in a similar stunt in the 1980s for the benefit of sinkerball pitcher Doyle Alexander. Trebelhorn discovered several inches of Diamond Dry—a material used to soak up excess water on a ball field—in front of home plate before the start of the game. After umpire Jim Evans ordered it cleared out for new soil, "three wheelbarrows of that stuff" was carted off.[23]

Another of Bossard's contributions to our subject was his implementation of the "frozen" baseball. (The term refers to treating the ball, not literally freezing it.) Roger later said that the concept originated with a conversation between his father, Gene, and White Sox manager Al Lopez in the early 1960s. It reached its zenith in 1967 when Eddie Stanky took over as manager.

The White Sox stored their game balls in two rooms at Comiskey Park—one on the first base side, the other on the third base side. The room on the first base side was just four brick walls and a humidifier, and the balls in the room would be damp and heavy. "If you went to the upper deck," recalled Roger, who was then just beginning his apprenticeship, "there was a walkway, and if you dropped a normal ball it would bounce up about 20 feet. If you dropped one of these balls, it would jump up maybe 10 feet. It was a huge difference."[24]

Opposing players complained about these leaden baseballs, and the league sent someone to check midway through the 1967 season. This is where the room on the third base side came in: Bossard showed the league the balls in the room without the humidifier, and the balls were fine. Nothing was done.

The White Sox of the time had outstanding ground ball pitchers and serviceable hitters, and they were generally competitive; their 17 consecutive winning seasons (1951–1967) comprise one of the longest streaks in history.

As a team the 1967 White Sox hit .225, including .207 at home. The pitchers had a 2.88 ERA on the road, but a 2.08 ERA at home. It was a low offense era (the league ERA was 3.23), but the White Sox games were at an entirely different level. The club was in the pennant race until the final weekend, eventually finishing 89–73, just three games behind the pennant-winning Red Sox.

In fact, baseball men were trying to deaden baseballs by freezing them (or at least cooling them) long before Bossard. As the science around building iceboxes developed during the second half of the nineteenth century, and as iceboxes grew in popularity, ballplayers and their coaches soon recognized an opportunity for cheating.[25]

Hall of Fame manager Connie Mack was possibly the first to freeze baseballs while managing the Pirates during the mid-1890s. "There used to be an icebox in the Pittsburgh club's office," the team statistician told sportswriter Fred Lieb, "and Connie got the idea of freezing balls in the box.… Connie contrived to work the balls into the game while the visiting team was at bat, and then substituted the unfrozen variety when the Pittsburgh club had its innings at the bat."

Many years later Lieb asked Mack about the episode. "An amused twinkle came into Mack's eye," Lieb wrote as Mack told him, "We had to use a lot of tricks to win games and maybe that was one of them."[26]

Cool Papa Bell similarly accused Rube Foster. "Before a home game," Bell recalled, "Foster would freeze the balls that were going to be pitched against the opposition. One of the big strong guys would come up and really connect. The ball would take off and then die like it had lead in it."[27]

While Bossard wasn't the first to treat a ball, he also may not have been the last. In 2010 the San Francisco Giants, including pitcher Tim Lincecum, accused the Colorado Rockies of supplying the home plate umpire with different balls depending on whether the Rockies or their opponents were batting. Specifically, it was alleged, the visitors would get balls that had been in the approved humidor, while the Rockies hitters got the non-humidor balls, which theoretically would travel farther. No proof emerged, but Major League Baseball changed its procedures so that umpires were present when balls were removed from the humidor and the bags of balls never left their sight.[28]

Players have also sought advantages through their equipment. Five-fingered fielders mitts were likely introduced as early as 1860. Initially, few saw a problem with this; it didn't appear to provide a meaningful advantage, and, in fact early glove wearers were often scorned for being unmanly. Once gloves started becoming larger and offering real benefits on the field, baseball began regulating their size.[29]

By 1989 they had grown so large that MLB had to limit their length to 12 inches from the tip of the index finger to the heel of the mitt.

Nonetheless, it was clear many players were using gloves significantly larger than this without repercussions. In September 1989, the two leagues sent letters to all teams, the Players Association, and the glove manufacturers announcing a crackdown starting in 1990. Opposing managers would be able to challenge a glove, and umpires could measure them independently as well. Some speculated that a recent *Sports Illustrated* article showing infielder Joel Youngblood's glove nestled within outfielder Herm Winningham's prompted the increased enforcement. Winningham later measured his now-notorious glove at 14 inches. Many other players were also breaking the rule. A spokesman for Rawlings, which manufactured roughly 55 percent of major league gloves, estimated one-quarter of their stock to be larger than 12 inches. Even with the new directive, penalties were minimal. If caught with an illegal mitt, the player would have to switch gloves but could remain in the game. Discipline was imposed only after multiple violations.[30]

In an example from decades earlier, New York Giants catcher Roger Bresnahan sported white cricket-type shin guards for Opening Day in April 1907. Shin guards had been used sporadically in the past but were makeshift and often smaller than cricket shin guards. They were generally worn under the player's socks or pants leg where they weren't visible. Bresnahan wore his on top of his pants where they were described as "picturesque." Spectators, noted one baseball scribe, "rather fancied the innovation."[31]

A month later while playing Pittsburgh, Pirates manager and center fielder Fred Clarke twisted his ankle on a play at the plate, while being called out on a squeeze play. Clarke blamed Bresnahan's shin guards. "As the matter stands at present New York has a big advantage over every other club," he claimed. "With Bresnahan the only catcher in the league wearing these guards, it will be next to impossible for any opposing player to touch the plate in a close play on the Polo Grounds. I am not stretching the truth a particle when I say that those shin guards cost us Saturday's game. Once when we tried the squeeze play Bresnahan ran fully six feet to the left of the plate and braced himself on the line so that it was impossible for me to get around him in my attempt to score on a bunt. Of course, I tried to slide but my spike caught in his shin guards and caused me to turn one of my ankles."[32]

Clarke and Pirates owner Barney Dreyfuss protested Bresnahan's advantage to NL President Harry Pulliam, demanding that shin guards be banned. Most observers ridiculed the complaint because the rule covering wearables did not exclude shin guards. Despite his antipathy toward the Giants and his friendship with Dreyfuss, Pulliam had little choice but to uphold the right to don shin guards, pointing out that no rule expressly prohibited them. Clarke sarcastically countered that he would up the ante, outfitting both his first and second baseman similarly. Over the next several years shin guards for catchers caught on throughout baseball. More recently, batters have begun to wear increasingly protective gear at the plate. To date, nearly all has been judged legal.[33]

Several years after Maury Wills had been the primary target of cheating by the Giants, he orchestrated some nefarious acts of his own. After finishing up a fine playing career in 1972, he was hired to manage the lowly Seattle Mariners in August 1980. His rule-breaking took place the following April.

Mariners outfielder Tom Paciorek had started the season hot, hitting .368 through April 25. On that day Seattle hosted the Oakland A's, who were led by skipper Billy Martin. The day before, Martin had complained that Paciorek was standing outside the front of the batter's box, something one might do in order to hit a curveball before it had finished its break.

Before the game on the 25th, Martin mentioned to umpiring crew chief Bill Kunkel that the batter's boxes looked funny. Kunkel measured, and determined that they were seven feet long rather than the six feet that the rulebook required. He summoned the groundskeeper, who told him that Wills had instructed him to lengthen the boxes. They were redrawn, and the game went on. Wills was fined and suspended, then fired by Seattle. He finished his one and only stint as a major league manager with a 26–56 record over parts of two seasons.

If the batter's box could be tampered with, why not the catcher's box? On a Friday night in June 2000, the Milwaukee Brewers complained that the Atlanta Braves had chalked too large a catcher's box.

A larger box would allow the catcher to set up wider than legally permitted, possibly increasing the likelihood of having a borderline outside pitch called a strike. The next night, umpire John Shulock called a balk on pitcher Greg Maddux because catcher Fernando Lunar had set up with his right foot outside the catcher's box. TBS broadcasters showed that game's batter's box superimposed on the one from the previous night. The Saturday night box appeared roughly four to five inches smaller than Friday night's, implying the Braves had shrunk an illegally enlarged box back to its regulation size after the Brewers objected. In retaliation for TBS's actions, the Braves banned their own TV announcers from the team flight, a move they reversed one day later.[34]

What about the on-deck circle? A batter who is "on deck" is supposed to await his turn at bat in a designated circle (sometimes chalked on the field, but often just a rubber mat). By rule, the circles must be 5 feet in diameter and placed 37 feet behind and to the side of home plate.

In reality, many batters do not stand in the circle. And there's a reason for that. "I try to get as close as I can behind the catcher so I can look at the pitcher," DeWayne Wise told the *New York Times* in 2010. "A lot of guys feel the same as I do; we want to get in a position where we can see the flight of the ball. Sometimes, you see guys who look like they're almost behind the catcher. It's crazy that the umpire doesn't say anything." Occasionally umpires do tell players to move, especially if they are within the pitcher's sight lines.[35]

Adrián Beltré preferred to stand closer to, and behind, the plate, supposedly because he thought he was less likely to get hit by a stray foul ball. In 2017, he was in his 20th season in the big leagues and had become a star third baseman for the Texas Rangers. Late in a game on July 26, second baseman umpire Gerry Davis asked the on-deck Beltré to move into the designated circle. Instead, Beltré walked over to the mat, dragged it to where he wanted to stand, and then stood on top of it. The Rangers were already losing 18–6 in a game they would drop 22–10, so it wasn't a high leverage moment. But Beltré was just four hits shy of 3,000 for his career, already tallying two doubles and a home run in this game. Davis ejected him.

Neither the home crowd nor manager Jeff Banister (also ejected) were happy. "I actually wasn't being funny," Beltré claimed. "He told me to stand on the mat so I pulled the mat where I was and stood on top of it. I was listening…. Why was that a problem today? I've been standing in the same spot the whole series."[36] Years later, this remains one of the most-played video clips of Beltré's storied career.

Although the groundskeeper has the largest role to play when trying to modify the park to a team's advantage, other officials have gotten involved. The advent of indoor stadiums, starting with the Houston Astrodome in 1965, offered additional means for the home team to modify playing conditions. In 2003 Dick Ericson, a former superintendent of the Metrodome in Minneapolis, described how he'd routinely adjusted the stadium's ventilation at the stadium late in games when he thought the Twins needed runs. "If they were down two runs and you're still hoping for them to have the advantage, you'd want to be blowing all the air out and up as much as you can," said Ericson. "I don't feel guilty…. It's your home-field advantage. Every stadium has got one."

Ericson, who said he acted alone, worked at the Metrodome from 1982 to 1995, a period that included two World Championships for the Twins. He claimed that his fans were blowing out when Kirby Puckett hit the most famous home run in team history, a walk-off in Game 6 of the 1991 World Series, though Puckett's home run was long enough that it likely needed no help.

Although Twins officials cast doubt on Ericson's claims, opponents had no difficulty believing them. Bobby Valentine recalled his years managing in the Metrodome with the Rangers when his players would report a strong breeze blowing out when they were in the field but coming in when they were batting. "I became very suspicious, maybe paranoid," said Valentine. "They had such an uncanny way of winning."[37]

This would not even be the earliest ethical breach involving air conditioning. Frank Lane, who ran several clubs over more than two decades, had a particularly dishonest way of dealing with the brutal Kansas City heat when he ran the Athletics in the mid-1960s: He put an air conditioner in the home dugout and a heater in the visiting dugout. Lane was flippant when confronted with the charge: "What's wrong? Players can bring their own air conditioners. We don't search them."[38]

Given the opportunity, fans could also help their teams in unsportsmanlike ways. In the 1930s Chicago Cubs third baseman Stan Hack earned the nickname Smiling Stan because of his cheery disposition and good looks. The Cubs had a promotion and handed out Smiling Stan mirrors to the crowd. The idea supposedly originated with Veeck, just 21 years old and working for the club that his late father (Bill Veeck Sr.) had served as team president. Whether instigated by the younger Veeck or not, home fans used their mirrors to shine reflected sunlight into the opposing batters' eyes. The umpires threatened to forfeit the game to the other team until an announcement was made to get them to stop. "Unsporting?" asked Veeck in his memoir, "Perhaps. Ineffective? Oh no. Awfully, awfully effective. And, until it happened too often, perfectly legal."[39]

Among the ways a manager can bend or break the rules are his actions when ejected from the game. As all baseball fans know, when a manager is kicked out, he is required to leave the dugout and to have no further involvement in the contest. That said, managers have been known to continue to run the team either by standing out of view just outside the dugout, or by using messengers to relay instructions from the clubhouse. Other than observing to make sure the skipper is out of sight, umpires do not police manager involvement.

The most-notorious recent violation of this rule involved New York Mets manager Bobby Valentine in 1999. On June 9 the Mets were locked in a tight extra-inning game with the Blue Jays. In the top of the twelfth Mets catcher Mike Piazza tried to throw out a Blue Jays baserunner, only to be called for interference for coming too far out of his crouch to catch the pitch. Valentine, furious, was ejected in the ensuing argument. The game continued.

A few minutes later, television cameras caught sight of a stranger standing in the back corner of the Mets dugout. In fact, it was Valentine wearing street clothes, a fake mustache, and sunglasses. The umpires didn't notice, but the Mets TV announcers could not help laughing at the strange sight and blew Valentine's cover. He was suspended for two games and fined $5,000. "I regret it," he later admitted. "It's going to cost me a lot of money. I don't regret the fact that it lightened the team." The Mets pulled out the game in the fourteenth and went on to make their first playoff appearance since 1988.[40]

Although Valentine got a lot of ink, other managers have been equally colorful in circumventing their ejections. In one of the most creative incidents, Boise Hawks (Northwest League) manager Mal Fichman was ejected from a game in 1989, only to return wearing the costume of the team mascot, Humphrey the Hawk. "The Hawk" spent the rest of the game wandering around the field, occasionally stopping by the Boise dugout to give instructions. When he was exposed after the game everyone agreed on Fichman's humor, but he still got suspended (just for one game).[41]

In August 1904, umpire Jim Johnstone ejected Giants manager John McGraw and catcher Frank Bowerman after they disputed a call at second base. Bowerman complied, but McGraw went to a small closet near the dugout used by the grounds crew for their equipment. Johnstone ordered a policeman to get him out, but instead pitcher Joe McGinnity locked McGraw in. Johnstone ordered McGinnity to leave the bench area, so the hurler simply went and sat in the seats right near the bench. Because he was wearing street clothes (he wasn't scheduled to pitch that day) Johnstone felt powerless to do more. In fact, there wasn't much McGraw could do from the shed or McGinnity from the stands, but McGraw likely took pride that he had defied an umpire yet again.[42]

President Pulliam suspended McGraw for three games. McGraw protested with high-toned officiousness. "Notice of your suspension received today," McGraw wrote Pulliam. "I don't think it is in keeping with the rule which covers removing players from the field. Umpire Johnstone ordered me from the field. I went and was not on the field again until the game was finished. Don't see what difference it makes whether I go to the clubhouse or some other place as long as I do not break the rule which covers this point."[43] Despite this specious response, McGraw's petition was successful, a testament to the Giants' strength within the National League.

For 150 years, baseball employees, in uniform and out, have pushed and bent and broken the game's rules to help their teams win. Many of these people—especially showmen like Bill Veeck—displayed intuition, creativity, and occasional humor. The successes encouraged copy-cat behaviors and remain integral to the lore of the game. The vaudevillian aspects, however, should not obscure the fact that these actions ignored the consensual ethic, and many brazenly violated the rulebook.

Chapter Seven

ROSTER SHENANIGANS

F ROM THE TIME BASEBALL CLUBS began to be organized in the 1840s, team management has concentrated on finding and keeping talented players. But building a championship baseball team is an extremely challenging job. One needs to scout, sign, and develop players better than all the other ballclubs. Perhaps no other area of the game has seen such determined, inveterate rule-skirting as building a team roster.

The rules guiding team building have changed repeatedly in the past 170 years, and many of the new regulations have been implemented because teams kept breaking the old ones. Smart, resourceful teams are no different than smart, resourceful players: They will do anything to win. So leagues frequently have had to reckon with the question of how to ensure compliance, and what to do with teams that flout the rules.

One of the earliest ethical dilemmas in baseball was the prevalence of "ringers" in the 1850s. The popularity of baseball matches between the top social clubs had exploded, and the competitive nature of these clubs led to their frequently poaching players from one another. In 1856, Joseph Pinckney caused a commotion among the New York clubs when he suited up for the Gothams against the Knickerbockers, despite being a member of the Union of Morrisania, a neighboring team from the Bronx. At the time, this violated no formal rule, primarily because there was no central authority governing the game. But even in those free-for-all times, the behavior was seen as ungentlemanly.[1]

In recognition of baseball's growing popularity in American culture, the National Association of Base Ball Players was created in March 1858—the first formal organization governing the sport. In addition to eligibility rules (requiring that players be members of a club for at least 30 days before playing against another team), amateurism was now codified: Paying players was prohibited. Though the association established a judiciary committee to oversee disputes, in truth it lacked any meaningful enforcement authority.[2]

Not surprisingly, many of the best teams ignored the rule prohibiting professionalism because it worked: The teams that paid players acquired the best talent. In 1860, the Brooklyn Excelsiors reportedly paid star hurler Jim Creighton, making him the first historically recognized professional. Other clubs also offered compensation, often more creatively. Al Reach, who later became a successful sporting goods manufacturer, received $25 per week from the Athletics of Philadelphia, who were paying additional players. Another future sporting goods magnate, Al Spalding, was given a grocery job sinecure at $40 a week by the Forest Citys of Rockford (Illinois), though this payment for nonwork was not considered cheating.[3]

By the late 1860s, instances of barely concealed professionalism were rampant across the National Association, as was "revolving," the practice of ringers jumping from team to team. At the 1868 winter meetings, Association officials threw in the proverbial towel. Forthwith, clubs would be allowed to pay players if they designated their professionals; all others would be considered amateurs. But the notion that clubs might function long-term with some paid players and some amateurs could not last—two years after the association allowed for pros, a squadron of mostly professional clubs split off, creating the National Association of Professional Ball Players, known to modern historians as the National Association.[4]

Five years later, the 1876 launch of the National League ushered in a new era in sports. With territorial rights, a defined set of teams, and a fixed schedule, owners created value through their franchises. Once they had this foundation in place, the owners began to spend their collective energy on minimizing expenses, principally player salaries. The infamous "reserve system," which effectively bound a player to his team for as long as the team wanted, was introduced in 1879 and expanded throughout the 1880s, with the concept enshrined in players' contracts by 1887. As players became more valuable to their teams, owners devised new rules to increase their control and avoid a free market.

In 1885, National League owners agreed to cap individual salaries at $2,000 annually. Much like the other rules, this cap was routinely ignored. Cincinnati star Bid McPhee signed a side letter that promised him an additional $300. Boston funneled Mike "King" Kelly an extra $3,000 for his photograph. Other owners skirted the rules by signing their star players to personal service contracts.[5]

Until the late 1880s there was no formal mechanism to sell or trade players. John B. Day, a principal in the group that owned the New York franchises in both the National League and the American Association (a major league between 1882 and 1991), wanted to transfer two of his stars, hurler Tim Keefe and third baseman Dude Esterbrook, from his American Association team to his National League team. But since contracts could not yet be transferred, he had to release the players from one team, then re-sign them with the other. As Day knew, the owners of the two leagues had agreed that any player who was released or became a free agent had to wait 10 days and be passed over by all the teams in his own league before he could sign with the other. To sidestep this rule, Day put both Keefe and Esterbrook on a cruise to Bermuda with manager Jim Mutrie, making them inaccessible. Mutrie then signed both players at the end of the 10-day waiting period. For this deceit the AA considered expelling Day, but in the end merely fined him.[6]

Another hullaballoo came at the tail end of the 1885 season, when the Detroit Wolverines purchased the entire Buffalo Bisons franchise in order to acquire Buffalo's "Big Four": Dan Brouthers, Hardy Richardson, Jack Rowe, and Deacon White. Now in control of two National League teams, the Wolverines owners released the stars from their Buffalo contracts and signed them for Detroit. The other owners, several of whom wanted these players for themselves, ruled that none of the Big Four could sign for 1886 until October 20. Amenable to joining Detroit, the four players went off to enjoy a clandestine fishing and hunting vacation in the isolated St. Clair flats, arranged by Detroit ownership so that they could not be approached by competing teams. On October 20, they returned, all signed up and ready for 1886.[7]

Although so-called "minor" leagues began forming in the 1880s, they still operated independently from the majors. Minor league teams competed for their leagues' pennants just as hard as major league teams, and their fans were just as rabid. If a player was good enough for the next level, his minor league team could sell him to a higher league or keep him. Under such a system, where players had no control over what team or league they played in, the potential for abuse was nearly limitless.

Eventually the various leagues banded together to create controls for player movement that offered small protections to the athletes and structured the relationship between major and minor leagues. The new arrangement started with a draft that allowed teams to claim players from lower leagues. This gave priority to the higher leagues in securing players and a mechanism for players to advance up the ladder. Additionally, provisions were made so that a team could send a player to a lower league for further development under an optional assignment. The higher-league team had the right to repurchase the player but with checks on how many times and for how long it could do so with any individual. There were further restrictions on how many players a team could control, keeping a team from signing dozens of prospects and farming them all over the country to friendly minor league owners.

The details of both the draft and optional assignments changed regularly. But inevitably, as soon as a new rule appeared, owners attempted to exploit its loopholes, engaging in all manner of chicanery to control as many players as possible, as cheaply as possible, and for as long as possible. Leagues redoubled their efforts, trying to make it harder to cheat. But as always, teams found innovative ways of bending or breaking the rules. During the first two decades of the twentieth century, the National Commission—baseball's governing three-person body—spent much of its time adjudicating player-control disputes. But it was all done rather loosely. When Kennesaw Mountain Landis became commissioner in 1920, he took a much harder line on abuses of covert player control.

There were many examples. In November 1921, Landis declared six players free agents for illegal "gentlemen's agreements" between major and minor league operators. All six had been sent to the minors without clearing waivers or a formal option agreement. This surreptitious farming of the players, Landis ruled, had cheated other ballclubs of a chance to claim them and allowed their own teams to control more than the officially allotted maximum. Of course, it also cheated the players out of a chance to move to another major league team.[8]

The following year, shortstop Ray French and pitcher Jess Doyle, both New York Yankee prospects, toiled for the Vernon Tigers in the Pacific Coast League under optional assignments. With no open spots on the Yankees and their option period expiring, Yankees GM Ed Barrow supposedly surrendered control and turned the players over to Vernon. Nevertheless, in January 1923 Barrow sent a telegram to several other Pacific Coast League clubs offering French and Doyle in trade, indicating that in reality he still controlled these players through a friendly agreement with Vernon. One of the PCL teams sent Commissioner Landis a copy of the telegram. Landis ruled that Vernon and New York had illegally conspired to control the two players and declared them free agents. This was typical of the era. If Landis found out about a violation, he acted, but he did not have the budget or staff to actively monitor every infraction.

In the early 1920s, with the costs of star players from the minors skyrocketing, St. Louis Cardinals GM Branch Rickey devised a strategic idea to circumvent some of the player-control constraints: baseball's first "farm system." Rickey rightly recognized this investment as a means to acquire more ballplayers cheaply.

Only a few years after Rickey's innovation, big league teams predictably began using their minor league clubs to skirt player-control rules. In fact, Commissioner Landis's first court challenge stemmed from such an action. The St. Louis Browns had optioned outfielder Fred Bennett to Tulsa early in 1928. Later that season they canceled their option—a team was limited to having eight players out on option, so these were valuable rights—meaning they no longer controlled him. Bennett ended up with Wichita Falls. But when the Pirates tried to acquire him, they were told that the Browns had first dibs. The Browns repurchased Bennett for less than the Pirates had offered, and then optioned him to Milwaukee.

Landis rightly found that St. Louis's control over Bennett was illegitimate, hurting Bennett's chance for a major league career and cheating other teams out of his skills. Browns owner Phil Ball sued Landis, claiming illegal interference in his business. It was not the strongest case to take to court, but the facts were not really in question. The issue was the reach of Landis's authority, and the court ruled that it encompassed matters of player control.

A few years later Landis faced a similar case of team overreach with a much more important player. In 1935, Cleveland general manager Cy Slapnicka signed Iowa high schooler Bob Feller, one of the nation's top prospects. This was against the rules, as only minor league teams could sign sandlotters. To get around that inconvenience, Slapnicka signed Feller to a Fargo-Moorhead contract, which was promptly transferred to New Orleans, and then to Cleveland. This was all a ruse, as Feller never appeared in the minor leagues. The transfers were prearranged, a blatant violation brought to light by the Des Moines club that had hoped to sign him. Despite his disdain for this practice, Landis allowed Feller to remain with the Indians, swayed by the fact that Feller did not want to be made a free agent. He also was likely influenced by big league owners, who had enacted a rule change permitting a major league team to recommend a player to the minors and act as a conduit.

Six months after his decision in the Feller case, Landis was not so generous with Slapnicka. He declared outfielder Tommy Henrich a free agent after Cleveland secretly orchestrated his transfer from New Orleans to Milwaukee to maintain extralegal control, a breach Henrich (unlike Feller) protested. Henrich subsequently signed with the Yankees and became one of baseball's top outfielders.

Rickey, one of baseball's greatest innovators, who is justifiably venerated for his role in integrating baseball after the war, also perpetuated one of the largest player control cheating operations in the sport's history. With baseball's most-extensive farm system, Rickey's Cardinals had an affiliate in nearly every minor league. To secure even greater coverage, beginning in 1936 Rickey created a second, shadow farm system through his relationship with the Single-A Cedar Rapids club. Cedar Rapids created working relationships with teams in the very same leagues where St. Louis had affiliates, allowing the Cardinals to control multiple teams that were supposed to be competing with one another. Confronted with this blatant rules violation, Landis declared 74 Brooklyn farmhands to be free agents, including outfielder Pete Reiser, who went on to star in the majors.

In 1940, the Tigers suffered a similar fate for a similar crime, in addition to other illegal arrangements. Landis placed the blame squarely on GM Jack Zeller, and in consequence, released nearly 100 players. This time, many of the players were at higher levels or even on the major league club—Detroit was left with only 78 players in their entire organization. A couple were significant losses, most notably Roy Cullenbine.

Landis realized that to end these violations he needed harsher penalties, and with his Detroit ruling he placed the accountability on front office executives. "Notice is hereby given all clubs, club offi-cials and employees," Landis wrote in his decision, "that the evils of common control of player dealings of two clubs in the same league, and perversion of 'working agreements' into arrangements ... for the wholesale 'covering up' of players must cease; and that all club officials and employees found to be involved in any such misconduct after this date will be placed on the illegible list [suspended], maximum files will be imposed on each club concerned, and all players mishandled therein will be declared free agents."[9] Landis's threat eliminated the most blatant player-control abuses.

Meanwhile, Landis and his small staff also tried to police scout-ing violations. Stories were widespread of scouts acting dishonestly to hide coveted players from other scouts, though many were likely apocryphal. Most have come down through history as part of the cat-and-mouse lore around scouting competition, though they clearly had consequences, for both players and teams. Longtime scout Hugh Alexander remembered getting called into Landis's office on suspicion that he had postdated contracts for young players. During most of Landis's tenure, a prospect was not eligible to be signed until either he or his high school class had graduated. Alexander and other scouts were often guilty of skirting this rule. "Mr. Alexander," Landis told him, "I understand that you have been signing some boys before they graduate from high school and then postdating the contracts.... If I catch you postdating contracts, Mr. Alexander, I'll throw you out of baseball. You understand me?"[10] Landis never followed through on this threat, but Alexander and his fellow scouts, for the most part, abided by the rules.

While the Negro Leagues didn't create extensive farm systems built around a hierarchy of leagues, they were not immune to player-control battles. In 1933, Homestead Grays owner Cum Posey signed two players from the cash-strapped Detroit Stars at midseason. Pittsburgh Crawfords owner Gus Greenlee, the Negro National League's most powerful executive and Posey's rival for the Pittsburgh market, was so angered at what he considered an unethical breach that he had the Grays expelled from the league. Publicly, Posey shrugged off this blow, claiming that he could better survive as an independent team anyway. But the dismissal clearly hurt. Two years later, in 1935, the Grays were back in the league.[11]

While some of these stories are well known, it is worth considering that Rickey, Zeller, Slapnicka, and others have largely been given a pass for their actions. They broke the rules repeatedly, to help themselves or their teams, often to the detriment of young players' careers and lives. Historians, however, have treated them merely as competitive men who carried things too far. This kid-glove treatment stands in sharp contrast to the way that twenty-first-century cheaters, especially players, are viewed.

After World War II, farm systems became more institutionalized, and the most brazen cheating receded. But the malfeasance had not vanished; it merely took on a new form. Now that amateurs were free to sign with whomever they chose, competition to recruit the best prep and college players was intense, and bonuses skyrocketed as postwar baseball attendance ballooned. To keep a grip on costs and minimize these bonuses, baseball began instituting disincentives.

The first bonus rule, introduced in 1947, required that any amateur signed for more than $6,000 (including his first-year salary) must be put on the major league roster after one season or be placed on irrevocable waivers. But cheating on bonuses was so prevalent that after the season baseball required that both the player and team sign an affidavit swearing no consideration had been paid outside of the stated terms of the contract. The Pittsburgh Pirates, for example, were fined $2,000 and the farm director $500 for hiring a signee's father as a part-time scout.[12]

Tired of all the chicanery, and the policing it required, the owners gave up on their bonus rule after the 1950 season. As a result, bonuses continued to balloon—one baseball official estimated that they totaled $4.5 million in 1952 alone.[13]

The owners tried again with a more restrictive rule. From 1953 to 1957, any player who received a bonus of more than $4,000 had to be kept on the major league roster for two seasons before he could be sent to the minors. If the player was assigned to the minors before the end of the two-year period, he was subject to an unrestricted draft and available to all other teams. There was the occasional payoff—Sandy Koufax, Harmon Killebrew, and Al Kaline—but their names were swamped by the Billy Consolos and Vic Janowiczes.

Nevertheless, enforcement again proved difficult, and cheating was rampant.

Longtime Orioles scout Jim Russo believed the behavior was nearly universal. "I think we're all cheating," farm director Jim McLaughlin told him, "except maybe two or three clubs." Russo recalled that Orioles GM Paul Richards "could cheat as well as anybody." According to Russo, Dutch Dietrich, an area scout for the Orioles, would pass a satchel of cash to a person riding on a train as it rode slowly through a Texas town, without the train ever stopping; that person would route the cash to the player. According to one story, Dietrich and the person on the train once missed the handoff, and $100 bills fluttered across the Texas countryside. Russo had few qualms about any of this behavior: "I didn't deny that we were cheating. We had no other choice. It was cheat or finish in last place, which would be cheating our fans as well as risking our whole business. This wasn't college. This was a fight for survival."[14] Although this attitude has persisted in baseball for 170 years, Russo enunciated it so clearly that we will call this rationale **the Russo Doctrine**.

Five years of the bonus rule and all of its attendant issues proved to be enough for the owners. After the 1958 season they instituted a new plan—the first-year player draft. If a player was not protected by being placed on the major league 25-man roster after his first year in the minors, he could be drafted by any team. The theory was that teams would not invest so heavily in youngsters if they were at risk of losing them after one year. No one liked this rule, and it didn't cut down on the biggest bonuses—it merely moved money from the middle class of prospects to the few at the top because teams could reasonably carry one or two on their 25-man squads. The owners tweaked the particulars several times but never succeeded in striking a balance they were happy with.

The amateur draft, finally introduced in 1965, slowed significant cheating over amateur players. It's surprising that baseball took so long to settle on this solution. The NFL started their draft in 1936, and the NBA in 1947, but baseball played around with several poorly executed half-measures before falling into line. Originally, there were three separate amateur drafts, the largest in June, for most players; another in August, for summer league players; and one in January for fall graduates. The August draft existed for just two years, and the January one until 1986.

In the first January draft, in 1966, the Atlanta Braves selected USC pitcher Tom Seaver. After the draft, Atlanta needed to act quickly because teams were not allowed to sign players once their college season started. In this case, the Braves (and Seaver) missed their deadline, signing after USC had played a couple of early season games. USC coach Rod Dedeaux, who naturally wanted to keep Seaver, reported the violation to Commissioner William Eckert.

Eckert voided Seaver's contract, and when the NCAA ruled Seaver ineligible because he had signed, Seaver suddenly had nowhere to go. Braves GM John McHale defended the signing, arguing that the USC season started earlier than most, and the team hadn't had enough time to negotiate with him. The system was brand new, so the Braves can perhaps be forgiven. But it is also likely they were aware of the rule and figured they could get away with it.

Fearing a legal battle, Eckert held a lottery for any team (except the Braves) that would meet the terms Seaver had signed for ($40,000 plus $11,000 to finish his education). For perspective, in the June 1965 draft only 13 players received bonuses of $40,000 or more. Seaver was highly regarded, but not necessarily viewed as a top talent. In any event, only three teams put their hats in the ring: the New York Mets, the Cleveland Indians, and the Philadelphia Phillies. The Mets won. The Braves were not disciplined further, but losing out on Tom Seaver was surely punishment enough.[15]

In 1978 the Seattle Mariners with the sixth pick in the draft selected outfielder Tito Nanni. But Nanni wanted more than the team was willing to pay, so the parties resorted to financial subterfuge. They agreed to a bonus below Nanni's price while forging a side agreement with him to make it up in salary during Nanni's first years in the minors. Such an agreement violated baseball's rules, which only permitted one-year contracts for draftees. When the deal came to light, the Mariners had to restructure the contract.[16]

After nearly five decades, the owners came to believe that their draft no longer sufficiently curbed signing bonuses. Accordingly, the 2011 Collective Bargaining Agreement capped bonuses that could be paid to draftees, and specified penalties for exceeding the cap. Each draft pick was assigned a "slot value" and the sum of these slot values totaled the bonus pool available to spend on draft picks. Although financial cheating has become harder to get away with, Braves GM John Coppolella offered a 2017 draft pick "impermissible benefits" to lessen his signing bonus, thereby leaving more bonus money for their other draft picks. As punishment, Commissioner Manfred docked the Braves their third-round pick the following year. This punishment was mild when compared with what the Braves would face in 2019.[17]

The rules governing non-U.S. players, who are not covered by the draft, have changed many times over the years as well, and front offices have violated those rules just as enthusiastically as they violated the previous ones. Ostensibly, all non-U.S. amateurs are free agents, but there have been policies in place regarding which countries can be scouted, the age of players in question, the size of their bonuses, and more.

In 1974, the Montreal Expos were the only non-U.S. team in the major leagues and therefore the only club not subject to the U.S.'s prohibition on traveling to Cuba. Regardless of the existence of flights from Canada to Cuba, U.S. citizens were still prohibited from traveling there. Nonetheless, Expos scouting director Mel Didier flew to Cuba to meet with the Cuban national team and exchange ideas for coaching and instruction. Didier attempted to convince Cuban authorities to allow the Expos to sign a few players, but he was turned down. In any case, it's doubtful that this would have worked. When Commissioner Kuhn learned of the trip, he threatened Didier with a two-year suspension if it happened again.[18]

New York Mets scout Red Murff held tryout camps in Puerto Rico in the mid-1960s, according to Murff a violation of Puerto Rican rules. Murff recalls finding several useful players in these tryouts, including hurler Ed Figueroa. Dodger scout Hugh Alexander was fined $500 by the commissioner's office for a tryout camp in the U.S. because one of the attendees didn't have the permission slip required of all participants.[19]

In the late 1970s and early 1980s, teams spent increasing time and energy trying to find players in the Dominican Republic and Venezuela, efforts that have dramatically transformed the game in the past 40 years. The Giants and the Dodgers had been active there for some time. But Toronto Blue Jays GM Pat Gillick dramatically increased MLB's presence when he teamed up with longtime colleague and Dominican scout Epy Guerrero to build the first rudimentary baseball academy in the Dominican Republic. As with Branch Rickey and the farm system, both the Blue Jays and Dodgers found ways to skirt the rules to their benefit.[20]

As Latin America became increasingly competitive, teams tried to sign players at ever younger ages, which had the advantage of providing a longer development runway while reducing a player's signing bonus. In 1984, when it came out that the Toronto Blue Jays had signed 13-year-old Jimy Kelly to a $5,000 bonus, baseball instituted a rule requiring that a player turn 17 by the end of his first professional season in order to be eligible.[21]

As soon as the age minimum was in place, teams began working to get around it, and many were caught. In 1999, Tommy Lasorda, then a Los Angeles Dodgers front office executive, said, "I bet you there's 50 ballplayers in the major leagues that have signed illegally."[22] Lasorda was expressing his frustration after Commissioner Bud Selig had voided the signing of two young Cuban signees, making them free agents, and fined the Dodgers $200,000. But the immediate cause of Lasorda's outburst was an impending ruling over another premature signee, young third baseman Adrián Beltré, whose birth certificate the Dodgers later admitted doctoring. Because Selig ruled that Beltré was, at the very least, complicit in the deception, Selig did not make him a free agent but barred the Dodgers from signing or scouting players in the Dominican Republic for a year. Nonetheless, one year later the Dodgers were fined $100,000 for signing underage Dominican Felix Arellan in March 1996 when he was 15. The Braves were also discovered to have signed two underage Dominican players, Winston Abreu and Wilson Betemit.[23]

Beltré notwithstanding, players discovered to have signed before they were of age were typically declared free agents. After the Marlins were caught in 1996 signing 14-year-old Dominican pitcher Ricardo Aramboles for $5,500, Selig released him. Later, Aramboles signed with the Yankees for $1.52 million (at this time the minimum signing age was 16).[24]

In 2002, Cleveland was penalized $50,000 and assessed a two-month suspension of their Venezuelan activities for the 1998 signing of 15-year-old Laumin Bessa. Scout Luis Aponte had inked Bessa to a blank contract, reportedly to be completed after the player turned 16. When confronted, Aponte replied, "In life, things happen that you can't explain." No doubt. To keep their rivals away, Cleveland stashed Bressa in their academy until he was 16. This was neither unusual nor egregious. "In a measure of the degree of corruption that exists in Latin American baseball," wrote a reporter, "the Indians opted not to fire Aponte after deciding he was following normal business practices."[25]

One of the first clubs to organize training in Venezuela, the Houston Astros, skirted the age restrictions in the late 1990s by opening their facility to players before they were eligible to be signed. But when the Astros found legitimate underage prospects, the temptation proved overpowering, and they took measures to prevent them from talking with competitors. Once the commissioner's office realized what was going on, the practice was banned; only players 16 or older could attend the academies.[26]

The next Latin American cheating scandal didn't erupt until the next significant policy change, in the mid-2010s. In the meantime, bonuses had exploded and baseball scouts from several teams were caught skimming money earmarked for the players. In yet another attempt to get control over bonuses, the owners resorted to a variation of their failed 1950s concept: a ceiling, this time in the form of a cap (bonus pool) on what each team could spend for international players. Teams with poorer records in the previous season were allocated more money. Teams could exceed the cap for one season but would have a reduced pool in subsequent years.

The Red Sox were the first team publicly exposed for evading the cap. After their 2015 signing of Cuban Yoan Moncada put them well over the ceiling, Boston was limited to a bonus of $300,000 for any individual player during the following signing period. No matter. The Red Sox skirted the threshold by bundling lesser prospects with stars, and instructing the agents to redistribute most of the money to the better prospects. As punishment, Commissioner Manfred declared five players free agents and barred Boston from signing any international free agents for a year.[27]

Attesting to the seriousness with which baseball viewed these violations, the 2016 CBA included a list of cap evasions that were now considered cheating and subject to discipline. The Atlanta Braves committed several violations anyway. First, they sidestepped the cap by paying inflated amounts to foreign professionals (defined as older players with professional experience who did not count against the cap), with the excess payments redirected to young prospects. In a dodge similar to Boston's, Atlanta also packaged bonuses to multiple players represented by the same *buscón* (a combination agent and trainer), with the bonuses redistributed. In a third ruse, the Braves signed several players represented by a *buscón* at above-market values so he would direct a different client, in this instance shortstop Robert Puason, to sign with them in the future. The Braves also signed South

Korean shortstop Ji-hwan Bae for $300,000, while agreeing to pay him another $600,000 on a side letter.[28]

Commissioner Rob Manfred lowered the boom. Thirteen players in Atlanta's organization, representing roughly $16.5 million in bonuses, were declared free agents. The Braves' international bonus pools were slashed for several years. Special assistant Gordon Blakeley was suspended for a year. Most dramatically, general manager John Coppolella was placed on baseball's permanently ineligible list. President of baseball operations John Hart was not implicated in the commissioner's report but left the organization to "pursue other opportunities." Manfred's severe penalties had finally made the costs associated with skirting bonus rules prohibitive.[29]

One final form of cheating must be noted here. Baseball has long had a rule prohibiting a team from "tampering," expressing interest in acquiring an opposing player, either to the player or even to a reporter. Until 1976 this didn't really matter—players were bound by the reserve clause, and what the player wanted was largely irrelevant. But when the players gained free agency following the 1976 season, tampering suddenly mattered. Not surprisingly, it was only a matter of weeks before the first case was exposed.[30]

In November 1976, the Atlanta Braves signed free agent outfielder Gary Matthews, but Commissioner Kuhn ruled they had had inappropriate conversations with Matthews prior to the free agent draft. Moreover, Braves owner Ted Turner had told Giants' owner Bob Lurie that "no matter what you offer Gary, we'll do better."[31] Kuhn leveled a stiff penalty: the loss of the Braves' two top draft choices (their first in both the June and January phases of the amateur draft), a $10,000 fine, and a one-year suspension for Turner. The team contested Kuhn's penalties in court and managed to salvage their June draft pick. Although accusations of tampering still occur now and again, Kuhn's stiff penalties have mostly prevented it.

The rules and restrictions around roster management have changed many times over the past 150 years, but one thing remains constant: teams trying to evade them. The people running teams are as competitive as their players, and no less likely to transgress. A cap on international bonuses, like virtually every rule discussed in this chapter, has the twin goals of reducing money going to players and keeping rich teams from signing more than their share.

But while rewards for cheating in roster building can be large—fame, money, championships—the risks have often been very low.

Chapter Eight

GREENIES

THOUGH MANY MODERN-DAY FANS ASSOCIATE BASEBALL'S doping issues with the scandals of the 1990s, the sport's history of using drugs to improve performance began much earlier. In early November 1951, the *Detroit Times* blared on its front page: "O'Neill Says Tigers Doped Newhouser." Another paper announced: "Drug 'Won' Tigers the 1945 Flag."[1]

The intrigue had begun a few days earlier when Cleveland catcher Birdie Tebbetts, an insurance agent during the offseason, spoke at the Massachusetts Association of Insurance Agents. Tebbetts told the story of a manager who urged a "promising young pitcher" to treat his sore back with an injection of novocaine. Approached after the talk by reporters demanding the identities of the pitcher and manager, Tebbetts did not elaborate.

Boston Post reporter Al Hirshberg decided to follow up on the matter with Red Sox manager Steve O'Neill. And O'Neill, who had also been the Detroit Tigers manager during their 1945 World Championship season, started talking. "Why sure, [Hal] Newhouser took a dozen shots of the stuff back in 1945," he told Hirshberg. (Newhouser had been the AL MVP that season.) "We had a trainer guy named Dr. [Raymond D.] Forsyth ... and he used to jab Hal in the clubhouse before the boy went out to pitch."[2]

"We were in the pennant race and brother, we needed Newhouser like we needed our legs," said O'Neill. "We just couldn't have won without him. Well, he had a lump in back of his left shoulder blade, and it irritated him something terrible. Every time he lifted his arm he nearly fainted. One day, somebody thought of giving him some kind of pain-killer. Hal said he'd take anything—just so he could pitch. So we had this Dr. Forsyth—he was an osteopath—give Newhouser novocaine whenever he needed it." O'Neill credited the championship entirely on the numbing agent. "Wasn't for that stuff, we'd never have won the pennant, because Hal never would have been able to pitch." O'Neill added that they had also injected first baseman Hank Greenberg's right hand during the World Series.

"Most ball players want to play ball if they can," said O'Neill, "and if they need something to keep them from having too much pain, why they're glad to take it."[3]

Newhouser agreed "My shoulder was hurting terribly," he said. "The way Forsyth put it, there would be nothing harmful at all in using these shots. I think very highly of him and took his word for it. The injections were made on my back between the neck and waistline."[4]

Hirshberg's story and O'Neill's revelations led to headlines throughout the nation. Many were damning, like the *Detroit Times* use of the word "doped" in its headline. Other papers gentler. The *Washington Evening Star* declared, "Doctor Says Drug Given Newhouser for Healing Only," and the *Cincinnati Enquirer* simply stated, "Novocaine Is Used by Tigers Players in 1945, Is Report."

Forsyth, who worked for the University of Detroit and had been on the staff of the Tigers and NFL's Detroit Lions, was distraught at the tone of the coverage. "There is no doping situation involved," he said. "The drug is merely used as an aid for healing."[5] Forsyth added that he had used novocaine "many times" on players at all three institutions. He went on to denounce Hirshberg. "The fellow who wrote that story doesn't know his drugs," Forsyth said. "The use of novocaine is accepted training room practice. You can ask any trainer about that. The Boston writer, however, implied that we used cocaine, Benzedrine, or some similar habit-forming drug."[6]

Newhouser also ridiculed those who took issue with the injections: "There were two or three reporters in the training room when Doc gave me an injection before the final World's Series game. They didn't think it was a story. That's how common the practice is." Newhouser guessed there were probably other instances of players using novocaine, though he couldn't come up with any.[7]

O'Neill disavowed any knowledge of recent drug use on the Red Sox. "No, we didn't have anything like that last year," he remarked. "But in Detroit it was different."[8] He did not expound on precisely what was different. Perhaps it was simply that the Tigers had a chance to win a championship, while Boston did not.

In his commentary a couple of weeks later, sports columnist Dan Parker asked two questions that continue to dog the drug debate today: What is the health impact on the player, and what precisely is the effect of the drug? "Does Dr. Raymond D. Forsyth, the University of Detroit trainer who recently defended his use of novocaine on Pitcher Hal Newhouser's sore arm in 1945 to kill the pain, on the grounds that is a healing aid and is used regularly in training rooms," wrote Parker, "know that medical books describe it as an anesthetic with less toxic [sic] than cocaine, and, far from having healing properties, would, in the case of Newhouser, cause him to aggravate his arm injury by pitching while he was numbed by the drug? ... Incidentally, if it is illegal to use drugs in a contest involving dogs or horses, why shouldn't the ban be extended to include athletes for their own protection?"[9]

In fact, a couple of earlier instances of novocaine use by baseball players had been noted, with little fanfare. During spring training in 1942, Red Sox manager Joe Cronin sent sore-armed hurler Tex Hughson to see a doctor in Coral Gables, Florida. Hughson received eight shots over two days, along with physical therapy. This may have awoken his dead arm, as Hughson went 22–6 that year. In the spring of 1949, Joe DiMaggio's swollen right heel led some to fear he would never play again. Doctors at Johns Hopkins concocted an injection consisting of novocaine and a saline solution. Whether because of the novocaine, other remedies, or rest, DiMaggio played in 76 games that year and a full season in 1950. After the 1950 World Series, it was revealed under large headlines that Phillies catcher Andy Seminick had taken 40 novocaine shots. He'd broken his left ankle late in the season in a home plate collision. Seminick required the shots to hobble through the final games of the season and the World Series. After the Series, Seminick's ankle was placed in a cast.

So why was there such a strong reaction to Newhouser, but not Hughson or DiMaggio? As we explore in this and later chapters, attitudes toward drug use in athletics have continually evolved. One possible distinction is that Newhouser received injections to deaden pain and allow him to pitch, while Hughson and DiMaggio were administered novocaine well prior to competition under a doctor's care as a way to recover from potentially career-ending conditions. Additionally, the Newhouser story broke at a time when there was a national controversy boiling around college football players being shot up with novocaine and sent back onto the field. Just a few days before the Newhouser revelation, headlines leveled these accusations at Michigan State Normal School (now Eastern Michigan).[10]

One constant in the drug story throughout the past several decades is that we (the game and its observers) have wrestled with differentiating between "restorative" drugs that permit injured athletes to perform to their "natural level," and "performance-enhancing drugs" (PEDs) that enable athletes to perform better than they could using only their natural talents. The distinction is often unclear, and the public has always displayed at least some level of discomfort with drugs in sports.

Much of the debate over restorative-type drugs revolves around player health. What are the risks to the athlete from taking a local anesthetic like novocaine or, more recently, anti-inflammatories like cortisone (first administered in 1948)? Use of these drugs to keep players on the field has burgeoned since the 1950s, but elevated injury risk, rather than cheating, is usually the concern.

The search for performance-enhancing ("ergogenic") substances is nothing new. Eating naturally occurring substances is how our species has managed the intake of energy and nutrients for thousands of years. For example, searching for ingredients to enhance athletic performance seemed in no way an unreasonable or unfair practice in the ancient world.

The original Olympians of antiquity experimented with a multitude of dietary innovations: huge portions of meat, consisting of up to 10 pounds of lamb per day; various herbal treatments; dried figs; wet cheese and wheat meal; psychoactive mushrooms; as well as brandy and wine as stimulants, possibly mixed with strychnine for added effect.[11]

Roman gladiators used edible performance enhancers in their competitions, too. The Roman physician Flanius systematically researched ingestible methods to boost performance from "coca leaves, hemlock, thistle, and lotus." Legend suggests that the ancient Nordic warriors, "Berserkers," augmented their strength by ingesting hallucinogenic mushrooms. West Africans used kola nuts for their caffeine before running races. Medieval knights often used naturally occurring stimulants to build stamina and courage for their jousts.[12]

The use of ergogenic aids remained little-changed until the middle of the nineteenth century, when three developments expanded what could be accomplished in performance enhancement, and eventually, how the expansion was perceived. First, the invention of the modern syringe provided for subcutaneous and intramuscular injections. Substances could now be delivered directly into the body without having to go through the digestive process and its diluting or modifying effects. Substances could also be administered locally, targeting a specific part of the body.

Second, advances in synthetic organic chemistry opened the door to systematic approaches around compounds that could modify human physiological reactions. Once scientists began to understand how atoms bonded with each other to form molecules, chemists could experiment with designing new ones or synthesizing those that they were already familiar with. No longer would one need to find herbs or dried figs. Now the chemicals that caused a desired reaction could be identified and synthesized.

Third, the emergence of a modern pharmaceutical industry and medical institutions with research and development capabilities created a favorable environment for the invention of new drugs. In due time, these developments forced a recalibration about what is fair in athletic competitions. Eating naturally occurring compounds—something humans have been doing for thousands of years—is one thing, but injecting synthetic compounds under the skin presents a new ethical dilemma.

As the modern athletic landscape formalized worldwide (the modern Olympics began in 1896), competitive athletes continued their search for ergogenic aids, focusing primarily on stimulants. Most commonly used were strychnine (a stimulant in small doses but highly toxic and fatal in larger ones), caffeine, and cocaine, often mixed with brandy. This was not generally seen as cheating, but the impact on the health of the athletes—there were a couple of tragic incidents—led to concern over their use.[13]

The increasing interest in sport science and perfecting human performance also led to the opening of several research laboratories at academic institutions in the 1920s, notably the Athletic Research Laboratory at the University of Illinois, the Harvard Fatigue Laboratory, and research centers at George Williams College (Chicago) and Springfield College (Massachusetts). The research soon split into two branches: psychology and physiology.

Dr. Coleman Griffith, director of the Athletic Research Laboratory and a pioneer of sports psychology, leaned in the direction of psychology (including scientific training and reconsidering performance limits), statistical research, and analytics. In his research Griffith examined both the psychology and physiology of sport and how they interacted. "There is only one way to be absolutely sure of selecting the right man for the right place," he wrote in *Psychology of Coaching*. "And that is to secure all the statistical data about him that can be gotten."[14]

Several years later, in late 1937, Cubs owner Phil Wrigley hired Griffith, who launched baseball's first proto-analytics department. He introduced a chronoscope and slow-motion camera to observe physical actions more closely. On the statistical side, he amassed and processed previously uncollected information on batter-pitcher matchups and pitch locations. Griffith believed this data could help in both the evaluation and training of Cubs players. Unfortunately, the Cubs' managers—first Charlie Grimm and later Gabby Hartnett—didn't take his suggestions seriously, and baseball's first attempt at serious analytics faded away.[15]

Harvard, on the other hand, focused more generally on fatigue research in industrial workers, and specifically as it pertained to human physiology. Their scientists introduced innovative methods for evaluating blood differences under fatigue, and in 1932 Harvard's science director found that some hormones could help reduce fatigue. Until analytics began its advance into baseball in the 1990s, athletes and sports organizations looking to gain an advantage would almost exclusively follow the Harvard model of ergogenic aids.[16]

When it comes to families of drugs currently associated with cheating, the two most significant are stimulants and steroids (along with related performance-enhancing drugs). We will tackle steroids in the next chapter.

Amphetamine (commonly referred to as "speed") was first synthesized in the late nineteenth century, but in 1927 it was rediscovered by the American chemist Gordon Alles, who was searching for relief of nasal congestion and asthma. He teamed up with pharmaceutical firm Smith, Kline & French to manufacture, market, and sell it.[17]

By the time America entered World War II, amphetamine (principally under the SKF trade name Benzedrine) was predominantly marketed in pill form as a remedy for depression, though it was also sold in an inhaler as a decongestant. Its stimulant and fatigue-inhibiting effects were quickly recognized, and college students and truck drivers were some of the first to use the drug extensively for nonadvertised purposes. Benzedrine in pill form became prescription-only in 1940, though the inhaler remained available over-the-counter.[18]

Throughout World War II, the militaries of all major belligerents experimented with amphetamines to improve the stamina and effectiveness of their soldiers and airmen. Various tests by the Allied forces indicated that in all but a few specific tasks, such as marksmanship, amphetamines did not elevate performance under fatigue conditions any better than caffeine. Nevertheless, the militaries issued it liberally to increase endurance. According to one scholar, the drug was also distributed "for its effects on optimism, aggressiveness, military comportment, and the other aspects of emotional condition that figure in morale."[19] In any case, many servicemen returned to civilian life desensitized to the regular use of amphetamines.

By the first postwar Olympics in 1948, reports of stimulant abuse were circulating. "I became suspicious that some competitors were receiving artificial stimulants at the Olympic games," wrote the official medical advisor to the British team. "A garrulous foreigner surreptitiously tried to show me his pet concoction of strychnine, caffeine, and Benzedrine," later adding that it was "more widespread than people think."[20]

Indeed, during the 1950s amphetamines exploded in popularity among U.S. civilians, ordinary people drawn to the idea of a "pep pill." Many were also marketed as diet pills. Total production increased from 16,000 pounds in 1949 (when the original patent expired) to 75,000 pounds in 1958—enough to produce 7.5 billion five-milligram tablets. Not surprisingly, the drug found its way into competitive sports, whose governing bodies were slow to address the problem. While one needed a prescription to obtain the pills, getting one was not difficult, nor was there much enforcement if you lacked the proper paperwork. In organized leagues in the U.S., the pills were often distributed by team trainers.[21]

On the rare occasions that their use was mentioned publicly, it attracted little attention. Star Boston Celtics guard Bob Cousy admitted to using pep pills before Game 7 of the 1960 NBA championship, and received no blowback. "We were ready for them psychologically," Cousy said. "I took pep pills and followed the advice of several friends in trying to get myself 'up' psychologically for the game. Every time I felt the team starting to go into a lull, I just put out a little extra and the team followed."[22] The Celtics victory might have helped soothe whatever doubts Cousy had.

Similarly, there was little negative reaction to the revelations in pitcher Jim Brosnan's classic *The Long Season*, published in 1960. Brosnan's book recounted his prior season with the Cardinals and Reds and was the first public acknowledgement of amphetamine use by baseball players. In one passage, Brosnan recounted a spring training conversation with St. Louis trainer Bob Bauman concerning diet, working out, and pep pills.

"You gonna order some of these pills that will make me 'go nine with little effort'? You want to keep in step with modern medicine and all that jazz, Doc," Brosnan said.

"Listen, I'll do my job. You do yours," Bauman countered. "Obviously, you don't need any Dexamyl to get you through the day, today. Get your sleep last night, did you?"[23]

Brosnan published another diary in 1962, after a season with the pennant-winning Reds. Once again, his casual conversation about amphetamine and prescription drugs testified to their prevalence in locker rooms.

"'Where in the hell's the Dexamyl, Doc?' I yelled at the trainer, rooting about in his leather valise. 'There's nothing in here but phenobarbital and that kind of crap.'"

"'I don't have any more,' said [the trainer]. 'Gave out the last one yesterday. Get more when we get home.'"

"'Been a rough road trip, huh, Doc?' I said. "How'm I to get through the day then? Order some more, Doc. It looks like a long season.'"

"'Try one of these,' he said."

"'Jesus, that's got opium in it! Whaddya think I am, an addict or something?'"[24]

Despite Brosnan's offhand admissions, at least one group was increasingly alarmed over amphetamines. In the late 1950s the American Medical Association began investigating the use of drugs in sports, holding hearings in 1957. In highly publicized comments, one of the leading crusaders against drug use even impugned the legitimacy of the many four-minute miles that rapidly followed Roger Bannister's historic 1954 feat: "The recent rash of four-minute miles is no coincidence. When I was a college boy, the four-minute mile was as unlikely as flying to the moon."[25] (No evidence was ever produced to implicate the milers, and the controversy quickly died down.)

The AMA endorsed a couple of large scientific studies to assess the impact of amphetamines on performance. Tested on swimmers, runners, and shot-putters, the results were released two years later: Amphetamine use resulted in a small but meaningful increase in performance.[26]

In response to the studies, in 1959 the AMA condemned the use of amphetamines in athletics, because of the unfair advantage they conferred alongside the potential health risks—one of the first instances of institutional censure for the performance-enhancing effect of drugs. Nevertheless, there was little public outcry against their use in professional sports, in part because high schools and colleges continued to deny their use. Of 1,800 coaches responding to an anonymous mail survey as part of the AMA investigation, fewer than 1 percent admitted using amphetamines to boost performance.[27]

In subsequent years there have been numerous studies on the effects of amphetamines. Perhaps the most noteworthy effects are "a sense of increased energy, self-confidence, and faster, more efficient thought and decision making."[28] And while much of those are psychological sensations, some research suggests that amphetamines can, in fact, improve some athletic performance, notably reaction time, speed, and endurance.[29]

The diverse results indicate that effects can fluctuate depending on factors such as "the responsiveness of the individual, the nature of the activity, the dose administered, and the timing of the administration."[30] These effects can even vary within the same person under different circumstances. As for baseball, one authority wrote that there remains at least some ambiguity as to precisely how much they enhance performance: "Although amphetamines appear to improve several physiological components thought related to athletic success, it cannot be concluded with certainty that they can enhance athletic performance. This is particularly true in complex sports activities such as baseball, basketball, and tennis."[31]

A consistent belief is that amphetamines act as an ergogenic agent most effectively when the user is suffering from fatigue because amphetamines "can extend aerobic endurance and hasten recovery from fatigue."[32] Oakland A's pitcher Chuck Dobson may have best summed it up best. "If you're rested and take a greenie," he said, "then you wouldn't feel anything. But if you're tired, it makes you anxious and you feel like you can pitch forever. Sometimes it makes you feel like you have more stuff than you really do."[33] Examples throughout this chapter reflect the pressure players have felt to ingest substances that keep them in the lineup. Because he articulated it so succinctly, we're going to label this **the Dobson Doctrine: Players and their teams will look at almost any treatment to stay in or return to the active roster.**

A new class of pharmaceuticals, tranquilizers, was introduced in the 1950s, and soon enough they made their way into baseball—and baseball headlines. Detroit Tigers third baseman Reno Bertoia, a 22-year-old bonus baby, was leading the league in batting average in mid-May 1957 when reports surfaced that he had been administered tranquilizers before games.[34] "He's young and naturally nervous about getting a chance to play regularly in the big leagues," manager Jack Tighe explained. "That's why we wanted him to take those pills to help him along. I don't think he needs them anymore."[35] Bertoia described his routine, "I take two pills a day. I don't get any physical or mental reaction, but just feel relaxed and calm."[36]

The stories did not criticize Bertoia or the Tigers for any undue advantage that came from taking the pills, and most were ambivalent about their efficacy. One headline asked, "Happy Pills ... Good or Bad?"[37] In a rare exception, the *Wall Street Journal* posed, "What will be the impact on the Record Books? They already are loaded with asterisks and daggers, besides the hallowed names, referring to such footnotes as: used spitball until 1922; sidelined for 40 games in 1933 with broken leg. Will the footnotes soon say something like this? Jones, Brooklyn, 1959: Played 30 games on Milltown, 20 on Equanil, 7 on Suavitil, and 40 on Thorazine."[38]

Despite the *Journal*'s editorial and a brief rehash of the episode when the AMA's drug concerns were publicized a couple of years later, the Bertoia story quickly receded. When his hitting faded—he hit .192 in June and .213 in July—so did the headlines. Tranquilizers were not viewed with the same concern as amphetamines and no longer appeared to be the magic pill they had in the spring. Jim Brosnan dismissed sedatives and tranquilizers as "kind of crap."

The use of amphetamines by baseball players, and other professional athletes, accelerated throughout the 1960s. At the time there were few public revelations, as players, trainers, and front office executives were happy to avoid any potential scandal. Whatever the studies might have said, taking drugs beyond their prescribed use carries the dual stigma of law-breaking and (supposed) unfair performance gains.

Toward the end of the decade, drugs in sports were garnering new headlines. In 1968 the Olympics introduced drug testing. One year later *Sports Illustrated* published a three-part exposé on drugs in sports by Bil Gilbert, observing that the problem "poses a major threat to U.S. sport even though the Establishment either ignores or hushes up the issue." Gilbert aired the first direct reference to amphetamines in baseball since Brosnan.

Among other revelations in Gilbert's piece was an astonishing admission. "We occasionally use Dexamyl and Dexedrine," Dr. I. C. Middleman, one-time team surgeon and physician for the Cardinals, told him. "We also use barbiturates, Seconal, Tuinal, Nembutal.... We also use some anti-depressants, Triavol, Tofranil, Valium.... But I don't think the use of drugs is as prevalent in the Midwest as it is on the East and West coasts." That seems like ... a lot?[39]

In 1970 pitcher Jim Bouton wrote about drug use in his revolutionary book *Ball Four*. Among many revelatory passages, Bouton recounts a conversation from June 1969 with Seattle Pilots teammate Don Mincher.

"Minch, how many major-league ballplayers do you think take greenies?" I asked. "Half? More?"

"Hell, a lot more than half," he said. "Just about the whole Baltimore team takes them. Most of the Tigers. Most of the guys on this club. And that's just what I know for sure."[40]

Mincher was unhappy with Bouton's book and disputed several of its stories but not, apparently, this one.[41]

Cincinnati's star catcher Johnny Bench commented in 1979 about the situation a decade earlier. "About the time [pitcher] Gary [Nolan] and I came up," Bench remembered, "using Dexamyls and Daprisals was very common.... The trainers had them and nobody thought twice about passing them out. A lot of pitchers popped. Gary would get a couple of daps in him and he'd start chirping away, just sitting in the dugout and talking a blue streak." Moreover, Bench added, "Popping uppers wasn't a vice of Gary's any more than anybody else. Pitchers popped them as a psychological way of getting around pain, a sore elbow, or something, and to get up for a start. They were misused, and not just by pitchers, and for that I blame the trainers as much as the players who took them. In the pros you look for any leg up, and a lot of guys, especially pitchers facing a tough start, thought daps and dexys were that edge."[42]

Mets hurler Tug McGraw later described the same period: "We were known for getting a buzz on even during games with the help of some pills and a shot of 'Listerine.' Back then it was different; you could get your treats from the trainers, and it wasn't like you had to sneak them. It was frighteningly easy. Amphetamines, red juice, and tranquilizers—they were all readily available. Red juice was a liquid amphetamine that you'd take by the capful from a Listerine bottle. We'd put trainers' tape all around the bottle, several layers, so we could put it in our kits and not have to worry about it shattering—at least, that's what the tape was supposed to do."[43]

As of 1969, baseball had no rule against amphetamines, nor any other drug. "Nothing has ever come to my attention that would require a special ruling," said NL President Warren Giles about the lack of drug-use regulations. "It has never come up, and I don't think it ever will." AL executive Bob Holbrook concurred even more explicitly (and ridiculously): "The American League has no rules regarding pep pills, pain killers, etc. Baseball players don't use those types of things."[44]

Dock Ellis, who notoriously pitched a no-hitter in 1970 after (by his own account) taking LSD, also downed eight to twelve amphetamines before that game. After sampling red juice early in his career, Ellis said he never pitched a game without first popping amphetamines.[45]

Under these circumstances—drugs dispensed by the team, enjoying widespread, accepted use, without prohibition—it is difficult to classify taking amphetamines or other drugs as cheating. At the time, the concerns about amphetamines were solely related to their illegality and their health risks, rather than the notion that they afforded an unfair advantage.

In *Sports Illustrated*, Bil Gilbert did acknowledge a difference between restorative drugs and additive ones, but mostly lumped all drug use together. Gilbert led off with the previous year's pennant winners, writing, "[The 1968 World Series] at times seemed to be a matchup between Detroit and St. Louis druggists."[46] He singled out the two teams' star pitchers: painkillers and cortisone for Detroit's Denny McLain, muscle relaxants for St. Louis's Bob Gibson. At the time, though, most observers considered using drugs in order to play through injuries as laudable. As one scholar wrote, "If players were using drugs in order to play through pain, in a fashion that made it impossible to ignore the effort, then they were deemed to be performing heroically."[47]

Baseball eventually reacted. In February 1970 Baseball Commissioner Bowie Kuhn hired a director of security, longtime FBI agent Henry Fitzgibbon. There was speculation that Fitzgibbon was principally hired in response to a federal investigation into sports gambling. But whatever the original reason, an experienced professional was now in a position to investigate drug use. Kuhn and Fitzgibbon soon expanded the security staff to three. In December 1970, baseball's team doctors created the Association of Professional Baseball Physicians, to better coordinate the care of ballplayers. Among their discussion points was improved oversight of team trainers, especially their role as distributors of drugs.[48]

In March 1971, baseball became the first major sport to publicly address the drug issue when Kuhn introduced an education and prevention program. It wasn't particularly stringent, and the players mostly scoffed. "When you have the flu and you have to pitch, what are you going to do?" Chuck Dobson asked. "I had to pitch last year with the flu. I took a greenie and threw a shutout. If Kuhn says we can't use them, then the next time I have the flu, somebody else can pitch."[49] Those remarks earned Dobson a reprimand from the commissioner's office. Despite this early resistance, once the players understood that their participation in the program was geared mainly toward preventing drug abuse among youth, they were more open to it.[50]

The program released a pamphlet entitled "Baseball vs. Drugs: An Education and Prevention Program," which focused on recreational drug abuse (including stimulants) and was distributed to officials in the major and minor leagues. In the straitlaced, rather cheesy publication, Kuhn pronounced that the clubs' general managers must report all instances of illegal drug use or involvement, known or suspected, to the commissioner's office or (for minor league clubs) the president of the minor leagues.

Furthermore, Kuhn reminded readers, the use or distribution of unprescribed amphetamines or barbiturates (including "greenies") violated federal and state laws. Accordingly, discipline would be handled by his office on a case-by-case basis.

In addition to baseball's actions, the U.S. government implemented greater restrictions on drug use in response to recreational abuse. Of interest to our subject, amphetamines and their derivatives were classified as Schedule II drugs, requiring that prescriptions could not be filled over the phone nor refilled without a new prescription. The government could also limit the manufacture of Schedule II drugs, curtailing the vast production of amphetamines in the U.S., significantly reducing the supply on the gray market, at least until foreign suppliers could fill this demand.[51]

The use of amphetamines, unless legally prescribed, was explicitly banned in baseball at this point. During the 1970s the casual admission of use went into decline, and players often had to get their supply elsewhere—most trainers were no longer dispensing them. "This has changed today," Johnny Bench wrote in 1979, "Not only because of new government regulations on amphetamines but also because players' attitudes about drugs and their effects have come a long way."[52]

Baseball's changing posture can be seen in its response to Reggie Jackson's casual mention of pep pills in his book on Oakland's 1974 season. Excerpts in the *Oakland Tribune*, from an uncorrected proof, garnered swift reaction. Jackson acknowledged that he had taken, "Boosters, greenies, bennies, whatever," and would "continue to take them unless I get so much (bleep) over this I am forced to stop."[53] Jackson and coauthor Bill Libby claimed this sentence didn't come out as intended. Jackson, nevertheless, discussed his rationale for stimulants in the released version of the book: "It's a long season without enough days off and with travel on most of the days you are off. Most of the time you travel without a day off in between games. Worst of all, you sometimes play a night game, then fly all night and have to play a day game the next day without any real rest or sleep. By August and September you are suffering from some things only rest will heal. And there's no rest to be had. We are paid to perform, and we have to play and we have to produce—so some players do what they have to do." Jackson added, however, that he "hadn't taken any for four or five years."[54] In Jackson's case, unlike with earlier revelations from Brosnan or Bouton, baseball's authorities reacted aggressively. Kuhn dispatched Fitzgibbon to California to interrogate the slugger. Times were changing.

Ron Bergman, The *Sporting News* baseball correspondent for Oakland, felt the commissioner's Jackson probe was more optics than substance: "The attitude of baseball's power structure seemed to be directed against the admission of taking pep pills rather than against their actual use, which is more widespread than most people in sports would like to have known." When Bergman checked with the commissioner's office about previous disciplinary action for drug issues he was told, "there had been 'no serious cases,' because of an 'ambitious drug program' Kuhn initiated after the Dobson disclosures."[55]

Several years later Pete Rose told *Playboy* a story similar to Jackson's. "Well, I might have taken a greenie last week," Rose was quoted in the interview. "I mean, if you want to call it a greenie. I mean, if a doctor gives me a prescription of 30 diet pills, because I want to curb my appetite, so I can lose five pounds before I go to spring training, I mean, is that bad? ... There might be some day when you played a double-header the night before and you go to the ball park for a Sunday game and you want to take a diet pill just to mentally think you are up. You won't be up but mentally, you might think you are up.... It won't help the game, but it will help you mentally. When you help yourself mentally, it might help your game."[56] Rose later denied making the statements.

Bergman was right; amphetamine use was not really being policed. The sport wanted to reduce stimulant usage, though the desire was driven almost exclusively by a wish to eliminate illegal drug use, not over concerns around any team or player gaining an unfair advantage. Stimulants were not considered cheating so much as law-breaking.

As for the players, they had adopted their own policy of "don't ask, don't tell."

In 1980, a Pennsylvania state drug investigator uncovered prescription slips for stimulants made out in the names of several Philadelphia Phillies and their wives at Reading, Pennsylvania, pharmacies. The prosecution that followed, by Pennsylvania officials, provided a unique lens into players' stimulant use in the late 1970s. If players wanted amphetamines, trainers were no longer handing them out; they needed to procure them on their own. Tug McGraw (a Phillies pitcher not named on the prescriptions) wrote years later, "Getting amphetamines was difficult unless you had established contacts."[57]

"The drug contact was the team doctor for our Double-A team in Reading, Pennsylvania," recalled McGraw. "He would write out prescriptions for diet pills in the names of the wives, the wives would give them to their husbands, and the husbands would take them and then they'd go out and play baseball." The doctor had gotten to know some of the players as minor leaguers, but kept up the operation after they reached the majors.

In July 1980, as Philadelphia was en route to its first World Series championship, a regional drug enforcement director and deputy attorney general interviewed several of the players and wives at the Phillies offices. They were not under oath and mostly denied receiving the stimulants under the prescriptions in question, though some acknowledged having received prescription amphetamines at other times.[58]

Based mainly on the players' denials, the state charged the doctor and two accomplices for writing prescriptions in the players' names and then diverting the drugs elsewhere. The Berks County District Attorney was uncomfortable with that posture, stating he would not prosecute the case unless polygraph tests were administered to the players, and his office could conduct its own investigation. "I certainly said the case rested on the credibility of the Phillies and from that perspective, I wasn't very comfortable with the case. I wasn't satisfied they were telling the truth."[59]

The state moved ahead with the prosecution anyway, holding preliminary hearings in January 1981. Under cross-examination, some of the player testimony raised suspicions. In fact, Randy Lerch admitted receiving amphetamines from the defendants. "I can't see a man going to jail five years because I won't stand up and say, 'I took a greenie,'" Lerch said after the hearing. "And they said he could have gone to jail for five years and have been fined and lose his practice and the whole bit. I can't see that." At the end of the hearings, the judge dismissed all charges.[60]

During a later investigation of the case by the *Philadelphia Inquirer*, Danny Ozark, who had managed the Phillies through the middle of the 1979 season, admitted that he knew about his players' drug use, but "What could I do?" he said. "They're all grown men."[61]

If the players had, in fact, asked for the stimulants, they likely denied their involvement for fear of a drug-related interaction with Commissioner Bowie Kuhn, and not because of any worries about being accused of cheating. In two contemporaneous cases, pitchers Bill Lee and Ferguson Jenkins had received disciplinary actions from Kuhn for drug-related incidents, and the Phillies players were doubtless anxious over the possible repercussions from their own use.

As for the cheating aspect, baseball's policy dealt only with amphetamines that were not legally prescribed. The drugs themselves were not banned by the sport. "Though the commissioner's office disapproves of the use of drugs to enhance athletic performance," the *Philadelphia Inquirer* reported, "it turns out that Kuhn has no clear policy against the use of prescription amphetamines in baseball. 'We have strongly urged the players against using amphetamines,' said Art Fuss, Kuhn's assistant director of security. 'That, however, does not prevent their use if they are legally prescribed.'"[62]

Phillies owner Ruly Carpenter expressed little concern. "Well, you know," he said. "I'm not stupid, and I would have to say there are players who take amphetamines in varying degrees on the Phillies, but other ballclubs as well. And I think any official in baseball will tell you that it does happen. It's a fact of life."[63] In another interview he concluded, "I don't think we have an image problem with the fans. We will probably still sell 22,000 season tickets. We don't consider our players drug addicts."[64]

During the 1980s, drug use became a highly public problem in baseball (and professional sports in general). Cocaine, considered a stimulant, was the predominant drug of choice and used almost exclusively as a recreational drug, not a performance enhancer. Any ergogenic benefit that a player might receive from taking the drug (and there is very little evidence one way or the other on possible performance enhancement) would have been dwarfed by the negative side effects and addictiveness.[65]

Although we don't consider cocaine use to be "cheating," as it more likely to hurt the player and his team, the way baseball dealt with this problem is instructive, considering what lay ahead with steroids.

Between 1982 and 1984, Commissioner Kuhn imposed suspensions on several high-profile players who had either been arrested or admitted to drug abuse, including Alan Wiggins, Willie Aikens, Jerry Martin, Willie Wilson, Vida Blue, Steve Howe, and Pascual Perez. These were a small minority of the users, the unlucky ones who were caught.

Baseball's cocaine problem reached its zenith in 1985, when a number of players, including high-profile stars, were called to testify in the trial of several Pittsburgh-area men charged with cocaine distribution. The players were merely witnesses, but the press and public acted as if they, and the sport itself, were the defendants. Over several days of wide-ranging cross-examination, players—Dave Parker, Dale Berra, Vida Blue, Keith Hernandez, and others—discussed pervasive cocaine use within baseball.

The trial touched on amphetamines as well. One former Pirate, John Milner, testified to their locker room prevalence several years earlier, while carefully avoiding too much detail. "I don't know who dispensed them," he said. "They'd always be in my locker. Not every game. Usually games in the second half of the season when the players are worn out and a little tired."[66]

Berra and Parker testified that they had received amphetamines from former Pirate captains Willie Stargell and Bill Madlock. In later testimony Berra walked back his accusation, saying, "If I asked for [an amphetamine] … I could get one. But I didn't ask for any, and they never gave me one."[67] Both Stargell and Madlock strongly denied the allegations. "I don't know what kind of friend Dale is," Madlock said. "But he's lying."[68] In 1986, Commissioner Peter Ueberroth exonerated both Stargell and Madlock, saying he did not believe the accusations.[69]

In the end, several defendants (not players) were convicted of varying counts of drug distribution and went to prison. New baseball commissioner Peter Ueberroth, embarrassed by the trial, named a total of 21 players who would be subject to random drug testing for the remainder of their careers.

Ueberroth also made a strong push for comprehensive drug testing. The target of his initiative was the illegal use of recreational drugs. Performance-enhancement issues were still not on baseball's radar. In many ways, baseball's perspective on amphetamines was illustrated by Madlock shortly after being cleared. "Even if I was doing that," he said. "it's still not in the same ballpark as cocaine. Way back, they used to hand out amphetamine in the clubhouse. All that testimony about amphetamines had nothing to do with the trial, but when names got mentioned, people thought all the names were involved in cocaine."[70]

In June 1984 the owners and union ratified a drug plan that called for an investigation by an independent panel if a team submitted evidence that a player was using prohibited drugs (notably, steroids and amphetamines were not included on the list of banned substances). If the panel determined that a drug problem existed, the player would be required to submit to treatment. If he balked at the process, the commissioner could discipline him, subject to the union's grievance procedure. As will be discussed in the next chapter, the owners quickly became disenchanted with this approach and abrogated the agreement in October 1985.[71]

Even without a formal drug agreement, the fines, suspensions, and terrible publicity from the Pittsburgh drug trials began to reduce cocaine use among ballplayers, with steroids becoming baseball's new drug problem shortly thereafter. Amphetamines were still no concern to the baseball establishment. Pharmacological innovation soon produced new prescription-only stimulants such as Ritalin and Concerta, commonly prescribed for Attention Deficit Disorder, that were gaining adherents among ballplayers. The use of these pills, even without a prescription, still didn't have the stigma of cocaine or steroids.

In June 2004, baseball began random testing for steroids with accompanying penalties. Amphetamines were not included in this initial testing, though pressure was building. A year earlier, Baltimore pitcher Steve Bechler had died during a spring training workout, and ephedra was found in his system. The medical examiner reported that "the toxicity of ephedra played a significant role."[72] A legal over-the-counter stimulant, ephedra combined with caffeine behaved like amphetamine. Already banned within the NFL and NCAA, the FDA prohibited supplements containing ephedrine alkaloids the following year.[73]

In November 2005 MLB and the players union agreed to test for amphetamines and related substances. The penalties were lighter for amphetamine use than for steroids, reflecting baseball's history of differentiating between the two. But amphetamines still played a role in the game, and one Phillies player reported anonymously that he used them nearly every day, receiving them from other players. Still, he wasn't concerned about the ban. "I'm sure there will be days I feel tired," he said. "I'll just have to deal with it."[74]

Other players weren't so sure. "Anybody who thinks you can go through the season normally and your body can just respond normally, after what we go through, is unreasonable," said Eric Chavez, the third baseman for the Oakland Athletics. "I'm not saying taking away greenies isn't a good thing, but guys are definitely going to look for something as a replacement."[75]

Despite their illegality under both U.S. law and baseball's rules over the past half-century, amphetamines had never really been considered cheating within baseball's consensual ethic. Although there is some evidence that the pills can aid performance, the players viewed the use of stimulants more as a restorative than as a performance-enhancing drug—they simply helped get you through a long, grueling season.

A meaningful minority of players could continue to use amphetamines or comparable drugs under the therapeutic use exemption for
"medically appropriate" prescriptions. Of the 1,349 players in the big
leagues in 2015, 113 (8.4 percent) were given a therapeutic use exemption. Of those, 111 were for attention deficit disorder. As always, these
professional athletes would do whatever they could to stay on the field
and perform.[76]

Chapter Nine

JUICE

IN JUNE 1889, Charles-Édouard Brown-Séquard, a renowned French physiologist and neurologist, announced that he had found an anti-aging elixir. The 72-year-old scientist had tested his discovery on himself, a not-uncommon practice. Over a two-week period, Brown-Séquard injected himself with a water-based extract made from the ground-up testes of dogs and guinea pigs. "I have regained at least all the force which I possessed a number of years ago," he reported. "Experimental work at the laboratory tires me little now. I can, to the great astonishment of my assistant, remain standing for hours without feeling the need of sitting down.... I can also now without difficulty, and even without thinking about it, go up and down stairs almost running, a thing which I always did before the age of 60. By using the dynamometer, I have established that there has been an incontestable increase in the force of my limbs."[1]

Brown-Séquard's claims quickly gained notoriety. Despite the skepticism of many colleagues, within six months of the physician's announcement more than 12,000 doctors around the world were dispensing Brown-Séquard's elixir. Their patients provided glowing testimonials.[2]

One person said to have taken the injection was 32-year-old Pittsburgh pitching star Pud Galvin. On Monday, August 12, 1889, according to the *Washington Post*, Galvin was administered the potion at a medical clinic in Pittsburgh. The next day he tossed a five-hit shutout against Boston. Given the notoriety of Brown-Séquard's concoction, it would not be surprising if other baseball players experimented with it. But no other players have ever been publicly associated with the substance, and no other papers picked up on the Galvin story—casting some doubt on the accuracy of the *Post*'s column. The *St. Paul Globe*, perhaps unaware of Galvin's supposed use of Brown-Sequard's formula, flippantly remarked in its game story, "Galvin acted to-day as if he had been partaking of new life elixir."[3] In any case, Galvin's career did not get any long-term boost—his days of stardom remained behind him.[4]

While Brown-Séquard was onto something—secretions of internal organs do affect and regulate the body—his discovery would not have provided a testosterone boost. A recent assessment in the *British Medical Journal* observed that there wouldn't have been any noticeable effect because such "little hormone would have dissolved in water."[5] Any improved performance was caused by a placebo effect, as argued by many physicians at the time.

Synthetic testosterone first became available in 1935; almost immediately researchers began exploring potential uses. Recognition that these synthetic derivatives could stimulate tissue growth suggested therapeutic possibilities. In the wake of general scientific progress during World War II, new and better drugs were seen as an opportunity to enhance well-being. Paul de Kruif, an early steroid advocate, wrote in *The Male Hormone* (1945) of the previous year's World Series participants, "We know how both the St. Louis Cardinals and the St. Louis Browns have won championships, super-charged by vitamins. It would be interesting to watch the productive power of an industry or a professional group that would try a systematic supercharge with testosterone—of course under a good hormone hunter's supervision."[6] In fact, The *Sporting News* printed advertisements for Defender Multivitamins, made by Grove Laboratories, the "same multivitamin formula issued American Soldiers," and touted that they were used by both the Cardinals and Browns.[7]

During the 1950s, weightlifters began experimenting with anabolic steroids that could help achieve previously unattainable muscle mass and strength. Their use spread to other sports where power and strength were paramount, particularly professional football. In the early 1960s the San Diego Chargers hired strength coach Alvin Roy, an early steroids advocate. The coach told offensive tackle Ron Mix, "I've learned a little secret from those Ruskies." The players were given large and regular doses. "Thereafter," Mix remembered years later, "there appeared on our training table for each meal cereal bowls filled with little pink pills."[8]

About this same time, stimulants and steroids were being dispensed by a celebrity doctor named Max Jacobson, dubbed Dr. Feelgood. His client list was a Who's Who of America in the 1950s and 1960s, including President John F. Kennedy. When New York Yankees star Mickey Mantle was worn down and ailing late in the 1961 season, as he and Roger Maris chased Babe Ruth's single season home run record, broadcaster Mel Allen referred Mantle to Jacobson. His concoction for Mantle "included steroids, placenta, bone, calcium, and a very small amount of methamphetamine."[9] This initial shot into Mantle's hip backfired, leaving Mantle limping, in agony, and running a high fever the next morning. Nevertheless, Mantle became a regular patient of Jacobson.[10]

While steroid use was becoming more popular in sports during the 1960s, it usually was not viewed as cheating. U.S. Olympic weightlifter Bill March recalled in 2005, "I never gave it any thought. I knew I was getting bigger and stronger. It was just another supplement."[11] Recent academic research pinpoints the start of the reaction against performance-enhancing drugs in the 1960s, and the reason for this, wrote one scholar, was "the framework of sporting idealism—that it should be a level playing field."[12]

Baseball players were among the last athletes to dabble in ste-roids. Muscle building was generally believed to impede flexibility and hinder overall batting ability. Pitchers initially led the way and began experimenting in the early 1970s. It was "common knowledge" on the Washington Senators that several pitchers were on a steroids program managed by the team physician. Iconoclastic hurler Tom House, who pitched for the Atlanta Braves in the early 1970s, used them in a much less regulated environment. "We were doing ste-roids they wouldn't give to horses," House recalled in 2005. "That was the '60s, when nobody knew.... We didn't get beat, we got out-milligrammed. And when you found out what they were taking, you started taking them."[13]

There is often no bright line that determines where cheating begins. Given their newness, it's hard to categorize early steroid users as cheat-ers: There was no rule against the substances; there was no test for them; they were not illegal under U.S. law; and the medical commu-nity mostly believed steroids offered little more than a placebo effect.

The World Anti-Doping Agency (WADA), whose code has been adopted by the International Olympic Committee—recommends that a substance be "banned" if it meets two of three criteria: "(1) It has the potential to enhance or enhances sport performance; (2) It represents an actual or potential health risk to the athlete; and (3) It violates the spirit of sport."[14] There is quite a bit of room for subjectivity around WADA's criteria, particularly the third, but they provide a reasonable guide to the current philosophy around banning drugs.

From our book's narrower perspective, only the use of prohibited substances that can enhance performance could be considered cheat-ing. As with stimulants, however, there is no bright line demarking drugs classified as therapeutic and restorative and others classified as performance enhancing. Many have both therapeutic and enhance-ment uses.

Throughout the 1970s and 1980s, there was little recognition by the medical community of steroids' potency and effectiveness. In 1972 the FDA required an information label on Dianabol, the trade name for the fundamental weightlifter anabolic steroid methandienone, stating "WARNING: Anabolic steroids do not enhance athletic ability." Despite anecdotal evidence, many researchers did not believe anabolic steroids increased muscle mass and strength. The labeling persisted up to 1988. But more-recent medical studies have validated beyond any reasonable doubt the effectiveness of steroids for building muscle mass and strength.[15]

When the U.S. Congress enacted the Federal Controlled Substances Act of 1970 to regulate the abuse of recreational drugs, anabolic steroids were not on the list. Among other ramifications, this meant that manufacturers of steroids would not have to submit production information to the FDA. Without the FDA's eyes on their operations, the companies were free to create quantities far beyond what was required to fulfill legal prescriptions.

Although there was a growing belief that using steroids violated the spirit of sport, this attitude was in stark contrast to the enthusiasm over groundbreaking surgical techniques. When Dr. Frank Jobe surgically replaced Tommy John's ulnar collateral ligament in his left elbow with a tendon from his right wrist in 1974, saving the pitcher's career, the procedure revolutionized the treatment of elbow injuries in sports. Similarly, many major league players have received laser eye surgery to improve their vision. The International Olympic Committee felt differently about PEDs and, armed with the first test that could detect steroids, banned them prior to the 1976 Olympics.[16]

Norwegian sports philosophy and ethics professor Sigmund Loland offered this case against doping: "Sport is not about any kind of performance; it is about performance developed by individuals' cultivation of talent primarily based on their own efforts. Sporting excellence becomes a kind of human excellence.... Doping becomes a 'short cut'; it overruns 'natural talent' and deprives athletes of developing sporting excellence as human excellence."[17] If one of the attractions of sport at the highest level is testing the limits of human ability, then artificially boosting that capacity somehow removes humanity from the contest. But is *any* enhancement over the line? Exactly how much is too much?

As long as baseball players eschewed weight training, steroids remained a nonissue. This began to change in the mid-1970s when Cincinnati's Big Red Machine gained notoriety for its weight-training program. Success breeds imitators, and by the early 1980s the Phillies, Astros, and others had their own regimens. Other than Tom House, there have been no disclosures of steroid use in baseball from this period.[18]

In 1981, a four-part examination of drugs in sports by Dave Nightingale in The *Sporting News,* entitled "Chemical Revolution," listed more than a dozen possible substances of abuse: cocaine, amphetamines, marijuana, LSD, peyote, PCP (angel dust), heroin, opium, Seconal, Librium, Valium, Quaaludes, and alcohol. But the series made no mention of steroids. Pitcher Ferguson Jenkins said, "It's a fallacy that one pill will make you a Superman (who can) strike out everybody and go nine innings.… I never took a pill before I pitched." NBA chief security officer Jack Joyce added, "I don't think athletes are using drugs to improve their performances."[19]

It's likely that only football had a significant PED problem at the time. The NFL soon realized this and acted: In 1983, Commissioner Pete Rozelle banned the use of anabolic steroids; in 1987 testing began, effectively legitimizing the ban; and in 1989 the first steroid-related suspensions were handed down. Agreeing to a testing program for drugs in baseball would prove much more difficult.

As we saw in Chapter 8, the dominant problem for baseball during the 1980s was the abuse of recreational drugs, particularly cocaine. Although cocaine is not performance enhancing and therefore not cheating by our definition, it is useful to examine how the fight over drug testing played out between owners and players. Their focus on cocaine, while ignoring amphetamines and steroid use, had significant consequences on the game over the next 20 years.

Commissioner Ueberroth and many owners soon became dissatisfied with the 1984 drug plan, in part because players received notice well before taking a test, making detection of relatively short-lived drugs almost impossible. Additionally, few front offices or field staffs had any interest in turning in suspected users and trying to prove one of their players was a drug user. Some owners, embarrassed by the drug trials and emboldened by the commissioner's new assertiveness, began to insert language around recreational drug testing in player contracts. The union filed a grievance, which it won. Ueberroth tried to reopen the joint drug agreement to introduce random testing, but he was unsuccessful. With the two sides entrenched, in October 1985 the owners withdrew from the agreement. The sport would remain without a formal joint drug agreement for nearly 20 years.[20]

In response to this impasse, owners acted unilaterally. Beginning in November 1986 clubs were required to disclose knowledge of a player's drug use to the commissioner's office or risk a $250,000 fine, the highest then permissible. The commissioner could then investigate and potentially discipline the player. But the union had never agreed to this plan, so any investigation or action by the commissioner was likely to be challenged—with attendant negative publicity and animosity. Nonetheless, the policy was restated in 1988 and regularly thereafter.[21]

The policy also called for testing minor leaguers for a specific list of illegal recreational drugs, again not including steroids. Eventually an informal arrangement emerged, in which players could be tested under a "reasonable cause" standard, negotiated between the commissioner's office and the union. Under the distrustful climate of the era, however, cases were rarely settled amicably. For one thing, by the time cause could be established and a test administered, any drug in the player's system was, almost always, already metabolized.[22]

Los Angeles Dodgers GM Fred Claire spoke of the difficulty of pursuing allegations against a player after Darryl Strawberry acknowledged his drug problem to the team in 1994. "He was asked about it numerous times," Claire said. "We did not sweep it under the rug. We confronted him. But unless you catch him or have hard evidence or the player steps forward you cannot accuse him."[23] Nevertheless, if a team suspected a player of using drugs, they did have some justification for approaching him, and furthermore, they were required to report it to the commissioner's office.

The owners continued to push for drug testing, and the players continued to resist, instead indicating a willingness to return to something like the 1984 agreement. In 1994 the owners again raised the issue as part of the Collective Bargaining Agreement (CBA) negotiations, but dropped the matter as the impasse hardened over larger economic concerns.[24]

Once again, it's important to remember that all of this attention was focused on illegal recreational drugs, not performance-enhancing ones.

Steroids made world headlines in September 1988, when Canadian sprinter Ben Johnson tested positive for stanozolol a few days after his record-setting 100-meter race, which won him a gold medal at the Olympic games in Seoul. Track and Field had been dogged by steroids accusations for years, but never had an athlete of Johnson's stature been caught. He was stripped of his record and his medal. Johnson's claim that he needed PEDs in order to compete with other drug users would presage similar comments from baseball players a decade later.

In the late 1980s, when anabolic steroids were being more widely introduced into baseball, their legal status was changing as well. In 1988 the U.S. Congress added criminal penalties for unauthorized distribution of steroids. And in 1990, after another round of hearings led by then-U.S. Senator Joe Biden, Congress added anabolic steroids as a Schedule III drug of abuse under the Federal Controlled Substances Act.

Though baseball still had no specific prohibition of steroids, the new legal classification made them drugs of abuse, which were prohibited. As stated in the 1988 major league drug policy: "The basic drug policy of the game is simply stated: There is no place for illegal drug use in Baseball." Later the policy states, "Any Major League player involved in the illegal possession or use of drugs or illegal trafficking with drugs of any sort will be subject to discipline.... The prohibition of drugs applies to all illegal drugs, including illegally obtained prescription drugs."[25] The use of steroids in baseball, still barely on the radar with the fans and press, had moved one step closer to closer to the line between permissible behavior and "cheating."

In 1991, Commissioner Fay Vincent issued a memo revising the drug language: "This prohibition applies to all illegal drugs and controlled substances, including steroids or prescription drugs for which the individual in possession of the drug does not have a prescription." Years later Vincent spoke of his frustration with the players: "The union, of course, wouldn't let me discipline players away from the federal statute. That is, unless the government enforced the statute, the union's position was I couldn't enforce the statute. That is, I couldn't ban players because of steroid use."[26]

Steroids' first meaningful use in baseball came during the mid-1980s. By his own account, Jose Canseco was the first modern position player to use the injections on a regular basis. He began in 1984 in the minor leagues and perceived a marked improvement in his strength, appearance, and most notably, his ability to hit a baseball. According to Canseco, the first player he introduced to steroids was teammate Mark McGwire in 1988, the year after the latter's Rookie of the Year campaign. "At that time," he later wrote, "as far as I know, Mark and I were the only ones using steroids."[27] Most baseball people still believed that too much muscle and bulk would impair baseball ability.

Washington Post columnist Thomas Boswell was the first to raise the issue in the press, appearing on CBS's Newswatch program in September 1988, just weeks after Ben Johnson's race. "Canseco's the most conspicuous example of a player who made himself great with steroids," Boswell said on the program, adding, "I've heard players, when they're talking about steroid use, call it a Jose Canseco milkshake."[28] At the time, Canseco denied the accusation and threatened legal action: "That's ridiculous. I don't know where he gets that," the slugger said. His denials impressed few. That October during the playoffs Boston fans serenaded Canseco with a chant of "Ster-oids! Ster-oids!"

Despite his disavowals, Canseco later admitted that he'd been evangelizing about the benefits of performance-enhancing drugs to other players around the league. "I was the godfather of steroids," he wrote. "I was the first to educate other players about how to use them, the first to experiment and pass on what I'd learned, and the first to get contacts on where to get them. I taught the players which steroid has which effect on the body, and how to mix or 'stack' certain steroids to get a desired effect."[29]

After years of mostly whispering in the press box, the first real exposé on the issue came in the summer of 1995. *Los Angeles Times* reporter Bob Nightengale spoke with players, team executives, and acting commissioner Bud Selig for his July 15 article. San Diego Padres GM Randy Smith estimated that 10 percent to 20 percent of major league players used steroids. An unidentified AL general manager thought it was more like 30 percent. Yet Selig professed not to see it. "If baseball has a problem, I must say candidly that we were not aware of it," he told Nightengale. "It certainly hasn't been talked about much. But should we concern ourselves as an industry? I don't know. Maybe it's time to bring it up again."

If the GMs and players saw it, it's hard to believe that Selig and the other owners didn't. As the AL GM said, "Come on, you just don't put on 50 pounds of muscle overnight and hit balls out of the stadium. I'm seeing guys right now who were washed up five years ago, and now they've got bat speed they've never had before. It's insane." Padres star outfielder Tony Gwynn echoed this from the players' perspective. "I'm just standing in the outfield when a guy comes up, and I'm thinking, 'Hey, I wonder if this guy is on steroids.'"[30]

Moreover, in 2005 FBI agent Greg Stejskal disclosed to the *New York Daily News* that he had told MLB's head of security in 1994 that the FBI had evidence that Canseco and other A's were being supplied with steroids. Another FBI agent confirmed the agency had records of the meeting. MLB disputed the meeting took place. But when pushed on the issue at the 2005 congressional hearings, Sandy Alderson, an Executive VP in the commissioner' office, acknowledged, "It's conceivable [that there may have been informal contacts], yes."[31]

In May 1997, Selig reissued baseball's drug policy memorandum, similar to Vincent's six years earlier. Once again, clubs were reminded that any "information concerning drug use by a player" must be reported; and the $250,000 fine for failure to do so was still in effect.

A focus on performance-enhancing drugs sharpened in 1998 during the pursuit of Roger Maris's single-season home run record by the St. Louis Cardinals' Mark McGwire and the Chicago Cubs' Sammy Sosa. That two players could mount a challenge to the hallowed 61 home runs, and ultimately obliterate it, seemed inconceivable. Everyone was having so much fun with the chase, however, that no one was eager to question it.

In August, AP reporter Steve Wilstein noticed a bottle of Androstenedione, Andro for short, on the top shelf of McGwire's locker. Although it has since been reclassified as a controlled substance, at the time Andro was a legal supplement and available over the counter. Chemically, it is a steroid precursor, meaning the body converts it into testosterone. At the time the substance was banned by the NFL, the NCAA, and the International Olympic Committee. But not by MLB or the NBA.[32]

Wilstein's article caused a brief dustup, but little critical analysis or further investigation about whether McGwire might also be using steroids (something he admitted 12 years later). Cardinal manager Tony La Russa defended his player, accusing the reporter of "snoop[ing] around"; he also demanded that AP reporters be barred from the locker room. (This was unsuccessful.) Canseco later conjectured that McGwire purposely placed the bottle where it was sure to be noticed to get reporters to focus on the Andro rather than the illegal drugs he was also taking. If this was McGwire's intent, it backfired, as the action only fueled speculation about steroids. In fact, Selig later marked this event as a seminal moment in his concern around PEDs. "I became concerned myself ... when I read about Mark McGwire and Andro, and that's when all these things started."[33]

Yet MLB did not immediately act—not even with minor league players, who were not shielded by a union. MLB had no trouble laying down the hammer when it wanted to, of course. In 1993 it had banned tobacco—both cigarettes and smokeless—in the minors.[34]

Some major league teams acted independently on the matter. In 1994 the New York Mets tested several minor leaguers they suspected of using steroids, but the initiative petered out after the 1994–1995 player's strike. The San Diego Padres began randomly testing minor leaguers in 1998—roughly 20 percent tested positive.[35]

Meanwhile, many players defended McGwire over the Andro revelation. "Anything illegal is definitely wrong," said Boston's star first baseman Mo Vaughn. "But if you get something over the counter and legal, guys in that power-hitter position are going to use them. Strength is the key to maintaining and gaining endurance for 162 games. The pitchers keep getting bigger and stronger."[36] Even so, a couple of years later McGwire claimed that he stopped taking Andro in 1999.[37]

We feel confident asserting that by the mid-1990s, using steroids was cheating. Once steroids became controlled substances they were prohibited under baseball's rules, and Vincent's and then Selig's memos specifically named steroids. Most important for our purposes, players were not taking them to enjoy a night on the town—they were using in order to help them hit or pitch better. Moreover, the code of silence and denial enveloping their use testified that users recognized that those drugs were forbidden.

In 2012 *Sports Illustrated* reported retrospective firsthand accounts of players' perspective on steroids in the 1990s. Twins hurler Dan Naulty, one of the few to admit his own use, expressed the players intrinsic understanding of sportsmanship. "I was a full-blown cheater, and I knew it," Naulty said. "You didn't need a written rule. I was violating clear principles that were laid down within the rules. I understood I was violating implicit principles." Minor league pitcher Brett Roberts, who was competing with Naulty for a shot at the majors, felt cheated by the users. "I was pretty upset," Roberts said. "Gosh, it's hard enough trying to make it in this profession. You want to make it on your own abilities and work ethic, and all of a sudden, when you think it's an even playing field, you've got somebody cheating. I was very upset, knowing my chance to get to the big leagues was cut short."[38]

Star first baseman Jeff Bagwell recognized the attraction of PEDs, especially for players struggling to make a roster. "One thing I know is I can go home after my career is over and say I did it myself," Bagwell said. "Now let me tell you, if I'm on the bubble, with the amount of money that's in the game, I probably would already have a needle in my butt. There's too much money out there. If it does make you better, why wouldn't you at least give it a shot to hang on? All you have to do is have one big year, and next thing you know you're around for five or six more."[39] With this type of temptation, meaningful disincentives were imperative if baseball was going to rein in steroid use.

Nonetheless, consequences for taking them were almost nonexistent. Without a formal drug agreement between players and owners, there was very little chance of management confronting a player, let alone proving he was using. And even if they could, unless the player was convicted of a drug crime in court, the penalties were likely to be nominal for a first-time offender. With little fear of being either caught or punished, no one should be surprised that steroid use was widespread among highly competitive professional athletes who had huge financial incentives for improved performance.[40]

It is instructive to look at the relative seriousness with which steroids and amphetamines have been viewed. As Hall of Famer Tony Gwynn said, "Guys feel like steroids are cheating and greenies aren't." This distinction, shared by many in the game at the time, can be called **The Gwynn Doctrine. Breaking the rules (by, say, downing a few "greenies") is not necessarily considered cheating if there is no perceived benefit to a player or team**, and a consensual ethic has evolved to tolerate (if not actually accept) the practice.

As steroid users began to be exposed, some observers made the case that the use of either steroids or amphetamines was cheating and that both substances should be treated the same way. By the 1990s, both had been banned under baseball's rules and included on the schedules of the Controlled Substances Act. So, why the difference?

From the players' perspective, there are at least three distinctions:

First, the benefit of amphetamines was generally perceived as more restorative—an aid to get through a long season—as opposed to performance *enhancing*. The sports world had been rocked by several high-profile PED scandals from record-setting athletes, including Johnson and cyclist Lance Armstrong, and baseball's record book had been laid to waste by newly muscle-bound sluggers. None of this happened in the 1960s and 1970s when greenies were prevalent in every locker room.

Second, the potential health problems associated with nonprescribed steroids were considered to be more severe than those caused by amphetamines. Observers point to former stars like Ken Caminiti, who admitted to a history of drug abuse (including steroids) two years before he passed away in 2004. Football defensive end Lyle Alzado, who died in 1992, blamed his brain cancer and related illnesses on many years of steroid use. The additional risks of negative side effects for young athletes added to their stigma.[41]

Third, greenies had become part of the game's consensual culture, behavior that most everyone believed was either acceptable or not worth complaining about, in a way that steroids never did. No one joked about taking steroids until the ever-talkative Canseco came along, and that was only after his career was over.

In June 2001, MLB and the players jointly issued a 15-page pamphlet entitled *Steroids and Nutritional Supplements* that listed 10 substances "believed to augment or enhance training routines or performance." The section on steroids echoed Vincent's 1991 memo: "All AASs [Anabolic-androgenic steroids] are controlled substances under federal law. The Anabolic Steroid Control Act of 1990 classifies AASs as Schedule III drugs, requiring a doctor's prescription for use. There are serious penalties for the illegal manufacture, distribution, and nonmedically prescribed use of AAS. They also are prohibited in baseball."[42] Despite the joint statement, the players union remained adamantly opposed to mandatory testing.

The 18-month period from June 2002 to November 2003 was the most consequential in baseball's PED journey, with several events provoking momentum toward drug testing that ultimately overwhelmed the player's intransigence. It started when the June 3, 2002, issue of *Sports Illustrated* published a bombshell exposé in which Caminiti admitted his use of steroids—the first baseball player to confess publicly—while estimating that half of all MLB players used. Caminiti also discussed the widespread abuse of other drugs, such as human growth hormone (HGH) and various stimulants.[43]

A couple of weeks later the U.S. Senate held hearings on steroids in baseball. MLBPA Executive Director Don Fehr, opposed to mandatory testing on privacy grounds, was in a challenging spot. "[Regarding the] merits of cause-based versus random testing," Fehr said, "the Players Association has always believed that one should not, absent compelling safety considerations, invade the privacy of an individual without a substantial reason—that is to say without cause—related to conduct by that individual and not merely to his status as an employed baseball player."

Fehr hoped that the educational programs and reasonable-cause testing would sufficiently placate the lawmakers: "With respect to steroids, the views of our physicians, which are entirely endorsed by the Players Association, as well as the clubs, are, in fact, reflected in the brochure or the booklet that is referenced in my testimony and that Mr. Manfred has referenced, entitled *Steroids and Nutritional Supplements*, which, as Rob [Manfred] has indicated, is the principal educational document that we utilize and has been distributed to all players. The Committee has copies. And as that document makes clear, all AAS's, as the document refers to it—anabolic androgenic steroids—are classified under Federal law as Schedule III drugs requiring a doctor's prescription to be lawfully used."[44] Fehr's testimony did not go over well on Capitol Hill.

Rob Manfred, then Executive Vice President of Labor Relations and Human Resources for MLB, told the Committee that a comprehensive-testing agreement was needed: "Contrary to the impression created by Mr. Fehr's written statement, we do not have an agreed-upon steroid policy in Major League Baseball. The Commissioner has unilaterally promulgated a policy on steroids that the union has consistently said is not binding on its players. While we have worked together in certain situations, the current regulation is ad hoc at best, and dysfunctional at worst."[45] The senators just wanted PEDs out of sports and were therefore much more sympathetic to the commissioner's position.

Under pressure from Congress, the union agreed to anonymous survey–testing in 2003: If more than five percent of players tested positive, mandatory drug testing would begin in 2004 with associated disciplinary actions: a first positive test would lead to treatment and education, with the player remaining unidentified; a second would result in a 15-day suspension or a $10,000 fine; subsequent positive tests had progressively longer suspensions and larger fines, marching up to a fifth, which resulted a one-year suspension or a $100,000 fine. On November 13, 2003, baseball and the union announced the results: more than 5 percent had tested positive. Baseball would have mandatory drug testing in 2004.[46]

In September 2003, as part of an unrelated investigation, federal law enforcement agents raided the Bay Area Laboratory Cooperative (dubbed "BALCO"), a company that supplied performance-enhancing drugs to world-class athletes. The evidence uncovered and interviews with the principals led to a grand jury investigation in which several baseball players linked to the facility, most notably Barry Bonds, Gary Sheffield, and Jason Giambi, were called as witnesses.

The BALCO investigation highlighted the rapid innovation in PED technology and its increasingly sophisticated administration. Baseball players were no longer taking the easily detectable drugs introduced decades earlier. BALCO created steroids that were undetectable in drug tests—infamous substances known as "the cream" and "the clear." While the use of steroids in baseball had largely been trial and error, several players were now clients of a company at the cutting edge of sophisticated chemistry that promised to beat drug tests.

"It was elaborate and systematic," wrote investigative reporters Mark Fainaru-Wada and Lance Williams, who'd spent months researching the story. BALCO executive Victor Conte created calendars to "list when athletes were scheduled to take which drugs, and they indicated the dates of competitions so the drugs' effects would be peaking at the right time. Conte also kept a ledger that detailed both the types of drugs athletes were using, as well as the results of their blood and urine tests."[47]

Lawmakers were unsatisfied with the nominal penalties management and the union had imposed. They claimed concern about the integrity of the game, the potential negative health effects on the athletes, and perhaps more significant, the example for youth athletes who might be enticed to use PEDs themselves. The U.S. Senate held new hearings in March 2004. Both Selig and Fehr were called to testify, and were told, in so many words, to clean up the game or federal legislation, with more stringent drug testing and penalties, would be forthcoming. Accordingly, in January 2005 baseball and the union agreed to new testing and punishment guidelines. The new agreement introduced random, year-round testing with increased penalties: an unpaid 10-game suspension for the first offense, 30 games for the second, 60 games for the third, one year for the fourth, and a punishment subject to commissioner's discretion for the fifth.

Congress remained unimpressed. In March, the House's Committee on Government Reform convened the now-infamous hearings that included Canseco, McGwire, Sosa, and Rafael Palmeiro. Canseco said that steroids were "as acceptable in the '80s and mid-to-late '90s as a cup of coffee."[48] McGwire did not deny steroid use, but repeatedly said he was not there to "talk about the past."[49] Palmeiro, under oath, denied using, then failed a drug test later that summer. In May, the House and Senate committee heads determined that the PED problem required federal oversight. They introduced the Clean Sports Act of 2005, under which sports' drug testing for the four major North American professional sports leagues—MLB, NBA, NFL, and NHL—would be federalized under a drug czar. Draconian penalties more in line with the Olympics would be instituted, including a two-year suspension for a first positive drug test.

In November, under continued pressure from the government and Selig, Fehr acquiesced to another significant revision to the PED drug policy. A first offense now led to a 50-day suspension, a second offense to a 100-day suspension, and a third offense resulted in a lifetime ban, with a right to appeal for reinstatement after two years. To bring an end to the government pressure, Selig and Fehr traveled to Washington to get an endorsement of their deal from key committee members in both chambers. The two were successful, thus ending a nearly four-year ordeal. In 2014, penalties were increased to the levels that stand today: 80 games for a first offense and a season-long 162 games for the second. Without the government's involvement, it's hard to imagine Selig ever gaining enough leverage to get union agreement on mandatory testing and severe punishments.

Riding high after the new drug policy, Selig hoped finally to close the matter by conducting an internal investigation around PED usage, and making recommendations based on its results. Such investigations are not uncommon in business, and Selig engaged a well-respected law firm as well as its best-known attorney, longtime U.S. Senator George Mitchell. There were two key differences, however, between MLB's investigation and most others of this ilk. First, its findings would be released publicly, warts and all. Second, Mitchell had no way to compel the most important sources—the players—to cooperate.

"You should be aware," Fehr and union attorney Michael Weiner wrote to the players, "that any information provided could lead to discipline of you and/or others.... Remember also that there are a number of ongoing federal and state criminal investigations in this area, and any information gathered by Senator Mitchell in player interviews is not legally privileged."[50] As the union had already ceded to random drug testing and agreed to penalties, the entire exercise seemed designed to place blame for the crisis on specific players.

But Mitchell and his team did not actually need the players' coop-
eration if his goal was to determine the extent of the problem—where
players were getting their drugs, how and when they were using, etc.
There was a vast amount of information available on PEDs already in
the public record. Moreover, Mitchell had access to all the nonplaying
employees in organized baseball, plus minor league players. But some
observers felt that unless Mitchell could name specific major league
players, the report would be a letdown. "Mitchell is running into serious roadblocks that threaten to undermine any chance of uncovering
the scope of the scandal this year," warned one newspaper article.[51]

Mitchell, however, found some outside help. Federal law enforcement was in the process of charging steroid dealer and one-time
Mets' clubhouse employee Kirk Radomski. As part of his plea deal,
Radomski met with Mitchell. Similarly, Brian McNamee, a trainer
whose name popped up in Radomski's records and who worked extensively with star hurler Roger Clemens, was reportedly compelled to
cooperate under threat of being charged with distribution. Of the
roughly 90 players named in the report, approximately two-thirds
were fingered by Radomski or McNamee, including Clemens, one of
baseball's all-time greatest pitchers.[52]

Released in December 2007, the Mitchell report brought anything
but closure. Much of the attention centered on Clemens, who vehemently rejected McNamee's accounts of injecting him with steroids.
In February 2008 the U.S. House held a four-hour hearing during
which Clemens and McNamee traded accusations. After Clemens
denied McNamee's claims, the government charged him with perjury,
resulting in a case that dragged on until 2012, when he was finally
acquitted.

Radomski later revealed how he perceived the report. "I felt bad for
the guys that dealt with me, that their names were being implicated,
but there were so many other guys out there that were so blatant, and
their names weren't mentioned," Radomski told ESPN.com. "That
was the biggest problem I had with the Mitchell report. If you're going
to name names, you had to do more digging, had to give yourself more

time to get names out there and not just depend on me and what was in the paper and BALCO. Listen, because these guys didn't deal with me, they're getting a free pass."[53]

Another player who faced federal prosecution regarding PEDs was star shortstop Miguel Tejada. Congressional investigators had questioned Tejada in 2005 as part of their investigation into whether Rafael Palmeiro had lied in his congressional testimony. In the interview, Tejada reportedly denied having discussions about or knowledge of use by teammates. He was identified in the Mitchell report, however, as having conversations about access to steroids. In February 2009 Tejada was charged with lying to the investigators and pleaded guilty. He was sentenced to one-year of probation, community service, and a $5,000 fine. Tejada was baseball's biggest name convicted of a PED-associated crime. (Barry Bonds had his obstruction of justice conviction related to the BALCO investigation overturned in 2015.)[54]

With the release of the Mitchell report, increased random testing, and stricter penalties, the use of PEDs began to subside. In 2012 baseball also began testing for HGH, which had been banned since 2005, becoming the first major North American sports league to do so. In 2013, no major league players tested positive for performance-enhancing drugs. In the years since there have been a handful of failures annually, the most notable names being Ervin Santana, Dee Gordon, Marlon Byrd, Starling Marte, and Robinson Canó. When the stakes are high enough, efforts to skirt the rules continue even at the risk of severe penalties.[55]

As presciently noted in the Mitchell report, anti-aging clinics would become another potential source for designer steroids and other PEDs. These clinics could create complex drug cocktails and sophisticated intake scheduling to avoid detection.

In January 2013, the *New Times*, a Miami weekly, reported that it had documentation that several star players, most notably New York Yankees third baseman Alex Rodriguez, had been receiving PEDs from Biogenesis, a Florida anti-aging clinic. Investigators from the commissioner's office hustled to Florida to secure the documentary proof and witness statements.

Even without positive drug tests, baseball can suspend players if there is other conclusive evidence. Of the fourteen players associated with Biogenesis, twelve were given 50-game suspensions and one a 65-game suspension. The biggest star, however, chose to contest the issue. Over the next twelve months, both baseball and Alex Rodriguez spent millions of dollars in a highly contentious struggle, culminating in a record 211-game suspension for Rodriguez, which was ultimately reduced to a full-season, 162 games.

With the culmination of the A-Rod saga, the journey from no-testing-no punishment to one of the strictest policies outside of the Olympics was complete. Still, some insiders continued to suspect widespread PED use. "I think we are back up to large scale use again," one former player told *Sports Illustrated* veteran reporter Tom Verducci in 2017. "It's all over, but folks don't want to see it. Many long-time baseball people are still oblivious."[56] One ex-member of MLB's Department of Investigations, Eddie Dominguez, suggested the number was "conservatively" 20 percent.[57]

By this time, however, drug-testing itself had become much more sophisticated, so it's hard to fathom how designer steroids could remain prevalent without somehow coming to public notice. While it is possible a few players may be using undetectable cutting-edge drugs, their on-field effects are likely smaller than those of traditional steroids. "We are testing way more than we have in the past," Dan Halem, MLB's chief legal officer, told Verducci in 2017. Halem claimed that MLB had run about 12,000 blood and urine tests the previous year, and that the tests were as good as anything available. He was convinced that usage had not returned to previous levels.[58]

It is important to keep in mind that most of the progress in testing and penalties for steroid use was because of intervention by the federal government. Both the BALCO investigation and congressional hearings—though theatrical—highlighted the problem and spurred the parties to implement a program with teeth. Without the threat of governmental oversight, it is doubtful that the players association ever would have acquiesced to a drug-testing program.

Even today there is debate about baseball's so-called "steroid era," a period spanning the 1990s and 2000s. Runs per game increased from 4.12 in 1992 to 4.92 in 1994, and stayed at that level for about 15 years, a period believed to coincide with the heaviest steroid use in the game. Many analysts have suggested, however, that changes to the physical baseball itself are more likely than drug use to cause such scoring spikes, and that smaller ballparks also have had an effect. Certainly, there are multiple issues at play.

But even if steroids had zero effect on run scoring (which seems unlikely), this does not prove they had no effect on the game. Both hitters and pitchers were using PEDs, deploying their benefits against one another. What is less ambiguous is that during this period there was a dramatic increase in high-quality "old" players.

Baseball has always been a young man's game. Studies consistently show that most players peak between 25 and 29 years old; after that point, performance declines. Using Wins Above Replacement (WAR) as the metric, "old" players (those 35 and over) have historically accounted for about 7.5 percent of the value in baseball annually. In the late 1990s this number rose rapidly, peaking at 14.2 percent in 2002. This was the highest total since World War II upended big league rosters. There were also more "old" superstars than ever before, players who performed at the highest level well into their 40s. This trend then reversed itself dramatically—by 2017, old players provided just 1.6 percent of the game's value.[59]

So while we can debate the effect that steroids had on the batter-pitcher balance, the era unquestionably was historic in the number of good players maintaining or even increasing their performance at ages when they'd normally be headed for retirement.

What we are left with is this: Most major league players of the 1990s were provided the opportunity to use drugs that could enhance their performances with little risk of being caught at first. Many of them—20 percent, 30 percent, more?—chose to cheat, and a small group was later accused or caught. Many of these users likely benefited from the drugs, but we can never know precisely which ones or how much.

It is nearly certain that many pre-1990s players would have made the same choice. Two of game's biggest former stars—Mike Schmidt and Bob Gibson—both said that they might have tried had they played in the late 1990s. Surely there are others.[60]

Robert Creamer, who wrote critically acclaimed biographies of Babe Ruth and Casey Stengel, later said that both would have used steroids if provided that choice. "Sure. Yes. Absolutely," he said. What did Creamer think of the users of the 1990s? "They were trying to get better, trying to improve themselves (foolishly), trying to win."[61]

Though neither Roger Clemens nor Barry Bonds played again after the release of the Mitchell Report, their stories continue. As two of the greatest players who ever lived, they would normally expect to enjoy decades as retired baseball heroes, the subjects of reverential documentaries, their playing numbers hanging on facades at baseball stadiums, and life as members of baseball's hallowed Hall of Fame, where their legacies would live forever.

Instead, they have spent the past 15 years as the stars of a grand baseball drama. How should baseball fans and historians treat players who have been associated with steroid use? Baseball is a game that takes its history seriously, and nothing symbolizes this better (or worse) than Hall of Fame debates. For Clemens, Bonds, Alex Rodriguez, Mark McGwire, Sammy Sosa, Manny Ramirez, and more, the arguments have nothing to do with baseball—their accomplishments are irrefutable—and everything to do with whether or not they used performance-enhancing drugs to achieve them. If so, exactly how should that affect their legacy?

Their cases are all different—from Clemens, who never failed a test and denies using, to McGwire and Rodriguez, who both confessed, to Ramirez, who failed two drug tests, to many others with their own stories. What is undeniable is that these players are a small subset of the players who may have used steroids, some of whom may be enshrined in the Hall of Fame already.

The story of PEDs in baseball followed the pattern of most of the other cheating stories we discuss in this book. Once players realized the advantages that could be gained from PEDs, many turned to them, particularly when the probability of getting caught or punished was almost nil. While at first glance it may be surprising when a minor leaguer or fringe major leaguer fails a drug test, these are the players who have the most to gain and the least to lose. Not so surprising, after all.

We will never know how many cheated beyond the handful who have confessed, or have been plausibly accused, or were named in the Mitchell report. Continued vigilance and innovation on the testing side plus severe penalties for getting caught appear to hold the upper hand. For now.

Chapter Ten

GREASE AND GLUE

O N JUNE 15, 2021, Major League Baseball announced a crack-down on pitchers putting foreign substances on the baseball, a long illegal practice that had been enforced only occasion-ally over the years. But starting June 21, umpires would search pitchers' hats, gloves, and uniforms for illegal material, and any violator would be immediately suspended for 10 games. "After an extensive process of repeated warnings without effect, gathering information from current and former players and others across the sport, two months of compre-hensive data collection, listening to our fans and thoughtful delibera-tion, I have determined that new enforcement of foreign substances is needed to level the playing field," commissioner Rob Manfred said.[1]

Very likely this crackdown was spurred by low-scoring games. The MLB-wide batting average was .238, the strikeout rate had reached an all-time high of 8.95 per nine innings, and there had been six no-hitters by early June. Several media outlets had been reporting on sticky baseballs for a few years, noting the apparent link between higher pitched ball spin rates and the inability of batters to make contact.

But the doctored-ball story, like most of the other cheating documented in this book, began more than a century ago.

A well-thrown major league fastball, a four-seam fastball or four-seamer, is thrown with the index and middle fingers extending across the seams, at maximum effort. The thumb, held beneath the ball, leaves the surface first, and the two fingers on top of the ball last, resulting in backspin for the roughly 55 feet of the ball's flight. The backspin keeps the ball's path stable, somewhat countering gravity. When thrown hard enough or with enough spin, the pitch is often called a rising fastball, though technically it just drops less than the human eye expects.

Most big-league pitchers employ at least two other pitches (for example, the changeup, curveball, or slider) that have less velocity and, often, more vertical or horizontal movement. And then there's that aberration, the knuckleball, that's a little bit of everything. With three or four pitches he can control, and a sequence that leaves the batter guessing which might be coming, a good pitcher can make any hitter look foolish.

Pitchers knew most of this by the 1880s, and most good pitchers knew they had to learn a breaking pitch and changeup to keep a batter off balance. The development of these new pitches was mainly trial and error—keep throwing with different grips and let's see what happens. Every arm is different, and many great pitchers have tried pitches that they cannot throw effectively before finding one or two they can master. If these can be presented to the hitter in the same way, by the time the ball begins to move it is too late for the batter to adjust. If a pitcher can throw a 96-mph four-seam fastball, and an 86-mph changeup, both seemingly with the same delivery, the batter practically has to guess the pitch before it is delivered. If the pitcher also has an 80-mph curveball that drops several inches, and a 92-mph slider or two-seam sinking fastball, and he can control all of these pitches, he will be very difficult to hit.

Inevitably, pitchers discovered that a ball's movement was affected by modifications to its surface. As usual, this innovation was ahead of the rulebook, and for many years pitchers were essentially free to tamper with the ball as they liked.

Roughly speaking, there are three ways a pitcher might want to doctor a baseball. The first is to add lubrication—saliva, sweat, Vaseline, etc.—either to the fingers or to the ball, to reduce the hand's grip. The ball is held without touching the seams, and it shoots out of the fingers like a watermelon seed. This pitch will have much less backspin, causing it to drop much more than an "untreated" fastball. These lubricated pitches, whether using saliva or another slippery substance, are usually lumped together as "spitballs."

A second method is to scuff the ball with sandpaper or dirt or even a sharpened belt buckle, which increases drag and causes the ball to move erratically, especially, according to practitioners, in the direction of the scuff.

Finally, recent years have seen a sharp increase in the use of pine tar, or other sticky concoctions, to give the pitcher a better grip on the baseball. The sticky pitched ball's behavior is roughly the opposite of the spitball—a higher spin rate, which causes fastballs to rise more (or, really, drop less), curveballs to sink more, and sliders to move more horizontally.

The purpose of all of this doctoring is to make the ball move differently than the hitter expects. If a pitcher can achieve this variety without changing his mechanics, so much the better. To pitchers in the early 1900s, all of this was legal—part of the trial and error each pitcher used when learning which pitches he could throw effectively.

Although several people later claimed to have thrown or faced the spitball as early as the 1890s, the pitch likely came to the major leagues in 1902. It became prominent in 1904 when Jack Chesbro, throwing his spitter on nearly every pitch, won 41 games for the New York Highlanders. Ed Walsh soon took it up and became, by the reckoning of Rob Neyer and Bill James, the best spitballer of all time. Over a seven-year period (1906–1912) he averaged 361 innings and a 1.71 ERA. That was most of his career, and it was enough to get him into the Hall of Fame. Many of the better pitchers of the next

20 years—Red Faber, Stan Covaleskie, Burleigh Grimes—threw the spitball as their primary pitch.[2]

Pitchers were also defacing the ball (or taking advantage of balls that had been defaced) in the nineteenth century, even if umpires would occasionally jettison severely damaged balls. Not too often, though. Hall of Fame outfielder Sam Crawford said, "Heck, we'd play the whole game with one ball if it stayed in the park."[3] Not surprisingly, many of the best pitchers learned to take advantage of an imperfect ball.

This came to a head in 1910 when a previously obscure New York Highlander pitcher named Russ Ford burst through with 26 wins and a 1.65 ERA. Batters claimed that his ball darted downward erratically, but no one could say why. Ford won 22 more games in 1911, but eventually his secret came out—he had sewn part of an emery board to the inside of his glove, and after a few scrapes against one side the baseball could achieve the desired movement. In the middle of the 1915 season, AL President Ban Johnson announced stiff fines and suspensions for anyone who scuffed the ball in this way. After the season roughening the ball was formally banned, which only meant that pitchers became sneakier about it.

The third category of doctoring—applying a substance to *increase* grip—came along around the same time. In the 1910 book *Touching Second,* by star Cubs second baseman Johnny Evers and Chicago sportswriter Hugh Fullerton, the authors wrote, "Slippery Elm, talcum powder, crude oil, Vaseline were used to lessen the friction of the fingers while other pitchers, to get more friction on the thumb, used gum, pumice stone, resin or adhesive tape."[4] With all this ball doctoring, it's a wonder that hitters ever saw a fresh baseball thrown from the mound.

Before the 1920 season, the spitball and all its unsavory variants were banned by the American and National Leagues and all affiliated leagues. Nonetheless, seventeen practitioners were allowed to continue using it until they retired; in 1934 Burleigh Grimes threw the last legal spitball in the American or National Leagues. Although the language has been modified many times since, according to today's Rule 6.02(c), there shall be no saliva, no foreign substances, no defacing of the ball in any manner. A pitcher cannot even rub the ball on his dry uniform.

For the purposes of this book, the first time an illegal spitball could have been used in the majors was in 1920, and we can assume that pitchers reacted as drinkers did to the Volstead Act, by taking the practice underground. For the next few decades, there appears to have been a downturn in usage, as very few pitchers became famous for using the spitter as a primary pitch. Tommy Bridges might be the most prominent. He had a fine career throwing with a conventional repertoire, but he reportedly relied more on the spitter by the early 1940s.

The Negro National League, the first major league in black baseball, began play in 1920. Although NNL officials claimed that their leagues used the same rules as the AL and NL, attempts to stop the spitball were nonexistent or futile. Defacing or cutting the ball was illegal and balls were often thrown out if a team complained. But catching players using saliva on a ball was no easier than it was in the white major leagues.

This account from a game in the Eastern Colored League is representative of the difficulty umpires faced.

"During a recent game in Baltimore," the *Pittsburgh Courier* wrote in 1925, "the batter asked to see the ball and the umps requested Pitcher [Joe] Strong, of the [Baltimore Black] Sox, to throw it in. Strong dropped the ball to the ground at his feet and told the umpire that if he wanted to see it he might come out and get it. The arbiter told the batter, [Charlie] Smith of the [Baltimore] Royal [Giants] that if he wanted to see the ball he might go out and pick it up. Smith accepted the invitation, inspected the sphere and threw it over the grandstand. Strong was permitted to remain in the game, but Smith and several other Royals were ejected."[5] Evidently it was impermissible to chuck even a damaged ball out of the park.

Many of the better pitchers in the Negro Leagues employed some form of ball doctoring, including Roosevelt Davis, Chet Brewer, and Johnny Taylor. Bullet Joe Rogan, one of the game's great pitchers, threw a spitball among his many pitches, and also cut the baseball on occasion. Bob Feller, who barnstormed against many of the best Black players of the 1930s and 1940s, said that Pat Scantlebury's spitter acted "like a pigeon coming out of a barn."[6]

When the second Negro National League was formed in 1933 (the first having folded after 1931), it more explicitly banned the spitball but grandfathered pitchers who had been throwing the pitch. The last two legal spitballers in major league baseball therefore survived until 1948: Neck Stanley of the New York Black Yankees, and Bill Byrd of the Baltimore Elite Giants. But it was never quite that simple: Both men were accused of doctoring the ball in other illegal ways. In July 1945 game against Kansas City, for example, Stanley was searched 13 times by the umpiring crew.[7]

By all accounts, the most famous Black pitcher in history did not throw a spitter. "I never threw an illegal pitch," said Satchel Paige. "The trouble is, once in a while I toss one that ain't been seen by this generation."[8] Paige was famous for a varied repertoire that only expanded as he got older, but all of his pitching seems to have been on the up and up.

Baseball officials have long acknowledged that new baseballs are too slippery to use fresh out of the box. To reduce their sheen, umpires originally rubbed the balls with some mixture of water, dirt from the field, and tobacco juice. This de-glossing was likely introduced after Ray Chapman was killed after being hit in the head by a pitch in 1920.[9]

In 1938 A's coach Lena Blackburne was talking to one of the umpires, who was griping about the unevenness and inconsistency from rubbing the balls with arbitrary substances. Blackburne had an idea, stemming from his youth. He dug up mud from the Pennsauken Creek, a tributary of the Delaware River in New Jersey, and tested it on some baseballs. The mud worked perfectly, removing the sheen, yet leaving the ball white and not hurting the laces. Over time, the teams and leagues agreed and adopted his mud for de-glossing baseballs. Blackburne kept the exact location secret and turned the rubbing mud into a family business.[10]

To this day, all baseballs are rubbed before every game by the equipment manager with the Delaware River mud supplied by Blackburne's original company. MLB would like to wean itself from the mud and have a ball that is ready for action right out of the box. In 2016 they started experimenting with Rawlings, the baseballs' manufacturer, to overhaul the surface texture and make the mud unnecessary. So far, the mud continues to win out.[11]

Of course, rubbing substances into a baseball isn't always perfect. Occasionally, one part of the ball may not get a full dose of mud, allowing a crafty pitcher to make the ball move unexpectedly. According to author Lee Gutkind, years ago the Wrigley Field stadium announcer, from his spot on field behind home plate near the backstop, would surreptitiously go through the bag of rubbed balls, reorganizing and removing the best ones so that they could be in play when the Cubs were batting, while the team's hurlers would throw those with blemishes.[12]

On July 20, 1944, St. Louis Browns pitcher Nelson Potter was ejected by umpire Carl Hubbard for licking his fingers while on the mound. "I warned Potter in previous games, and I feel I have given him every break possible," Hubbard said. "[Browns manager Luke] Sewell forced the issue by kicking about [Yankees pitcher Hank] Borowy's pitching methods. Warnings to Potter were not prompted by any protest from the Yankee side until after Sewell asked me to warn Borowy."[13] Potter claimed innocence. But he became the first player to be ejected for throwing a spitter and was suspended for 10 games.

The spitball story got another boost in 1955, when pitching star Preacher Roe, soon after his retirement from the Dodgers, sold his story to *Sports Illustrated* for $2,000. "I threw spitballs the whole time I was with the Dodgers, seven years in all."[14]

"A pitcher will take any little advantage he can today," Roe said, "and I don't blame him. I'd pitch in front of the rubber when I had a chance. I never used to cut the ball much, but I wasn't too proud to— and neither are a lot of the other guys around the league." He reported that hitters put "molasses and soda" on their bats, and "nobody says nothing." Roe said he would wipe off his brow, and when the meat of his hand passed in front of his mouth he would spit on it.

He asked the writer not to blame his teammates, all of whom knew and helped him, including catcher Roy Campanella. "I don't need any sign," Campy told him. "I caught spitters in the Negro Leagues for years."

The point of the confession, Roe said, was to help make the case that the pitch should be legalized, an effort that had the backing of Commissioner Ford Frick and many umpires. Roe credited the spitball for much of what he had attained in life—three World Series shares, a home, a grocery business. "Not bad for a little ol' country boy. I'm for spitballs. I like 'em."

Whatever his motives, Roe's story caused a sensation in baseball that summer, and many people stepped up to dispute his account. Umpire Larry Goetz, whose profession stood accused by implication for letting Roe off the hook for seven years, claimed that Roe made it all up to get in the batters' heads. "Spitter … bah. I worked a lot of games behind the plate when Roe was pitching. I never once saw him throw a spitter and I've seen them thrown by real experts."[15]

Teammate Carl Erskine claimed that Roe could have won without the pitch. Other teammates also felt Roe was successful without the need to resort to the spitball. Campanella said, "All I know about spitballs is that I swung at a lot more of them than I ever had to catch." And Jackie Robinson added, "So many guys are doing it that I don't think Roe should be criticized. I could name five pitchers in the league who throw 'em—but I won't."

NL president Warren Giles seemed impressed. "If Roe [threw the pitch], he covered it so very cleverly, because no club ever registered any complaint about Roe with the league office since I came into the office [1951]." Commissioner Frick suggested Roe "had done a little bragging."[16]

Roe came to regret the article, downplaying how often he threw the pitch and how much it actually helped him. He need not have worried. His reputation as one of the better pitchers of the era has held, and he was soon eclipsed by many more notorious practitioners of the spitball.[17]

Just one year later in a *SPORT* article, major league batters were asked about the subject and 14 pitchers were called out by name, including stars like Lew Burdette, Bob Lemon, Sal Maglie, and Ellis Kinder. Burdette was the most named pitcher, and he openly admitted to having relied on the pitch. But those admissions did not come until after his career was over. "Burdette threw the spitter and I caught him," said Joe Torre many years later, "but I couldn't tell you where he got it because he never told anybody. I knew what it was going to do."[18]

Roy Campanella thought it was overblown. "I'd rather catch the spitter than the knuckler, as well as hit against it. The spitter's more predictable. I caught Bill Byrd on the old Elite Giants when I was only 14 years old and he made the ball do tricks with slippery elm. With that stuff or chewing tobacco on that ball, you never see a pitch hanging up there."[19]

According to Dodger hurler Clyde King, Campanella once helped him with a less subtle substance. "I was pitching for Brooklyn against the Giants," King recalled. "Whitey Lockman was the hitter and the tying and winning runs were on base. The pitch I threw to strike out Lockman had three pieces of bubble gum on it ... not one, but three." With a smile, King added, "I don't know how the gum got there, but when (Roy) Campanella caught the ball and when umpire yelled strike three to end the game, Campy fired the ball into left field before anybody could look at it."[20]

With the controversy around illegal substances playing out regularly in the media, a significant minority agreed with Roe that baseball should legalize the spitball. Hall of Fame catcher Ray Schalk, who caught some of the most famous spitballers—Faber, Walsh, and Eddie Cicotte—said, "If they'd legalize the spitter again, the pitching would be helped and a lot of cheating would be stopped."[21] Many executives felt the same way, particularly in the National League. President Frick, Giants owner Horace Stoneham, and Pirates owner Frank McKinney supported legalizing the pitch. Much of the opposition came from the AL.[22]

The 1960s and 1970s were peak years for the illegal spitball. In a cover story on the pitch in 1967, *Sports Illustrated* claimed that 25 percent of all big-league pitchers were throwing the pitch, and that 100 percent of umpires "look the other way." Managers complained when it grew blatant, but they had their own pitchers to worry about. "[Jack Hamilton] made a farce of the game," said Senators manager Gil Hodges. "Everyone knows that 90% of pitchers in our league have thrown the spitter, but no one continues to break the rule like Hamilton." What got managers out of the dugout was usually the "volume" of the saliva or Vaseline, more than the frequency.[23]

Many hurlers were named, including Don Drysdale (praised for how fast he threw it), John Wyatt, and Dean Chance, who was once caught with sticky fingers and forced to wash them during a game. Phil Regan, whose performance in Detroit had landed him in the minor leagues, was picked up by the Dodgers in 1966 and went 14–1 with a 1.62 ERA as a reliever. "I can't come right out and tell you that I now throw the spitter," said Regan, "but I'd say this: I don't use it nearly as much as everyone thinks." Maybe not. But in a 1968 game Regan was on the base paths when a tube of Vaseline fell out of his pocket. "I've never seen it before in my life," he said. He was not punished.[24]

In August 1967 Mets hurler Calvin Koonce admitted throwing a spitter. "Sure, I throw a spitball," Koonce said during a postgame interview. "What's wrong with admitting it? I don't throw a spitter often. I threw only two against the Pirates." Reportedly, he did not receive any disciplinary follow up from the league office.[25]

In *Ball Four*, Jim Bouton writes matter-of-factly about pitch doctoring, and expresses particular admiration for his old Yankees teammate Whitey Ford. According to Bouton, Ford could take advantage of any imperfection on the ball, and often gouged it with his sharpened wedding ring. "Ford could make a mud ball drop, sail, break in, break out, and sing 'When Irish Eyes are Smiling.'"[26] All of Ford's Yankee teammates came to Whitey's defense, though he later admitted to the doctoring and more in his 1977 memoir. Ford also reminisced about coming up with a grip-enhancing concoction well before Spider Tack: "Well, what I did was make a sticky stuff from a few well-selected ingredients. I took some turpentine, some baby oil and some resin, and mixed them all together in a jar. It turned out like Elmer's Glue. It was white stuff, not black, so you couldn't see it on my fingers."[27]

The most famous spitballer of the past century was Gaylord Perry, who won 314 games and struck out 3,524 men in a career that stretched from 1962 to 1983. Perry also had a great fastball and slider, and he always claimed that his biggest weapon was psychological—hitters became so worried about the spitball that he didn't actually have to throw it. Perry wrote a book in midcareer detailing how he learned the pitch, how he threw it, and when he threw it, while also claiming that he had reformed and did not throw it anymore. Years later, he changed his story again; the book was part of his ruse, and maybe he had never thrown the spitball at all. Perry reveled in his role as a magician, and he sold the mystery.[28]

In his book, *Me and The Spitter*, Perry claimed that he learned the pitch from Bob Shaw, one of the more famous spitballers of the era, who had been Perry's teammate in the mid-60s. Braves' skipper Bobby Bragan once ordered his pitchers to throw nothing but spitballs in a game against Shaw, trying to force the umpires to act. Bragan may also have been the first to complain publicly about Perry, in a 1966 game. After a few years of inconsistency, Perry became a star for the Giants that season, when he won 21 games as well as the All-Star game. Perry saw a connection between the complaining and the winning—it meant that he had arrived but also that the managers and batters would always be on edge if they were thinking about his hand.

At the time, pitchers were allowed to lick their fingers as long as they wiped them off on their uniform. (Crazy that this didn't work.) In 1968, largely because Perry licked his fingers on virtually every pitch, baseball finally outlawed the practice. According to Perry, this killed the pure spitter—from that point on, he used Vaseline or hair tonic.

"I reckon I tried everything on the old apple but salt and pepper and chocolate sauce toppin'."[29]

Perry's between-pitches ritual included the touching of his nose, his neck, behind his ear, his glove, his chin, all in full view of the umpire, batter, and fans. Where did he hide it? When the All-Star teams visited the White House in 1969, President Nixon asked Perry this very question. "Mr. President," he said, "there are some things you just can't tell the people for their own good."[30]

Over the next few years, mound invasions grew more frequent when Perry was pitching. Umpires would bring out a towel and make Perry wipe his entire face, they'd ask him to remove his shirt, roll up his pants legs. Al Barlick, umpiring at second, once sneaked up behind him and pulled his cap off, revealing a closely held secret: Perry was almost bald.

The vaudevillian quality of these umpire/pitcher confrontations added some humor but also kept the crime from being taken seriously. The home plate umpire/detective would walk to the mound in all his gear where the pitcher/suspect would be waiting, a picture of wounded innocence. Other interested parties—players, managers, other umpires—joined them at the mound, talking and gesticulating wildly, one side making accusations, the other protesting. With the full focus of spectators and TV cameras, an umpire would try to body search the pitcher without losing too much dignity. One can see why the umpires had little interest in acting like cops. If he found anything, the pitcher would feign ignorance—where could that have come from?

The charade became a part of Perry's identity. During an NLCS game in 1971, a television reporter found the Perry family in the stands and talked to them during a game Gaylord was pitching. Allison Perry, his five-year-old daughter, was asked, "Does your daddy throw a grease ball?" Unruffled, she responded, "It's a hard slider."[31]

A trade to the American League's Cleveland Indians in 1972 led to some of Perry's greatest seasons, and a new set of protagonists. (Leagues did not share umpires in those days.) Billy Martin, managing the Detroit Tigers, told reporters after a game against Perry that he had ordered his pitchers to throw nothing but spitters to dare the umpires to act. He called AL President Joe Cronin and Commissioner Bowie Kuhn gutless for their handling of Perry. Cronin suspended Martin for three games, and the Tigers fired him before he returned.

In 1974, the spitball rule was strengthened once more—again, thanks to Perry. An umpire could now call a pitch a ball if he felt it behaved like a spitball—the umpire didn't have to catch the pitcher with the foreign substance. A second infraction would result in ejection. On Opening Day, the home plate umpire used this rule to call a ball on Perry.

The Indians, alarmed at the implications for their best player, arranged a session for the umpires before a game at Boston's Fenway Park. Perry threw forkballs while several umpires watched. The umpires were impressed, and AL President Lee MacPhail sent a note to all teams letting them know that Perry's forkball indeed behaved just like a spitter.

The mannerisms, and the complaints, did not stop. "I watched Gaylord like a hawk," said umpire Bill Haller after one outing. "He never goes to his mouth. I never see him get any foreign substance. I'll tell you what he's got: a good curve, a fine fastball, a good change, and a fine sinker. I'll tell you what Perry is: he's one helluva pitcher, a fantastic competitor."[32]

Be that as it may, many umpires still believed that Perry was cheating. Tom Gorman once found a tube of Vaseline in Perry's warmup jacket, "but it was considered circumstantial, not enough to convict."[33] Doug Harvey said, "He could load the thing up. We know he was putting some kind of shit on the ball. We just couldn't catch him."[34]

Ken Kaiser wrote, "There was never any doubt he threw a spitball, or a Vaseline ball, or a vodka and tonic ball." He remembers a game in Texas where the temperature was "about 130 degrees," and Billy Martin was demanding home plate umpire Ron Luciano search Perry. While searching Perry, the pitcher told Luciano, "Don't look under my armpits." Luciano had no intention of doing so. After a fruitless search Martin screamed at Luciano, "You didn't look under his armpits!" As Kaiser recalled, "Ronnie looked at Billy and nodded knowingly."[35]

Durwood Merrill exiled Perry from a game in 1980, though not officially. After the seventh inning Merrill told Perry, "Mr. Perry, now you're going to make me have to take a stand. I'm going to have to come out and start hunting for your K-Y Jelly. Or, if you're so tired that you have to throw the greaseball at every batter, then you need to get out of the game." And Merrill recalled, "By gosh, he took himself right out of the game."[36]

Merrill and Kaiser also talked about another Perry specialty, the "puff ball," where Perry took advantage of a substance legally available on the mound. He would coat his hands with rosin from the ubiquitous rosin bag located on the back of the pitcher's mound. When he released the ball, "it would just explode out of a bank of white smoke, and there was no way a hitter could hit it, or the umpire could call it."[37] Kaiser once put a stop to it by calling two pitches that found the strike zone balls. When Perry glared at him, Kaiser told him, "You keep putting that stuff on there, I can't see the pitch. It's distracting, you know what I mean?"[38]

Perry won his 300th victory for the Mariners in 1982. Later that season, while Perry was warming up, umpire Dave Phillips—prompted by a player—asked to see one of the warm-up balls. "I noticed my fingerprints appear on the ball," Phillips recalled. "I could see my fingerprints in the grease." Phillips went out to the mound where he warned Perry and manager Rene Lachemann. A couple innings later, when Perry threw a pitch that looked as if it rolled off a table, Phillips ejected him. It was the first and only time Perry, a 21-year veteran approaching his 44th birthday, had been kicked out of a ballgame for his famous pitch, and the first for any pitcher since 1944. Though Perry was embarrassed in the moment, he subsequently threatened legal action, before eventually backing down.[39]

After Perry finally retired, the spitball mainly faded from the news.

The demise of the spitter likely owes a lot to the advent of another pitch: the split-fingered fastball, which behaved in much the same way. Bruce Sutter started throwing it in the late 1970s, and *Sports Illustrated* later called it "The Pitch of the '80s." Roger Craig preached its virtues when he coached the Tigers in the early 80s, and again when he moved to manage the Giants. Jack Morris, Mike Scott, and Jack McDowell are among the many who mastered this pitch.[40]

But if the pure spitball was dying, ball doctoring was not. With the Astros playing at Wrigley Field in May 1985, Cubs first baseman Leon Durham found a piece of sandpaper on the mound while heading out to his position. Mike Scott was pitching for Houston, and the Cubs immediately thought something was fishy. Cubs manager Jim Frey sent the sandpaper to the league office, though he realized the evidence was only circumstantial. "The players know who they are and the umpires know who they are," Frey said. "The problem is enforcing it."[41]

In August 1987, Minnesota Twins pitcher Joe Niekro was ejected from a game for using an emery board and sandpaper to scuff the baseball, after a comical attempt secretly to toss away the evidence. When the umpires went to the mound to confront Niekro, the pitcher quickly found himself surrounded by a cast of gesticulating, arguing men—the umpiring crew, Twins manager Tom Kelly, catcher Sal Butera, and first baseman Kent Hrbek. While umpire Tim Tschida was examining Niekro's glove, crew chief Dave Phillips ordered Niekro to empty his back pockets. As Niekro turned his pockets inside out, he surreptitiously tossed a small object to the side. The umpires spied the movement and picked the item up. It turned out to be a piece of emery board, and Niekro was promptly ejected.

Niekro, nearing the end of a 22-year career as a knuckleball pitcher, claimed that he used the equipment to keep his fingernails short. Just a week later, Cubs manager Gene Michael, asked the umpires to check the glove of Phillies pitcher Kevin Gross. During an earlier game, Michael had collected a number of scuffed baseballs but didn't call Gross out because, "we were hitting him pretty good." Now, the umpires found a piece of sandpaper glued into Gross's glove. Like Niekro, he was ejected and given a 10-day suspension.[42]

Reaction to the two incidents varied widely. Niekro decided to explain himself to David Letterman on *The Late Show*. While proclaiming his innocence, Niekro walked onto Letterman's set wearing a tool belt equipped with an electric sander. Fans and media got a big kick out of this, and Niekro's reputation as a man willing to go to any length to get batters out won the PR battle. The absurdity of the oft-replayed video, rather than the dishonesty, became the central story.

Many in baseball decried the apparent epidemic of cheating about this time (including several corked bat incidents). Cubs pitcher Rick Sutcliffe said, "Something needs to be done. If they don't do something, they ought to let everyone do it. If they suspend a pitcher for only two games (10 days) and they have a chance to win four or five more games [by cheating], anybody would. They should make it two months. I don't know how many people would take a chance at losing that kind of money."[43]

Cardinals manager Whitey Herzog was even more outraged. "I don't know how they're going to go about it," Herzog said, "But somewhere down the line there have got to be rules to stop the cheating. You either play by the books or you don't play, whether you're a pitcher or a hitter. The only thing I can say is ban them for life if they get caught doing it."[44] Once again, the potential benefits seemed to outweigh the likelihood of getting caught or penalized. In the near term, increased vigilance seemed to reduce the problem to tolerable levels.

A year later baseball was faced with cheating during the NLCS. Dodger reliever Jay Howell was ejected after he was found with pine tar on his glove, which he later admitted to putting on his fingers before every pitch—especially in bad weather. When he was tossed, it was 43 degrees and raining. "I thought at the time they would throw the glove out of the game and let me continue," he said. "I didn't think they'd throw me out. I've used it in cold-weather situations when the rosin bag doesn't work. I know a lot of pitchers who use pine tar, because when the weather's cold like it is today, rosin makes the ball slick."[45]

When the story broke on television during the ALCS, commentator Reggie Jackson downplayed Howell's actions. "I could name 10 or 15 pitchers in the [AL] who use pine tar on the breaking ball. I don't think it's that severe," said Jackson.[46] Originally given a three-day suspension, it was reduced to two after Howell met with NL president Bart Giamatti.

Nearly two decades later, the 2006 World Series pitted two managerial friends against one another, the Cardinals' Tony La Russa and the Tigers' Jim Leyland. In the top of the first inning of Game 2, announcers Joe Buck and Tim McCarver noticed that Detroit pitcher Kenny Rogers had a large brown spot on the palm of his left (pitching) hand. The crew discussed this throughout the first inning, the camera zoomed in, and the news traveled down to La Russa in the Cardinals' dugout. The manager strolled out to talk to the umpires but did not ask that Rogers be checked. Instead, he merely wanted Leyland to ask Rogers to wipe the substance off his hand and resume the game. This happened, all very gentlemanly, and Rogers threw eight shutout innings in the Tigers' 3–1 victory. This turned out to be the only Tigers win of the Series, but La Russa could not have known that. When presented with evidence that the Tigers might be violating the rules in order to cheat him out of a career-defining achievement, La Russa chose not to press punishment. Quite a contrast compared to Billy Martin's strategy when confronted with George Brett's illegal bat in 1983.[47]

Although pitchers had long known about the importance of spin (or lack of spin) on all their pitches, it wasn't until Statcast and its embedded TrackMan technology came to all big-league stadiums in 2015 that they could precisely measure their spin rates. An average four-seam fastball, for example, had a spin rate of about 2,265 rpm (revolutions per minute). Not long after analysts obtained access to spin data, we learned that high revolution fastballs resulted in more missed swings and more fly balls, consistent with the notion that they resist gravity throughout their path to the plate. Once pitchers and teams had this data, it followed that they would want to learn how to achieve higher spin rates.

That May, two pitchers were ejected for having a mixture of sunscreen and rosin on their nonthrowing arm which they touched before pitching: the Brewers' Will Smith and the Orioles' Brian Matusz. Defending his pitcher, Baltimore manager Buck Showalter drew a distinction between grip enhancement and cheating. "Why is the rosin on the field? Why is it there?" Showalter asked. "It's a deeper issue than that. You've all heard me talk about the crux of the problem; same reason hitters have pine tar. We all understand the crux of the problem is gripping the ball; it's not trying to doctor the ball."[48]

Trevor Bauer, in the years before allegations of sexual assault derailed his career, may have studied spin rate more than any other pitcher in the game. He had trained at a Texas ranch since he was a child and built his own pitching lab there—with his own TrackMan system and high-speed cameras. He taught himself to replicate other pitchers' grips, training himself to learn certain pitches.

When Tom Verducci asked Bauer how a pitcher could modify his mechanics to achieve higher spin rates, Bauer said it was impossible. "He explained," wrote Verducci, "that when you backspin the ball with your hand directly behind the ball—not to the side, or not with any degree of side spin—there's nothing you can do about making it spin appreciably faster. Your spin rate on your best fastball is like your fingerprint—it is what it is."[49] Physicist Alan Nathan agrees. "It's probably pretty hard to change that [fastball spin] ratio for an individual," Nathan said. "I can see that you could do it for a curveball because a curveball involves some technique whereas a fastball is pure power. There is no finesse."[50]

There is only one way, implied Bauer: cheat.

When several Houston Astros pitchers began collectively achieving much higher spin rates in early 2018, especially recently acquired Gerrit Cole, Justin Verlander, and Charlie Morton, Bauer took to Twitter and essentially accused them of cheating: "If only there was just a really quick way to increase spin rate. Like what if you could trade for a player knowing that you could bump his spin rate a couple hundred rpm overnight; ... imagine the steals you could get on the trade market!"[51] Bauer had a long-standing feud with Cole, his former UCLA teammate, which made these claims even more salacious.

"My fastball is about 2250 rpm on average," he had written a few weeks earlier. "I know for a fact I can add 400 rpm to it by using pine tar." He then presented a chart showing batting average against various spin rate fastballs, including .213 at the "2600 and up" level.[52] He also claimed that 70 percent of all big-league pitchers were using something for their grip.

As if to make his point, in the first inning of his April 30 start, Bauer averaged 2600 rpm on his fastball, compared with an average of 2,280 in all his prior first innings. Bauer knew this would be noticed—spin rates are instantly monitored during games by analysts. In the second inning he returned to his usual self, and later declined to comment on how he had achieved those first-inning results. For the season, Bauer's average fastball spin rate was 2,322, which ranked 80th among all pitchers who faced at least 250 batters.

He had a fine 2018 (12–6, 2.21 ERA), but during a lackluster 2019 he was traded to the Reds. For the season, his fastball spin rate was 2,412 (47th best in the majors) though in September it was more than 2,700 in each start. Again, the man who often seemed so willing to talk about anything, would not talk about this.

Bauer's claims were given a fair bit of backing in March 2020 when the Angels fired Brian Harkins, their longtime visitors' clubhouse attendant, after they confirmed MLB's allegation that he was supplying a ball-doctoring substance (a melted-down pine tar solution mixed with rosin) to several visiting pitchers. Harkins did not deny the charge, and even provided the names of several clients, including Cole and Verlander (both Bauer targets), Max Scherzer, Corey Kluber, and Adam Wainwright. Harkins later sued for defamation, claiming that what he'd done was a widespread and open practice, and that the controversy had made him unemployable. As of this writing, an initial dismissal was reversed and the case sent back for trial.

The new testing labs and equipment have become popular throughout the sport, and many pitchers have derived completely honest benefits from them. Pitchers can now test multiple new grips and release points and get immediate feedback on movement and velocity, allowing them a more efficient way to improve their repertoire. But they can also allow them to test different ways to doctor the baseball.

"I've tested all sorts of different stuff in the lab up at Driveline," Bauer said in 2018 when he went public on the issue. "I've tested sunscreen and rosin. I've tested pine tar sticks. I've tested the liquid pine tar. I made my own non-Newtonian fluids. I sat down with a chemical engineer to understand it. I've melted down Firm Grip and Coca-Cola and pine tar together. I've tested a lot of stuff."[53] If the wood-repellant substance from *It Happens Every Spring* were available, you can be sure it would be on Bauer's list.

Beyond Bauer's experiments, another new substance gained traction among pitchers during 2020. Spider Tack had been invented just over a decade earlier to help carry Atlas Stones, an event in the World's Strongest Man competition. "I started seeing a lot of orders to major league stadiums," co-inventor Jeff Defflinbaugh said. "Just, you know, things that are clearly baseball-related. I Googled a couple names and they were starting professional pitchers."[54]

Meanwhile, in the pandemic-shortened 2020 season, Bauer's fastball kept spinning, reaching an average of 2776 rpm, the highest by a fair margin since Statcast began measuring in 2016. Cole was fourth, but at a comparatively measly 2505.

In that shortened season, Bauer posted a 1.73 ERA in 73 innings, with 100 strikeouts, winning the NL Cy Young Award. After the season, he signed a three-year contract with the Dodgers for $102 million, including an all-time best $40 million for 2021.

In the wake of the Brian Harkins charges, prior to the 2020 season MLB issued a memo reminding clubs of a 100-year-old truth: Putting foreign substances on the baseball was illegal. In the spring of 2021, baseball announced there would be compliance officers at the park

on game days, that baseballs would be randomly inspected, and that
Statcast spin rates would be monitored. As usual, the pitchers did not
seem to mind.

"In every case a pitcher would ask his pitching coach, 'Does this
mean they're cracking down?'" an unnamed MLB source told *Sports
Illustrated*. "And the answer was always, 'No. Keep on doing what
you're doing.' You can't change behavior without enforcement."[55]

After spin rates increased for the fourth consecutive year, MLB
informed the owners of their impending crackdown, which they
publicly announced on June 15 and began implementing the following
week. With the increased scrutiny, it looked at first as if baseball would
have a larger problem on its hands. Umpires began randomly checking
the pitcher's glove, hat, and uniform as he left the field at the end of
an inning, or at the opposing manager's request. A few pitchers were
angry about it, including Max Scherzer, who threw his glove and hat
to the ground and had to be stopped from taking off his pants. After
a few days, the angst died down and the between-innings checks did
not seem to affect the pace of the game.

The inspections seemed to have the desired effect. Two pitchers—
the Mariners' Hector Santiago and the Diamondbacks' Caleb Smith—
were caught with substances on their gloves, ejected from their games,
and given 10-game suspensions. At the same time, pitched ball-spin
rates declined dramatically.

According to one study, the average spin rate for a four-seam fastball
dropped from 2,318 rpm (when the crackdown was first announced),
to 2,229 rpm (from June 21 to 30, after the crackdown was fully implemented). Over the final three months of the season, the four-seam
fastball spin rate was 2,247 rpm. This was a massive reduction, a level
slightly below the 2018 spin rate, effectively negating the gains in spin
rate over the previous three years. Strikeout rates also declined to pre-
2019 levels.[56]

Interestingly, by the end of the season some of these effects had dis-
sipated. According to a study by Rob Arthur, four-seam fastball spin
rates recovered half of their initial decline calculated for July, and the

rise continued into the postseason. Arthur surmises that pitchers had likely figured out what they could get away with, what levels of substance umpires would not check for, or would tolerate. Alternatively, they could have discovered a natural way to achieve spin gains, though one wonders why they had never discovered this before. On the other hand, this trend reversal is much less apparent for curveballs and sliders, where the postcrackdown spin rates held relatively constant over the final three months of the 2021 season.[57]

What remains is this: The story is not done. Whether legitimate innovation or over-the-line cheating, pitchers finding new techniques to help them shut down batters, batters devising new ways to crack a ball farther, and managers manipulating anything they can—the story of creative people searching for innovative ways to gain an edge will never be finished.

EPILOGUE

IN THE 1958 FILM *DAMNED YANKEES*, and the 1955 Broadway musical on which it is based, a middle-aged fan of the hapless Washington Senators watches his team lose yet again to the New York Yankees and declares, "I'd sell my soul for one long ball hitter!" At which point the Devil appears and accepts the deal. Our hero will join the Senators as an out-of-the-blue ringer, and, after clinching their season, will then belong to the Devil.

Left unsaid: If a fan is willing to take this extreme step, imagine what the players and management might do.

Competitive people, in sports or any other high-stakes environment, will always seek out an advantage, legal or otherwise. Rogers Hornsby, as we have seen, believed this attitude was necessary to succeed in baseball. That attitude is widely shared. We have seen it in players doctoring pitchers, stealing signs, and taking pills. We have seen it among general managers exceeding bonus limits, forging birth certificates, and signing ineligible players. We've even seen cheating from groundskeepers, clubhouse attendees, trainers, and stadium employees. Baseball is a culture that, more often than not, rewards rule-breaking.

We do not mean to imply that baseball people are bad people, or even generally dishonest. They are simply competitive people, doing whatever they need to do to win. Nor are we attempting to exonerate those who cheat. For the most part baseball has clear rules over what is and isn't allowed. But there has always been a large gray area, and the "consensual ethic" among baseball people constantly evolves.

Four of the "Doctrines" we invoke in this book attest to that bare-knuckle competitiveness and the ways the consensual ethic has shifted and developed over time. The Hernandez Doctrine speaks to the idea of gamesmanship, the notion that since umpires are there to enforce the rules, trying to fool them is acceptable. Similarly, the Veeck Doctrine encourages the idea of shaping an environment to your benefit if you can get away with it. The Dobson Doctrine recognizes the players' imperative to stay in the lineup no matter what, in order that their teams might continue to benefit from their abilities. What we define as the Russo Doctrine may be the broadest of all: You are "cheating" your fans and your organization if you don't do everything you can to win.

This type of pressure to succeed under any circumstance will naturally nudge players toward testing the boundaries of fair play and, often, jumping over them. It seems illogical to expect otherwise. If the game wants to cut back on pitch doctoring, relying on the honor system is not going to cut it. If balls aren't inspected, or if the penalty for an infraction is nothing more than calling a pitch a ball, clever hurlers might calculate that the potential gain is worth the risk. Similarly, if the goal is to stop players from taking steroids, you can't simply disseminate pamphlets about their health risks. Recall the words of Jim Bouton in *Ball Four*: "If you had a pill that would guarantee a pitcher 20 wins but might take five years off his life, he'd take it."

Occasionally, unwritten understandings take hold that make certain actions acceptable or unacceptable, counteracting the rulebook. The

McGraw Doctrine underlines the difference between sign stealing with and without mechanical support, despite lack of any formal rule on this for many years. The Gwynn Doctrine differentiates between steroids and amphetamines, despite similar prohibitions on each. These instances of different perspectives on their seriousness can lead to controversy. When the consensual ethic is deemed to have been violated, yet no punishment results, trouble often follows.

One of the issues we wrestled with throughout this book is the public's perception of rule-breaking and its seriousness, whatever the rules may say. Why are some schemes viewed humorously, as boys being boys, while others fuel debate around a player's Hall of Fame candidacy or the legitimacy of a World Championship?

There are no clear-cut answers, but several themes emerge. First, cheating that involves fooling an umpire tends to be judged less harshly. This is closely related to the pervasive acceptance of the Hornsby Doctrine.

Second, fans and participants view athletic competition as a test of human performance limits. Anything that artificially stretches these limits causes concern. Spider Tack seems to have a larger effect than saliva, just as steroids are seen differently from amphetamines. Recreational drugs are, of course, prevalent throughout all segments of society and not generally credited with athletic benefits.

Third, rule-breaking that moves players around rosters does not change the action of the game on the field and therefore does not evoke the same moral outrage. The irony is that these violations likely affect games and pennant races *more* than something like sign stealing and have led to harsh punishments, even jail time. But because the game on the field does not play differently, these transgressions don't tarnish baseball's reputation in quite the same way.

The intricacy and complexity of the cheating also matters. Calculated schemes masterminded by multiple individuals are often viewed more harshly than one-offs. Reaction to the determined use of manufactured foreign substances, for example, feels different to baseball fans than saliva. In the same way, complicated, electronically aided, multiperson sign-stealing schemes have been regarded differently than opportunistic, but short-term, undertakings.

Whatever your attitude about rule-breaking, we see that it is often engineered by the most innovative people and organizations, searching for new advantages within baseball's gray areas. "Cheating" is a frequent outgrowth of these innovations. Before their sign stealing scheme was exposed, the Houston Astros had been widely hailed as one of baseball's most inventive organizations—even before winning the World Series in 2017. Gaylord Perry was a brilliant hurler with a large arsenal of excellent pitches; the spitball was just another tool in his arsenal. Barry Bonds was a once-in-a-generation player before he ever got involved with BALCO.

If there is an innovation that can increase individual, team, or organizational performance—whether that's binoculars, new drugs, surgical procedures, or ever-sharper digital video—someone will find it. Sometimes, such as with early baseball gloves or the farm system, the advantage is not immediately apparent, and the game adapts to absorb the new intelligence. Other times, as with PEDs or using real-time video to decipher catcher signs, the actions are recognized as out-of-bounds and eventually confronted. Baseball—or any organized athletic endeavor—must define, and constantly redefine its limitations.

ACKNOWLEDGMENTS

IN PREPARING THIS BOOK, we received a lot of help from friends and colleagues. First and foremost, we need to thank two people who read an early version of the entire manuscript: Rob Neyer and Marc Gullickson. Both improved the copy considerably, while providing fresh ideas for revisions. Several others read and improved one or more chapters, including Rob Arthur, Nathaniel Grow, Ben Lindbergh, Eno Sarris, Bob Tholkes, and Jason Turbow. Each of them has written on some of these subjects themselves and helped light the path for our research. We'd also like to thank Jim Linn, Arnold Witt, and Mark Witt for reading one or more chapters and offering valuable suggestions. Cliff Blau performed his usual first-rate fact check of the book.

We are both longtime members or SABR and reached out to many fellow-members in the last couple of years for ideas on this subject. At the risk of forgetting someone, we thank Gary Ashwill, Jeff Bower, Kevin Braig, Stephen Bratkovich, Scott Bush, Dan Fradl, Gary Gillette, Doron Goldman, Derrek Goold, Leslie Heaphy, Tim

Jenkins, Ted Knorr, Larry Lester, Art Mugalian, Alan Nathan, Todd Peterson, Jacob Pomrenke, Tom Shieber, Steve Steinberg, and Stew Thornley.

We have written several previous books, together and separately, but never on a subject as relatable to so many people. Not many of our friends could offer insight into Ed Barrow or Joe Cronin, but anyone who has ever played sports on the playground might have an opinion of cheating or gamesmanship, and we asked many of them. These conversations are too numerous to list here, but we thank all of you.

Thanks to Mike Noren, @gummyarts on Twitter, for the amazing illustrations. Everyone should follow him and check out his great art. David Israel helped us put together the website for the book.

The folks at Clyde Hill Publishing have been enthusiastic, encouraging, and helpful every step of the way. We would like particularly to thank Greg Shaw, who believed in the book from the beginning and shepherded it for more than a year, Claudia Rowe, who made a number of substantial suggestions to the manuscript, and Barbara Bonner for her marketing support and insights.

Finally, we would like to thank our families: Suzy, Charlie and Joey for Dan; and Jane, Maya, and Drew for Mark. Their love, kindness, and understanding has always been appreciated.

NOTES

Introduction

1. Lloyd Bacon, director, *It Happens Every Spring*, 20th Century Fox, 1949
2. Dick Zehms, "Chandler Frowns on Milland Plot," *Long Beach Press Telegram*, January 24, 1949.
3. Rogers Hornsby as told to Bill Surface, "You've Got to Cheat to Win in Baseball," *True*, August 1961.
4. Maury Allen, "The Cheating in Baseball Today," *SPORT*, January 1966.
5. Lindsay Adler, "How will Yankees ace Gerrit Cole respond on the mound as MLB plans sticky stuff crackdown?" *The Athletic*, June 8, 2021.
6. Tyler Kepner, "Once Again, M.L.B. Faces a Crisis of Its Own Making," *New York Times*, June 16, 2021.

1. Deception

1. Hornsby, "You've Got to Cheat to Win in Baseball."
2. Tim Kurkjian, *I'm Fascinated by Sacrifice Flies: Inside the Game We All Love* (New York: St. Martin's Griffin, 2017), 97.
3. Maury Allen, "The Cheating in Baseball Today," *SPORT*, January 1966.
4. Lee Gutkind, *The Best Seat in Baseball, But You Have to Stand!* (New York: The Dial Press, 1975), 135. After publication, Harvey charged that the book "is

199

full of untruths, it's a flock of lies." Jack Murphy, "Gutkind's Revealing Book on Umpires Sheds a Tainted Light," *Camden (NJ) Courier-Post*, June 3, 1975.

5. Peter Morris, *A Game of Inches—The Game on the Field* (Chicago: Ivan R. Dee, 2006), 22–25.

6. "Around the Bases," *Chicago Tribune*, June 17, 1887.

7. "Turning Balls Into Strikes With Subtlest of Motions," *New York Times*, March 22, 2014.

8. Joe Sheehan, newsletter, August 19, 2014.

9. Connie Mack, "Memories of When the Game Was Young," *Sporting Life*, June 1924.

10. John Holway, *Voices from the Great Black Baseball Leagues* (New York: Dodd, Mead & Company, 1975), 212.

11. "Derek Jeter Fakes Getting Hit By Pitch, Claims 'It's Part of the Game,'" NESN.com, September 16, 2010.

12. "Max Scherzer Loses Perfect Game with HBP in 9th But Completes No-Hitter," 6abc.com, June 21, 2015.

13. Paula Duffy, "Reggie Jackson and Tommy Lasorda Look Like Fools During Yanks-Dodgers Game Telecast," *Huffington Post*, May 25, 2011.

14. Ken Denlinger, "Jackson: Hip, Hip Hooray," *Washington Post*, October 15, 1978.

15. *Detroit News*, March 18, 1907.

16. Andres Chaves, "Mets: Michael Conforto explains what happened the game-winning 'hit by pitch,'" empiresportsmedia.com, April 9, 2021.

17. David Voight, *The League That Failed* (Lanham, MD: 1998), 63.

18. Peter Morris, *A Game of Inches*, 472.

19. Hornsby, "You've Got to Cheat to Win in Baseball."

20. Jason Turbow, "Todd Frazier, Master Magician, Makes Baseballs Appear Out Of Thin Air," thebaseballcodes.com, September 6, 2018.

21. Rick Talley, *The Cubs of '69* (Chicago: Contemporary Books, 1989), 15-16.

22. Allen, "The Cheating in Baseball Today."

23. Bill Shaikin, "Casey Blake accuses Cubs pitcher Ted Lilly of cheating," *Los Angeles Times*, May 27, 2010; Rob Neyer, "Cubs' Lilly cheats, busted by Twitter," espn.com, May 27, 2010.

24. Tim Kurkjian, *Is This a Great Game*, Kindle location 2828.

25. Allen, "The Cheating in Baseball Today."

26. William J. Ryczek, *Baseball's First Inning: A History of the National Pastime Through the Civil War* (Jefferson NC: McFarland, 2009); Richard Hershberger, *Strike Four: The Evolution of Baseball* (Washington: Rowman and Littlefield, 2019).

27. Hershberger, *Strike Four*, 171–172.

28. Ibid., 174.

29. Holway, *Voices from the Great Black Baseball Leagues*, 35.

30. J. Roy Stockton, "Balk Decision Called on Dizzy Dean Leads to 3 New York Runs," *St. Louis Post-Dispatch*, May 20, 1937.

31. "Dizzy and Frick Remain Deadlocked Upon 'Apology,'" *Boston Globe*, June 4, 1937.

32. Martin J. Haley, "Diz, With Victory of Frick, Seeks One on Mound Tomorrow," *St. Louis Globe-Democrat*, June 5, 1937.

33. Les Biederman, "Yanks Flouted Balk Rule, Says Rickey," *Sporting News*, October 15, 1952.

2. Binoculars and Telescopes

1. "Mad Mr. Magee," *Sporting Life*, October 21, 1899.

2. "Murphy's Shrewd Trick," *Washington Times*, September 12, 1899.

3. "Fake Batting Averages," *Washington Evening Star*, September 25, 1900.

4. "A Grotesque Joke Was the Buzzer, Says the Colonel," *Philadelphia Inquirer*, October 3, 1900.

5. "Rogers Knows Naught of Alleged Buzzer," *Philadelphia Inquirer*, October 1, 1900.

6. Peter Morris, *A Game of Inches—The Game on the Field* (Chicago: Ivan R. Dee, 2006), 232–234.

7. "Baseball Game Is Beastly Bore, Says Shaw When McGraw Snubs Him," *Spokane Spokesman-Review*, October 29, 1924.

8. "Intimate Stories of the Big Leaguers by John J. McGraw," *Pittsburgh Gazette Times*, April 13, 1913.

9. Fred Lieb, "Cloak-and-Dagger Men Nothing New, first Spies in '98," *The Sporting News*, July 13, 1960.

10. "Closing Sensation in American League," *Buffalo Times*, September 30, 1909.

11. "Magnates Delaying National Election," *St. Louis Globe-Democrat*, December 15, 1909.

12. "Ban Johnson Says Signal Tipping Stories Untrue," *Washington Herald*, July 15, 1910.

13. "Challenge to Pres Johnson," *Boston Globe*, July 27, 1910.

14. Dan Daniel, "When Stengel Was a Baby-Sitter," *The Sporting News*, October 17, 1951. This story seems a little exaggerated. While McGraw was not averse to using youngsters in pressure situations, it's unlikely he would have used a rookie for signaling in such pressure-packed games. More likely he used Maguire occasionally to throw off the Yankees. Moreover, Daniel is remembering this event more than thirty years later.

15. Rogers Hornsby and Bill Surface, *My War with Baseball* (New York: Coward-McCann, 1962), 176–177.

16. Dick Young, "Majors Ban Mechanical Pilfering of Enemy Signs," *New York Daily News*, April 1, 1962.

17. Hank Greenberg, *Hank Greenberg: The Story of My Life* (New York: Times Books, 1989), 140.

18. Hornsby and Surface, *My War with Baseball*, 162.

19. Bill Veeck with Ed Linn, *Veeck as in Wreck* (New York, Fireside, 1989), 162.

20. Jayson Jenks, "Binoculars and buzzers, telescopes and whistles: What won't they use to try to try to steal signs?" *The Athletic*, October 22, 2019.

21. *St. Louis Globe Democrat*, May 10, 1955.

22. Joshua Praeger, "Was the '51 Giants Comeback a Miracle, Or Did They Simply Steal the Pennant?" wsj.com, January 31, 2001.

23. Ibid.

24. Dan Daniel, "Daniel Traces Signal-Swiping History to '76," *The Sporting News*, April 4, 1962.

25. Daniel; Bob Broeg, "Sports Comment: On Stealing Signs," *St. Louis Post-Dispatch*, May 25, 1962; Praeger, "Was the '51 Giants Comeback a Miracle."

26. Dan Holmes, "George Kell Designed an Electric Sign Stealing Operation More Than 60 Years Age," vintagedetroit.com, November 20, 2019.

27. Lou Hatter, *Boston Globe*, July 22, 1956.

28. Ed Sainsbury, "ChiSox Not Guilty of Sign-Thefts," *Jackson (MS) Clarion-Ledger*, July 1, 1956.

29. Levitt interview with Al Worthington, May 20, 2020.

30. John Devaney, "A Bible in the Bullpen," *Saturday Evening Post*, May 2, 1964.

31. Jim Murray, "Twins Worthington Wouldn't Even Steal Signs," *Boston Globe*, October 8, 1965.

32. Hornsby, "You've Got to Cheat to Win in Baseball."

33. Milton Richman, "Harsh Question: Do You Cheat?" *Boston Globe*, January 29, 1965; John Devaney, *Saturday Evening Post*, May 2, 1964.

34. Arthur Daley, "Sports of the Times: Grand Larceny," *New York Times*, June 25, 1962.

35. Edgar Munzel, "Tepee 'Cub Scouts' Touch Off New Chi 'U-2' Turmoil," *The Sporting News*, July 13, 1960.

36. Daley, "Sports of the Times: Grand Larceny."

37. Dick Young, *New York Daily News*, April 1, 1962.

38. "Claims 1951 NL Winners Helped by Sign Stealing," *Richmond (IN). Palladium-Item and Sun-Telegram*, March 23, 1962.

39. Dan Daniel, *Knoxville News-Sentinel*, July 2, 1962.

40. Max Greenwald, "The Indian Sign on White Sox," *Indianapolis Star*, June 20, 1971.

41. Joe Goddard, "Retired Harrelson Admits to Bat Doctor," *Idaho Falls Times News*, June 6, 1982.

42. Ross Newhan, "Some of Baseball's Best Thieves Have Done a Peach of a Job," *Los Angeles Times*, September 12, 1991.

43. Mike Shropshire, "Whitey Challenges Brewmaster Integrity," *Fort Worth Telegram*, July 9, 1973.

44. "Herzog Fumes as Brewers Win Pair," *Appleton (WI) Post-Crescent*, July 9, 1973.

45. Sid Bordman," For Openers—Royals 3, A's 1," *Kansas City Times*, September 22, 1976; Joe McGuff, "Sheriff Whitey, Royals Get Drop on Bad Guys," *Kansas City Star*, September 22, 1976.

46. Del Black, "And Who Says Baseball Isn't an Emotional Sport," *Kansas City Times*, September 22, 1976.

47. "No More Close-Ups," *Passaic (NJ) Herald-News*, July 14, 1959.

48. Joe McGuff, "Yanks Clear Walkie-Talkies; Herzog Still Fumes," *Kansas City Star*, October 12, 1976.

49. "Kuhn Gets the Final Word in Walkie-Talkie Trouble," *Albuquerque Journal*, October 17, 1976; Bob Hertzel, "Yankees Disobey Kuhn's Ground Rules, But Get O.K. to Resume Practice," *Cincinnati Enquirer*, October 17, 1976; Dick Young, "Yank Electronic Spy System Gets Final OK," *New York Daily News*, October 17, 1976.

50. Lowell Reidenbaugh, "Kuhn Silences Yank Voice in Stands," *The Sporting News*, October 30, 1976.

51. Mel Durslag, "Walkie-Talkie Stirs Dispute in Series," *Scranton (PA) Tribune*, October 21, 1976

52. Tim Kurkjian, "Sign Language Hidden Cameras."

3. Espionage

1. Ramona Shelburne, "How the Astros Built a Winner," espn.com, October 5, 2003.

2. Matthew Futterman, "Baseball After Moneyball," *Wall Street Journal*, September 23, 2011.

3. Joe Torre and Tom Verducci, *The Yankee Years* (New York: Doubleday, 2009), 442–445.

4. Ben Reiter, "What Happened to the Houston Astros' Hacker?" si.com, October 4, 2018.

5. Evan Drellich, "Astros' formula for success builds on its own data bank," *Houston Chronicle*, March 8, 2014.

6. *USA v. Correa*, Sealed Responses to Defendant's PSR Objections (Redacted version unsealed January 25, 2017); *USA v. Correa*, Sentencing Memo of the United States (Redacted version unsealed January 25, 2017); Brian Walton. "The Comprehensive Cardinals Correa Chronicle on Houston Hacking," thecardinals nation.com, February 3, 2017.

7. Plea Agreement; Tyler Kepner, "Former Cardinals Official Pleads Guilty to Hacking," *New York Times*, January 9, 2016; Derrick Goold and Robert Patrick, "Ex-Cards Official Admits Hacking Astros' Database, *St. Louis Post-Dispatch*, January 9, 2016; *USA v. Correa*, Sealed Responses to Defendant's PSR Objections (Redacted version unsealed January 25, 2017); Derrick Goold, "Cards' Punishment Near," *St. Louis Post-Dispatch*, January 30, 2017.

8. Plea Agreement; Tyler Kepner, "Former Cardinals"; Goold and Patrick, "Ex-Cards Official."

9. Evan Drellich, "Astros GM Jeff Luhnow addresses trade leaks," Deadspin.com, June 30, 2014; Evan Drellich and David Barron, "Astros defend Ground Control and take breach seriously," ultimateastros.com, June 17, 2015.

10. Barry Petchesky, "Who Leaked The Astros' Hacked Data, And Why?" deadspin.com, June 17, 2015; Barry Petchesky, "Leaked: 10 Months Of The Houston Astros' Internal Trade Talks," deadspin.com, June 30, 2014.

11. Sentencing memo; Sealed Responses to Defendant's PSR Objections.

12. Ibid.

13. *USA v. Correa*, Rearraignment document, January 8, 2016.

14. Howard Megdal, *The Cardinals Way: How One Team Embraced Tradition and Moneyball at the Same Time* (New York: Thomas Dunne, 2016), 262.

15. "Astros' GM Luhnow disputes details related to hacking probe," si.com, June 18, 2015.

16. Evan Drellich, "Astros' formula for success builds on its own data bank," *Houston Chronicle*, March 8, 2014.

17. 2017–2021 Basic Agreement (Collective Bargaining Agreement), Attachment 56, p. 335, https://docs.wixstatic.com/ugd/b0a4c2_95883690627349e0a520 3f61b93715b5.pdf.

18. Stephanie Springer, An Update On Wearable Baseball Technology, fangraphs.com, August 7, 2018; Darren Rovell, "MLB approves device to measure biometrics of players," espn.com, March 6, 2017; John A. Balletta, "Measuring Baseball's Heartbeat: The Hidden Harms or Wearable Technology to Profeesional Baseball Players," *Duke Law and Technology Review* 18 (2020); company websites.

19. Barbara Osbourne and Jennie L. Cunningham, "Legal and Ethical Implications of Athletes' Biometric Data Collection in Professional Sport," *Marquette Sports Law Review* (Fall 2017).

20. Eno Sarris and Brittany Ghiroli, "Baseball's new frontier: Inside the looming battle between players and teams over the new data," *The Athletic*, March 21, 2019.

21. Attachment 56, 2017–2021 Basic Agreement; specifically, "Any and all Wearable Data shall be treated as highly confidential at all times, including after the expiration, suspension or termination of this Agreement, shall not become a part of the Player's medical record, and shall not be disclosed by a Club to any party other than those persons listed in this Paragraph 4 without the express written consent of the Player and the Association."

22. Buster Olney, "Padres' A.J. Preller suspended 30 days after investigation of Drew Pomeranz trade," September 15, 2016; Tim Healey, "Marlins send injured right-hander Colin Rea back to Padres for minor leaguer," *South Florida Sun Sentinel, August* 1, 2016.

23. Bob Nightengale, "MLB suspends Padres GM A.J. Preller for his conduct in trade," *USA Today*, September 15, 2016.

24. Buster Olney, "MLB executives: Preller suspension not enough," espn.com, September 17, 2016.

4. Smart Watches and Trash Cans

1. Alex Speier, "A brief history of video and technology in baseball, and how it helped teams steal signs," msn.com, May 3, 2020.

2. Murray Chass, "Electronic Larceny at Shea?" *New York Times*, August 19, 1997.

3. Ken Rosenthal, "Red Sox crossed a line, and baseball's response must be firm," *The Athletic*, September 5, 2017.

4. Gordon Edes, "Gillick's accusations hit home," archive.boston.com, November 20, 2003.

5. "Buehrle Says Rangers Cheat in Stealing Signs," *Detroit Free Press*, August 31, 2005.

6. "Mets claim Phillies cheated by stealing signs," *New York Daily News*, September 2, 2007.

7. "Manuel: Phils not trying to steal signs," espn.com, May 12, 2010.

8. Troy E. Renck, "Rockies miffed at Phillies' use of binoculars," denverpost.com, May 12, 2010.

9. "Manuel: Phils not trying to steal signs."

10. Amy K. Nelson and Peter Keating, "Signs of trouble in Toronto," espn.com, August 5, 2011.

11. "Decision and Findings of the Commissioner in the Red Sox Investigation," April 22, 2020, https://img.mlbstatic.com/mlb-images/image/upload/mlb/scn5xwigcottcbte7siw.pdf; Emma Baccellieri, "Sign Stealing and the Unintended Consequences of Replay," si.com, January 8, 2020; Tom Verducci, "Why MLB Issued Historic Punishment to Astros for Sign Stealing," si.com, January 13, 2020.

12. "Decision and Findings."

13. Ian Crouch, "What to Make of the Red Sox's Apple Watch Scandal," *New Yorker*, September 15, 2017; Michael S. Schmidt, Red Sox Used Apple Watches to Help Steal Signs Against Yankees," *New York Times*, September 5, 2017.

14. "Commissioner's statement regarding Red Sox-Yankees violations," mlb.com, September 15, 2017.

15. Alex Speier, "A brief history of video and technology in baseball, and how it helped teams steal signs," msn.com, May 5, 2020.

16. "Statement of the Commissioner," January 13, 2020, https://img.mlbstatic.com/mlb-images/image/upload/mlb/cglrhmlrwwbkacty2717.pdf.

17. "Major League Baseball statement," mlb.com, October 6, 2017.

18. Jeff Passan, "The shocking history of sign stealing in baseball," yahoo.com, September 6, 2017.

19. "Statement of the Commissioner."

20. "Decision and Findings of the Commissioner in the Red Sox Investigation," April 22, 2020, https://img.mlbstatic.com/mlb-images/image/upload/mlb/scn5xwigcottcbte7siw.pdf.

21. Ben Reiter, The Edge: Houston Astros (podcast), Episode 1: Bang Bang, September 11, 2020.

22. Danny Picard, "Metro Exclusive: Astros may have been cheating in Game 1 against Red Sox," metro.us, October 16, 2018; "MLB clears Astros of sign stealing: 'We consider the matter closed,'" sportnet.ca, October 17, 2018.

23. Tom King (@TomKing50 tweet, January 15, 2020, "Cheating is Wider Than We Think," wsau.com, January 15, 2020.

24. Robert Murray, "'Something looks a little bit off': In a postseason of paranoia, some Brewers suspect the Dodgers are stealing signs," The Athletic, October 18, 2018; Andy Martino, Cheated: The Inside Story of the Astros Scandal and a Colorful History of Sign Stealing (New York: Doubleday, 2021), 194.

25. Tom Verducci, "Exclusive: MLB Set to Pass New Rules Designed to Crack Down on Sign Stealing," si.com, February 19, 2019; Andy Martino, Cheated.

26. Mark Townsend, "Yu Darvish comment fuels Brewers' sign stealing speculation; Christian Yelich fires back," yahoo.com, November 15, 2019.

27. Jeff Passan, "Sources: Red Sox were warned by Indians about Astros attempting to steal signs and information," yahoo.com, October 16, 2018.

28. Ken Rosenthal and Evan Drellich, "The Astros stole signs electronically in 2017—part of a much broader issue for Major League Baseball," The Athletic, November 12, 2019.

29. Jared Diamond, "Astros Players Cheated. Baseball Wanted Answers. So It Made a Deal," wsj.com, January 22, 2020.

30. Jared Diamond, "How the Houston Astros Cheated," Wall Street Journal, February 8, 2020; Jared Diamond, "Rule-Breaking Permeated the Astros," Wall Street Journal, February 13, 2020.

31. Tom Verducci, "Astros' Cheating Haunts Clayton Kershaw's Memory of 2017 World Series," si.com, February 20, 2020.

32. "Statement of the Commissioner."

33. Jared Diamond, "How the Houston Astros Cheated"; Marly Rivera, "Memo details new MLB rules to discipline electronic sign stealing," espn.com, July 30, 2020.

34. "Statement of the Commissioner."

35. "Ex-Astros GM Jeff Luhnow again denies role in Houston Astros' sign stealing scandal," espn.com, October 19, 2020.

36. "Statement of the Commissioner."

37. Chandler Rome, "Jeff Luhnow's lawsuit vs. Astros dismissed after sides 'resolved differences,'" houstonchronicle.com, February 5, 2021.

38. Ken Rosenthal and Evan Drellich, "MLB's sign stealing controversy broadens: Sources say the Red Sox used video replay room illegally in 2018," *The Athletic*, January 7, 2020.

39. "Decision and Findings of the Commissioner in the Red Sox Investigation," April 22, 2020, https://img.mlbstatic.com/mlb-images/image/upload/mlb/scn5xwigcottcbte7siw.pdf.

40. Tom Verducci, "Why MLB Issued Historic Punishment to Astros for Sign Stealing," si.com, January 13, 2020.

41. Dick Young, "Majors Ban Mechanical Pilfering of Enemy Signs," *New York Daily News*, April 1, 1962; Tim Kurkjian, "Can you read the signs?"; Billy Evans, "Tipping the Signals," *Pearsons Magazine*, July 1914.

42. Bob Broeg, "Sports Comment: On Stealing Signs," *St. Louis Post-Dispatch*, March 25, 1962.

43. Terence Moore, "Former Miami Marlins President Details History Of Cheating In Baseball: Where Astros Went Wrong," forbes.com, March 6, 2020.

44. Jayson Stark and Eno Sarris, "Does electronic sign stealing work? The Astros' numbers are eye-popping," *The Athletic*, January 31, 2020.

45. Tom Verducci, "Astros' Latest Scandal Demands Quick Action From MLB," si.com, November 13, 2019.

46. Tony Adams, signstealingscandal.com; see Jared Diamond for background on Tony Adams's research, https://www.wsj.com/articles/an-astros-fan-spent-50-hours-listening-for-banging-he-heard-a-lot-of-banging-11580394165. A number of analyses were based on this and other data to determine the value the Astros received from the sign stealing. One suggested a large theoretical benefit but acknowledged the complexity of actual play: Ben Clemens, https://blogs.fangraphs.com/the-hypothetical-value-of-an-ideal-frictionless-banging-scheme/. One emphasized the inconclusiveness of the data: Jake Mailhot, https://blogs.fangraphs.com/how-much-did-the-astros-really-benefit-from-sign-stealing/; one looked at high leverage situations: Jake Mailhot, https://blogs.fangraphs.com/the-most-important-bangs-of-the-astros-scheme/; others simply took a deep dive into Adams's data: https://www.reddit.com/r/baseball/comments/exkkoz/i_went_through_the_footage_provided_by_uatadams/; one was as short analysis on the benefit by player: Bill Petti, https://twitter.com/BillPetti/status/1222931646372089857; Adam Gilfix, "Analyzing Astros Trash Can Banging Signal Accuracy and Corresponding Batter Swing," reddit.com, February 25, 2020.

47. Robert Arthur, "Moonshot: The Banging Scheme Hurt the Astros As Much As It Helped Them," BaseballProspectus.com, January 30, 2020.

48. Ben Lindbergh, "There's No Virtue in Signaling. But Is There Any Benefit?" theringer.com, November 22, 2019.

49. Ross Newhan, "Some of Baseball's Best Thieves Have Done a Peach of a Job," *Los Angeles Times*, September 12, 1991.

50. Todd Dybas, "MLB Looking into New Technology to Prevent Theft of Pitch Calls," nbcsports.com, March 19, 2019.

51. Mark Demsky, Jordan Radach, "MLB to test pitcher-catcher transmitter with Ports, Nuts to combat cheating," fox40.com, August 4, 2021.

52. Hannah Keyser, "Sources: MLB discussing on-field technology to prevent sign stealing," yahoo.com, January 6, 2020.

5. Penny Nails and Cork

1. William Asher, director, *Bewitched*, "Twitch or Treat," American Broadcasting Company, October 27, 1966.

2. Seymour Robbie, director, *Bewitched*, "I Confess," American Broadcasting Company, April 4, 1968.

3. "Pine Tar Game: An oral history of the most controversial home run ever hit," si.com, July 22, 2016.

4. Thomas Boswell, "Justice is Done with a Sticky Wicket," *Washington Post*, July 29, 1983.

5. Joe Soucheray, "Twins Split Two Games With Yanks," *Minneapolis Tribune*, July 20, 1975; "Oily Bat Costs Cub Hit," *Kenosha News*, August 19, 1975.

6. Bill Christine, "Illegal Bats Pop Up in Majors," *Pittsburgh Post*, September 2, 1975.

7. "Met Rookies Boost Team's Title Chances," *Hackensack (New Jersey) Record*, August 27, 1975.

8. "Text of League President's Ruling," *New York Times*, July 29, 1983.

9. Jimmy Stamp, "The Past and Future of the Baseball Bat," smithsonianmag.com, July 2, 2013; *Official Baseball Rules*, 2019 Edition.

10. Peter Morris, *A Game of Inches—The Game on the Field* (Chicago: Ivan R. Dee, 2006), 475.

11. John H. Gruber, "The Rules and Tools of the National Game," *The Sporting News*, November 11, 1915.

12. "The Readers Take Over," *Sports Illustrated*, May 4, 1981; Dan Gutman, *It Ain't Cheatin' If You Don't Get Caught* (New York: Penguin, 1990), 72.

13. F. C. Lane, *Batting* (Baseball Magazine, 1925), 70. Reprinted by SABR, 2001.

14. Bill Shirley, "Maybe Baseball Ought to Have a Corkage Fee," *Los Angeles Times*, September 1, 1982; "Braves Pine Over Johnstone's Tar," *Philadelphia Daily News*, August 13, 1976; Bill Christine, "Illegal Bats Pop Up in Majors," *Pittsburgh*

Post, September 2, 1975; Bob Hertzel, "Cheating Frowned On, But Still a Part of Baseball," *Baseball Digest*, September 1984.

15. Peter Gammons, "Fans in Boston Shudder at Trade Prospects," *Boston Globe*, September 22, 1974.

16. Gutman, *It Ain't Cheatin'*, 70.

17. Jim Hawkins, "Tigers Ticked by Nettles' Cork Bat," *The Sporting News*, September 28, 1974.

18. Steve Wulf, "Tricks of the Trade," *Sports Illustrated*, April 13, 1981.

19. Ibid.

20. "Otis Confesses Use of Corked Bats to Help Hit .277 as Major Leaguer," *Los Angeles Times*, April 28, 1992.

21. Bob Sudyk, "Discarding Cork-Filled Bat Thornton's Biggest Moment," *The Sporting News*, December 16, 1978.

22. Bruce Markusen, "Card Corner Plus: Dan Ford and the Disco Revolution," *Hardball Times*, November 9, 2018.

23. John Strege "Ford's Bat Ploy isn't Better Idea," *The Sporting News*, September 26, 1981.

24. Terry Pluto, *The Earl of Baltimore* (Piscataway, NJ: New Century Publishers, 1972), 181.

25. "Hatcher Ejected for Using Illegal Bat," *Washington Post*, September 2, 1987.

26. Damon Hack, "Baseball; Sosa Ejected for Using Corked Bat In a Game," *New York Times*, June 4, 2003.

27. Buzz Bissinger, "A Darker Shade of Rose," *Vanity Fair*," September 2001.

28. Jerry Crasnick, "Rose Denies New Set of Allegations," *Sun Sentinel*, August 8, 2001.

29. Danny Gallagher, "Pete Rose alleged to have used a corked bat while playing for Expos," *Montreal Gazette*, May 1, 2020.

30. Joe Capozzi, "He called me 'Corky': Jupiter man says he corked baseball bats for Pete Rose in 1984," *Palm Beach Post*, June 5, 2020.

31. Keith Hernandez and Mike Bryan, *Pure Baseball* (Harper Collins: 1994).

32. Alan M. Nathan, et. al., "Corked Bats, Juiced Balls, and Humidors: The Physics of Cheating in Baseball," *American Journal of Physics* (June 2011).

6. Rakes and Hoses

1. Bill Veeck with Ed Linn, *Veeck as in Wreck* (New York, Fireside, 1989), 160.

2. Ray Gillespie, "Short Career for Midget in Brownie Uniform," *Sporting News*, August 29, 1961.

3. Victor O. Jones, "Are Midgets People?" *Boston Globe*, August 23, 1951.

4. Gillespie, "Short Career for Midget."

5. Bill Veeck, "Gamesmanship Helped Indians Win 1948 Pennant," *Mansfield (OH) News-Journal*, September 14, 1952.

6. Veeck with Linn, *Veeck as in Wreck*.

7. Danny Peary, *We Played The Game* (Westport, CT: Hyperion, 1994), 420.

8. Arthur Daley, *Inside Baseball* (New York: Grosset & Dunlap, 1950), 63.

9. Veeck with Linn, *Veeck as in Wreck*.

10. Veeck, "Gamesmanship."

11. Veeck with Linn, *Veeck as in Wreck*.

12. Gayle Talbot, "Cleveland Indians' Groundskeeper Tells of Tailoring His Diamond," *Freemont (NE) Guide and Tribune*, May 19, 1955.

13. Veeck with Linn, *Veeck as in Wreck*, 159.

14. Mrs. John McGraw, edited by Arthur Mann, *The Real McGraw* (New York: David McKay Company, 1953), 94.

15. Peter Morris, *Level Playing Fields: How the Groundskeeping Murphy Brothers Shaped Baseball* (Lincoln, NE: University of Nebraska Press, 2007), 37, 57.

16. "Inside Baseball as Played by Orioles, *Weatherford (OK) Diplomat*," June 7, 1923.

17. Larry Lester, *Rube Foster in His Time: On the Field and in the Papers with Black Baseball's Greatest Visionary* (Jefferson, NC: McFarland, 2012), 105.

18. Noel Hynd, "Giant-Sized Confession: A Groundskeeper's Deeds," *Sports Illustrated*, August 29, 1988.

19. "It's Dirty Pool, Says Dodgers' Bavasi," *Santa Rosa (CA) Press-Democrat*, August 15. 1962; Art Rosenbaum and Bob Stevens, *The Giants of San Francisco* (Coward-McCann, 1963), 25–27.

20. Lee Gutkind, *The Best Seat in Baseball, But You Have to Stand!* (New York: The Dial Press, 1975), 41.

21. Annie Sweeney. "Bossard Dead at Age 80," *Chicago Tribune*, February 1, 1998.

22. Paul Sullivan, "'The Sodfather' recalls a time when skirting the rules in baseball was just part of a groundskeeper's job," *Chicago Tribune*, March 9, 1990.

23. Tom Trebelhorn, "Dugout Wisdom," *Memories and Dreams*, Summer 2021.

24. Paul Sullivan, "Frozen baseballs and the 1960s White Sox," *Chicago Tribune*, March 8, 2020.

25. Jonathan Rees, *Refrigeration Nation: A History of Ice, Appliances, and Enterprise in America* (Baltimore: The Johns Hopkins University Press, 2013), 124–125, 133; Joseph C. Jones, Jr., *American Ice Boxes : A Book on the History, Collecting and Restoration of Ice Boxes* (Humble, TX: Jobeco Books, 1981), 38–75.

26. Fred Lieb, *Connie Mack: Grand Old Man of Baseball* (New York: G. P. Putnam's Sons, 1945), 45.

27. Lester, *Rube Foster in His Time*, 105.

28. Jim Armstrong and Troy E. Renck, "Giants accuse Rockies of cheating with humidor," *Denver Post*, September 25, 2010.

29. Peter Morris, *A Game of Inches A Game of Inches—The Game on the Field* (Chicago: Ivan R. Dee, 2006), 294.

30. "Taking off the Kid Gloves: Baseball to Enforce Mitt Rule," *Binghamton (NY) Press & Sun-Bulletin*, May 1, 1990; Michael Paolerclo, "Gargantuan Gloves Come Under Scrutiny," *Burlington (VT) Free Press*, March 27, 1990; Hal McCoy, "Baseball Orders Players: Put Up Your Mitts," *Dayton Daily News*, March 25, 1990.

31. "Baseball Crowd Causes Forfeit," *New York Times*, April 12, 1907; Peter Morris, *A Game of Inches*, 302–303.

32. "Shin Pads of Bresnahan Bring Forth a Protest," *St. Louis Post-Dispatch*, May 14, 1907.

33. "Clarke Orders Armor," *Pittsburgh Daily Post*, May 22, 1907.

34. Michael Lee, "Maddux Suffers a Painful, Rare Loss," *Atlanta Constitution*, July 25, 2000; Carroll Rogers, "TBS Announcers Denied Seats on Braves' Plane," *Nashville Tennessean*, June 27, 2000; Paul Newberry, "Announcers Allowed Back on Braves' Plane," *Wilkes-Barre (PA) Times Leader*, June 28, 2000; Furman Bisher, "Catcher's Box Flap Flares, Fades," *Atlanta Constitution*, June 28, 2000.

35. Mark Viera, "Batters Search For Edge Outside On-Deck Circle," *New York Times*, October 4, 2010.

36. Sam Butler, "Adrian Beltre was asked to go back to the on-deck circle, so he dragged it to where he was standing," mlb.com, July 27, 2017.

37. Associated Press, "Ericson admits to adjusting ventilation system," espn.com, July 26, 2003.

38. Hornsby, "You've Got to Cheat to Win in Baseball."

39. Veeck with Linn, *Veeck as in Wreck*, 159.

40. Andrew Mearns, "Bobby Valentine was ejected and wore a disguise in the dugout 18 years ago today," mlb.com, June 9, 2018.

41. Kevin T. Czerwinski, "Fichman recalls his feathered fame," milb.com, January 29, 2020.

42. Memo from Jim Johnstone to NL President Harry Pulliam, August 19, 1904.

43. Letter from John McGraw to NL President Harry Pulliam, August 23, 1904.

7. Roster Shenanigans

1. Bob Tholkes, telephone interview, March 4, 2021; John Thorn, "New York Base Ball Club (a.k.a. Washington BBC, Gotham BBC)," in Peter Morris, William J, Ryczek, et al., *Baseball Founders: The Clubs, Players, and Cities of the Northeast that Established the Game* (Jefferson, NC: McFarland, 2013), 58; Aaron W. Miller, "Union Base Ball Club of Morrisania," Morris, Ryczek, 96; Harold and Dorothy Seymour, *Baseball: The Early Years* (New York: Oxford, 1960), 51.

2. Tholkes, telephone interview.

3. Harold and Dorothy Seymour, *Baseball: The Early Years*, 47–48; Peter Morris, *A Game of Inches—The Game on the Field* (Chicago: Ivan R. Dee, 2006), 462–463; William J. Ryczek, *Baseball's First Inning* (Jefferson, NC: McFarland, 2009), 210; John Thorn, *Baseball in the Garden of Eden: The Secret History of the Early Game* (New York: Simon & Schuster, 2011), 122–124; Bob Tholkes, email correspondence, June 2, 2021.

4. Mark Pestana, "Pivot to Professionalism: The 1869 Winter Meetings," in Jeremy K. Hodges and Bill Nowlin, *Base Ball's 19th Century "Winter" Meetings: 1857–1900* (Phoenix: Society for American Baseball Research, 2018), 89–90.

5. Harold and Dorothy Seymour, *Baseball: The Early Years*, 120.

6. Charlie Bevis, "Tim Keefe," SABR's Baseball Biography Project, sabr.org; Harold and Dorothy Seymour, *Baseball: The Early Years*, 166.

7. Brian Martin, *The Detroit Wolverines: The Rise and Wreck of a National League Champion, 1881–1888* (Jefferson, NC: McFarland, 2018), 119-126.

8. "Two Superbas Are Made Free Agents," *Pittsburgh Press*, November 16, 1921.

9. House Judiciary Committee, Study of Monopoly Power: Hearings before the Subcommittee on the Study of Monopoly Power, Serial No. 1, Part 6, "Organized Baseball," 82nd Cong., 1st sess., 1951, 685.

10. Dan Austin, *Baseball's Last Great Scout: The Life of Hugh Alexander* (Lincoln, NE: University of Nebraska Press, 2013), 40.

11. Mark Ribowsky, *A Complete History of the Negro Leagues 1884 to 1955* (New York: Citadel Press, 1995, 2002), 176; Neil Lanctot, *Negro League Baseball: The Rise and Ruin of a Black Institution* (Philadelphia: University of Pennsylvania Press, 2004), 41; James E. Overmyer, *Cum Posey of the Homestead Grays: A Biography of the Negro Leagues Owner and Hall of Famer* (Jefferson, NC: McFarland, 2020), 139–140; Leslie A. Heaphy, *The Negro Leagues 1869 to 1960* (Jefferson, NC: McFarland, 2003), 108.

12. Shirley Povich, "Mr. Chandler a Tough Boss," *The Sporting News*, September 15, 1948.

13. Wynn Montgomery, "Georgia's 1948 Phenoms and the Bonus Rule," *Baseball Research Journal* (Phoenix: SABR, 2010).

14. Jim Russo with Bob Hammel, *Super Scout: Thirty-Five Years of Big League Scouting* (New York: Bonus Books, 1992), 43–44.

15. Alan Simpson ed., *Baseball America's Ultimate Draft Book* (Durham, NC: BA Books, 2016), 32; Giants scout George Genovese remembered liking Seaver even when he was pitching at junior college in Fresno. When he asked why the Giants didn't participate, he was told "Chub [Giants front office executive Feeney] felt that since we already had Marichal and Perry, we don't need another pitcher." Genovese with Taylor, 144.

16. Hy Zimmerman, "Farm Director Fired in M's Clash," *The Sporting News*, October 14, 1978; Mel Didier and T. R. Sullivan, *Podnuh: Let Me Tell You A Story—A Baseball Life* (Baton Rouge LA: Gulf South Books, 1997), 105–110.

17. Jerry Crasnick, "Ex-Braves GM John Coppolella 'disgraced and humbled'," si.com, December 5, 2017.

18. Didier and Sullivan, *Podnuh,* 17–22.

19. Red Murff with Mike Capps, *The Scout* (Dallas: World Publishing, 1997), 108.

20. Thomas McKenna, "The Path to the Sugar Mill or the Path to Millions: MLB Baseball Academies' Effect on the Dominican Republic," *Baseball Research Journal* (Phoenix: SABR, Spring 2017); Mark L. Armour and Daniel R. Levitt, *In Pursuit of Pennants* (Lincoln: University of Nebraska Press, 2015), 309.

21. Roger Bruns, *Finding Baseball's Next Clemente: Combating Scandal in Latino Recruiting* (Santa Barbara, CA: Praeger, 2015), 119–120; Melissa Segura, "Drafted at 13, How One Player Changed International Signing Rules," *Sports Illustrated,* July 2, 2012.

22. "Lasorda defends Dodgers' actions," espn.com, November 16, 1999.

23. "Dodgers fined for signing young Beltre," espn.com, December 21, 1999; Jason Reid, "Dodgers Under Microscope Again," *Los Angeles Times,* June 17, 2000; Jayson Stark, "Age Issues Brought on by Sept. 11," espn.com, February 23, 2002; Arturo J. Marcano Guevara and David P. Fidler, *Stealing Lives: The Globalization of Baseball and the Tragic Story of Alexis Quiroz* (Bloomington, IN: Indiana University Press, 2002), 34.

24. Steve Fainaru, "Baseball's Minor Infractions," *Washington Post,* October 26, 2001.

25. Steve Fainaru and Dave Shenin, "Indians are Hit with Penalties," *Washington Post,* February 27, 2002; Guevara and Fidler, *Stealing Lives,* 33–34.

26. Fainaru, "Baseball's Minor Infractions."

27. Jeff Passan, "Source: Red Sox banned from signing international amateurs for a year," yahoo.com, July 1, 2016; Boston was not restricted on its ability to sign international free agents that qualified as professionals, dubbed foreign professionals (Jeff Passan, "Source"). Major League Baseball distinguishes between amateur international free agents and professional ones. The latter, generally defined as those who are least 23 years old and have played professionally for at least five years do not count against the cap.

28. Passan, "Source:"; "Commissioner's Statement Regarding Braves' Violations," November 21, 2017; Tyler Kepner, "Baseball Bars a Former Braves Executive for Life" *New York Times,* November 22, 2017.

29. Mark Bowman, "Braves penalized for int'l signing violations," mlb.com, November 21, 2017; "Ex-Braves GM John Coppolella permanently banned; team loses prospects," espn.com, November 21, 2017; "Commissioner's Statement Regarding Braves' Violations," November 21, 2017; Jerry Crasnick, "Ex-Braves GM John Coppolella 'disgraced and humbled'," espn.com, December 5, 2017; Mark Bradley, "Going, going, gone: The Braves had no further need of John Hart," *Atlanta Journal Constitution,* November 17, 2017.

30. Roger Abrams, "Arbitrator Seitz Sets the Players Free," *Baseball Research Journal* (Phoenix: SABR, Fall 2009).

31. Wayne Minshew, "Kuhn Suspends Turner for Year," *Atlanta Constitution*, January 3, 1977.

8. Greenies

1. "O'Neill Says Tigers Doped Newhouser," *Detroit Times*, November 2, 1951; "Drug 'Won' Tigers the 1945 Flag," *St. Cloud Times*, November 3, 1951.

2. Ibid.

3. Al Hirshberg, "Never Would Have Won Flag Without 'Pain-Killer,' Steve O'Neill Insists," *The Sporting News*, November 14, 1951.

4. George Puscas, "Drug Newhouser Took a Harmless Pain-Killer," *Detroit Free Press*, November 3, 1951.

5. "Pain-Killing Drug Helped Bring Tigers Flag," *Dayton Daily News*, November 3, 1951.

6. Watson Spoelstra, "Novocain Accepted Training Practice—Trainer Blasts Hub Shot at Newhouser," *The Sporting News*, November 14, 1951.

7. Ibid.

8. Al Hirshberg, "Never Would Have Won Flag Without 'Pain-Killer,' Steve O'Neill Insists," *The Sporting News*, November 14, 1951.

9. Dan Parker, *Camden New Jersey Courier-Post*, November 22, 1951.

10. See for example, *Detroit Free Press*, October 31, 1951.

11. Terry Todd, "Anabolic Steroids: The Gremlins of Sport," *Journal of Sport History* (Spring, 1987): 90; Sally Jenkins, "Winning, Cheating Have Ancient Roots," *Washington Post*, August 3, 2007; Charles E. Yesalis and Michael S. Bahrke, "History of Doping in Sport," *International Sports Studies* 24, no. 1 (2002): 42–45; Richard I. G. Holt, Ioulietta Erotokritou-Mulligan, and Peter H. Sönksen, 'The history of doping and growth hormone abuse in sport," *Growth Hormone & IGF Research 19* (2009): 320–326; Robert Voy, *Drugs, Sport and Politics* (New York: Leisure Press, 1991), 5.

12. Will Carroll, *The Juice: The Real Story of Baseball's Drug Problems* (Chicago: Ivan R. Dee, 2005), 31; Andre McNicoll, "Breakfast of Champions," *MacLean's*, September 19, 1977; Yesalis and Bahrke, "History of Doping in Sport," 45; Voy, *Drugs, Sport and Politics*, 6.

13. Yesalis and Bahrke, "History of Doping in Sport," 45–46; Voy, *Drugs, Sport and Politics*, 6.

14. C. R. Griffith, *Psychology of Coaching: A Study of Coaching Methods* (New York: Scribner's and Sons, 1926), 28, quoted in Kornspan, "Cubs Use of Statistics," NINE 23, no. 1 (Fall 2014).

15. Christopher D. Green, "Psychology Strikes Out: Coleman R. Griffith and the Chicago Cubs," *History of Psychology* 6, no. 3 (2003); Christopher D. Green,

"The Chicago Cubs and 'The Headshrinker': An Early Foray into Sports Psychology," *Baseball Research Journal* (Phoenix: SABR, Spring 2011).

16. Robin Wolfe Scheffler, "The Power of Exercise and the Exercise of Power: The Harvard Fatigue Laboratory, Distance Running, and the Disappearance of Work, 1919–1947," *Journal of the History of Biology* 48 (2015): 391; Paul Dimeo, *A History of Drug Use in Sport, 1876–1976: Beyond Good and Evil* (London: Routledge, 2007), 35.

17. Nicolas Rasmussen, *On Speed: The Many Lives of Amphetamines* (New York: New York University Press, 2008), 22–24; "History, Pharmacology, and Prevalence Methamphetamine Overview: Origin and History," methoide.fcm.arizona. edu. Recently, other families of stimulants have overtaken amphetamine, but we will often use "stimulants," "speed," and "amphetamines" interchangeably to improve the readability of the text.

18. Rasmussen, *On Speed*, 41, 50, 101.

19. Ibid., 82.

20. "Alleges Stimulation of Olympic Athletes," *New York Times*, October 1, 1948.

21. "'Wake Up and Die': The Pep Pill Menace," *Readers Digest*, October 1960.

22. "'Pepped Up' Cousy Leads Celtics Romp," *Long Beach Press-Telegram*, April 10, 1960; "Cousy 'Pepped' Up," *Cincinnati Enquirer*, April 10, 1960.

23. Jim Brosnan, *The Long Season* (New York: Penguin Books, 1983), 48. Dexamyl was an amphetamine spiked with a low-dose barbiturate introduced about 1950 that became highly popular.

24. Jim Brosnan, *Pennant Race* (New York: Penguin Books, 1983), 27–28.

25. Robert K. Plumb, "A.M.A. to Study Drugs in Sports: Use in Four-Minute Mile Hinted," *New York Times*, June 6, 1957.

26. "Amphetamine in Athletics," *British Medical Journal*, December 26, 1959; "Pep Drugs Found to Spur Athletes," *New York Times*, May 28, 1959.

27. "Pep Drugs Found to Spur Athletes"; "'Wake Up and Die': The Pep Pill Menace," 57; "Pep Pills for Athletes," *Des Moines Register*, June 3, 1959.

28. John L. Ivy, "Amphetamines," in Melvin H. Williams, ed., *Ergogenic Aids in Sport* (Champaign, IL: Human Kinetics Publishers, 1983), 103.

29. For a summary of amphetamine research see Ivy, "Amphetamines"; Robert K. Conlee, "Amphetamine, Caffeine, and Cocaine," in David R. Lamb and Melvin H. Williams, *Ergogenics—Enhancement of Performance in Exercise and Sport* (Traverse City, MI: Cooper Publishing, 2001), 290–295; Alan J. George, "Central Nervous System Stimulants," in David R. Mottram, ed., *Drugs in Sport*, 4th ed. (London: Routledge, 2005), 64–73; David R. Mottram, "Stimulants," in David R. Mottram and Neil Chester, *Drugs in Sport* (6th) (London: Routledge, 2015), 166–176; Amit Momaya, Marc Fawal, and Reed Estes, "Performance-Enhancing Substances in Sport," in Arthur L. Caplan and Brendan Parent, *The Ethics of Sport: Essential*

Readings (New York: Oxford University Press, 2017), 478–480; Gary I. Wadler and Brian Hainline, *Drugs and the Athlete* (Philadelphia: F. A. Davis Co., 1989), 75–86; Avois, L., Robinson, N., "Central nervous system stimulants and sport practice," *British Medical Journal of Sports Medicine*, 2006, 40 (Supplement I): i16–i20.

30. Conlee, "Amphetamine, Caffeine, and Cocaine," 291.

31. Ivy, "Amphetamines," 120.

32. Ibid., 112.

33. Ron Bergman, "Sure Dobson Takes Greenies, But Not as a Regular Practice," *Sporting News*, March 13, 1971.

34. Jerry Nechal, "Reno Bertoia," SABR's Baseball Biography Project, sabr.org.

35. "Bat Leader Takes Tranquilizer Pills," *Fort Worth Telegram*, May 18, 1957.

36. Tommy Devine, "Bertoia's 'Happiness Days May End," *Detroit Free Press*, May 17, 1957.

37. *Pittsburgh Sun-Telegraph*, May 17, 1957.

38. *Wall Street Journal* editorial syndicated in Lancaster (PA) *New Era*, May 23, 1957.

39. Bil Gilbert, "Problems in a Turned-On World," *Sports Illustrated*, June 23, 1969.

40. Jim Bouton with Leonard Shecter, ed., *Ball Four* (World, 1970).

41. Al Hirshberg, "7 Ballplayers Answer Jim Bouton," *SPORT*, October 1970, 55, 93.

42. Johnny Bench and William Brashler, *Catch You Later: The Autobiography of Johnny Bench* (New York: Harper and Row, 1979), 125–126.

43. Tug McGraw with Don Yaeger, *Ya Gotta Believe! My Roller-Coaster Life as a Screwball Pitcher and Part-Time Father, and My Hope-Filled Fight Against Brain Cancer* (New York: New American Library, 2004), 67–68.

44. Bil Gilbert, "High Time to Make Some Rules," *Sports Illustrated*, July 7, 1969, p. 34.

45. Kevin McAlester, "Balls Out," dallasobserver.com, June 16, 2005.

46. Bil Gilbert, "Problems in a Turned-On World," *Sports Illustrated*, June 23, 1969, p. 66.

47. Nathan Michael Corzine, *Team Chemistry: The History of Drugs and Alcohol in Major League Baseball* (Urbana, IL: University of Illinois Press, 2016), 75.

48. "Kuhn Appoints Ex-FBI Agent Security Chief," *The Sporting News*, February 21, 1970; "Kuhn Adds FBI Agent to His Security Staff," *The Sporting News*, May 16, 1970.

49. Wells Twombly, *The Sporting News*, March 13, 1971, p. 30.

50. Ron Bergman, "Pep Pill Whirlwind Revolves Around Reggie," *The Sporting News*, July 12, 1975, p. 20.

51. Rasmussen, *On Speed*, 215–219; William N. Taylor, *Anabolic Steroids and the Athlete* (Jefferson, NC: McFarland, 2002), 110.

52. Bench and Brashler, *Catch You Later*, 126.

53. Bergman, "Pep Pill Whirlwind," 9.

54. Reggie Jackson with Bill Libby, *Reggie: A Season with a Superstar* (Chicago: Playboy Press, 1975), 197.

55. Bergman, "Pep Pill Whirlwind," 20.

56. "Playboy Interview: Pete Rose," *Playboy*, September 1979, 108.

57. McGraw with Yaeger, *Tug McGraw: My Roller-Coaster Life*, 141. The *Philadelphia Inquirer* published an extensive investigative report of this case in three installments from July 12 to July 14, 1981. *Sports Illustrated* published a brief summary, "The Continuing Saga of Dr. Mazza and His 'Good Friends,'" February 16, 1981. Another good summary appeared in *The Sporting News*, "Phils-and-Pills Story Blazes as a Hot Item" by Hal Bodley, February 28, 1981.

58. Robert J. Rosenthal and Vernon Lamb, "At the Start of Inquiry, 4 Phillies," *Philadelphia Inquirer*, July 13, 1981.

59. Robert J. Rosenthal and Vernon Lamb, "The Evidence Crumbles and the Case Collapses," *Philadelphia Inquirer*, July 14, 1981.

60. Ibid.

61. Rosenthal and Lamb, "At the Start of Inquiry."

62. Robert J. Rosenthal and Vernon Lamb, "How the State Created a Sham Phils Investigation," *Philadelphia Inquirer*, July 12, 1981.

63. Ibid.

64. Hal Bodley, "Phils-and-Pills Story Blazes as a Hot Item," *The Sporting News*, February 28, 1981.

65. Wadler and Hainline, *Drugs and the Athlete*, 87–98; George, "Central Nervous System Stimulants," 76-83.

66. "Player Claims Mays Kept Speed in Locker," *Great Falls (Montana) Tribune*, September 13, 1985.

67. Aaron Skirboll, *The Pittsburgh Cocaine Seven: How a Ragtag Group of Fans Took the Fall for Major League Baseball* (Chicago: Chicago Review Press, 2010), 174.

68. "Baseball's Image Could Take a Further Beating," *Great Falls (Montana) Tribune*, September 15, 1985; Michael Goodwin, "Stargell and Madlock Accused by Berra," New York Times, September 11, 1985"; Michael Goodwin, "Cocaine Sale Is Put in Pirate Clubhouse," *New York Times*, September 13, 1985; Aaron Skirboll, *Pittsburgh Cocaine Seven*, 174–178.

69. Michael Goodwin, "Stargell and Madlock"; Goodwin, "Cocaine Sale Is Put in Pirate Clubhouse"; Skirboll, *Pittsburgh Cocaine Seven*, 174–178; Dave Anderson, "Madlock Sees No Hard Drug Discipline," *New York Times*, February 23, 1986; Michael Goodwin, "Baseball Orders Suspension of 11 Drug Users," *New York Times*, March 1, 1986.

70. Dave Anderson, "Madlock Sees No Hard Drug Discipline."

71. George J. Mitchell, "Report to The Commissioner of Baseball of An Independent Investigation into The Illegal Use of Steroids and Other Performance Enhancing Substances by Players in Major League Baseball," DLA Piper US LLP, 25, 26, 34; Thomas Rogers, "Baseball Players Ratify Drug Plan," *New York Times*, May 24, 1984.

72. Murray Chass, "Pitcher's Autopsy Lists Ephedra as One Factor," *New York Times*, March 14, 2003.

73. A timeline of steroids in baseball," denverpost.com, December 13, 2007; "A timeline of MLB's drug-testing rules", usatoday.com, March 28, 2014; Wadler and Hainline, *Drugs and the Athlete*, 101.

74. Jim Salisbury, "Current Phillie Took Speed 'Every Day,'" *Philadelphia Inquirer*, March 5, 2006; Jim Salisbury, "Baseball's Problem with Pills" *Philadelphia Inquirer*, March 8, 2006; Mitchell Report, 58.

75. Jack Curry, "With Greenies Banned, Up for a Cup of Coffee?" *New York Times*, April 1, 2006.

76. "Annual drug testing report: 111 of 113 Therapeutic Use Exemptions for ADD," espn.com, December 1, 2015.

9. Juice

1. J. M. D. Olmstead, *Charles-Edouard Brown-Sequard: A Nineteenth Century Neurologist and Endocrinologist* (Baltimore: Johns Hopkins Press, 1946), 207; Merriley Borell, "Brown-Sequard's Organotherapy and Its Appearance in America at the End of the Nineteenth Century," *Bulletin of the History of Medicine* (Fall 1976): 312; Theodore C. Rich, "Charles Edouard Brown-Sequard (1817–1894)," *Yale Journal of Biology and Medicine* 10, no. 4 (March 1938): 234.

2. Olmstead, *Charles-Edouard Brown-Sequard*, 209.

3. *St. Paul Globe*, August 14, 1889.

4. *Washington Post*, August 14, 1889. This article was unearthed by law professor and baseball arbitrator Roger I. Abrams in researching his book, *The Dark Side of the Diamond* (Burlington, MA: Rounder Books, 2007), 105–108.

5. Tony Delamothe, "Monkey Business," *British Medical Journal*, July 28, 2012, p. 29. See also John M. Hoberman and Charles E. Yesalis, "The History of Synthetic Testosterone," *Scientific American*, February 1995, p. 77.

6. Paul de Kruif, *The Male Hormone* (New York: Harcourt, Brace and Company, 1945), 223.

7. Charles E. Yesalis, *Anabolic Steroids in Sport and Exercise* (Champaign, IL: Human Kinetics, 2000, 1993), 1, 2; Charles D. Kochakian and Charles E. Yesalis, in Charles E. Yesalis, ed., *Anabolic Steroids in Sport and Exercise* (Champaign, IL: Human Kinetics, 2000, 1993), 25; "A Miracle in Sports," advertisement, *The Sporting News*, October 12, 1944, p. 27.

8. Robert Dvorchak, "NFL Tests Frequently to Keep Out Steroids," *Pittsburgh Post Gazette*, October 4, 2005, A-7; T.J. Quinn, "Pumped-up pioneers: the '63 Chargers," espn.com, February 1, 2009,

9. Richard A. Lertzman and William J. Birnes, *Dr. Feelgood: The Shocking Story of the Doctor Who May Have Changed History by Treating and Drugging JFK, Marilyn, Elvis, and Other Prominent Figures* (New York: Skyhorse Publishing, 2013, 2014), 106.

10. Jane Leavy, *The Last Boy: Mickey Mantle and the End of America's Childhood* (New York: HarperCollins, 2010), 225; Lertzman and Birnes, *Dr. Feelgood*; Jane Leavy, *Last Boy*, 226.

11. Robert Dvorchak, "Experiment Turns Epidemic," *Pittsburgh Post Gazette*, October 2, 2005, A-11.

12. Paul Dimeo, *A History of Drug Use in Sport, 1876–1976: Beyond Good and Evil* (London: Routledge, 2007), 13. Also see Daniel M. Rosen, *Dope: A History of Performance Enhancement in Sports from the Nineteenth Century to Today* (Westport, CN: Praeger, 2008), 28–29.

13. Shelby Whitfield, *Kiss it Goodbye* (New York: Abelard-Schuman, 1973), 204; Ron Kroichick, "House a 'failed experiment' with steroids," *San Francisco Chronicle*, May 3, 2005.

14. Amit Momaya, Marc Fawal, and Reed Estes, "Performance-Enhancing Substances in Sport," in Arthur L. Caplan and Brendan Parent, *The Ethics of Sport: Essential Readings* (New York: Oxford University Press, 2017), 468; "WADA Prohibited List," usada.org.

15. Robert Dvorchak, "Officials Bungled Steroid Rules from Start," *Pittsburgh Post-Gazette*, October 3, 2005; William N. Taylor, M.D., *Anabolic Steroids and the Athlete* (Jefferson, NC: McFarland, 2002), 111–126; for research on the effectiveness of steroids, see Martin Enserink, "Does Doping Work," in Arthur L. Caplan and Brendan Parent, *The Ethics of Sport: Essential Readings* (New York: Oxford University Press, 2017), 498; Karl E. Friedl, "Effect of Anabolic Steroid Use on Body Composition and Physical Performance," in Charles E. Yesalis, ed. *Anabolic Steroids in Sport and Exercise* (Champaign, IL: Human Kinetics, 2000, 1993), 144–154; Amit Momaya, Marc Fawal, and Reed Estes, "Performance-Enhancing Substances in Sport," in Caplan and Parent, *The Ethics of Sport*, 473; Neil Chester, "Anabolic Agents," in David R, Mottram and Neil Chester, *Drugs in Sport*, 6th ed. (London: Routledge, 2015), 70. Two studies commonly cited are Shalender Bhasin, M.D., Thomas W. Storer, Ph.D., et al, "The Effects of Supraphysiologic Doses of Testosterone on Muscle Size and Strength in Normal Men," *New England Journal of Medicine* 335 (1996): 1–7, and A. Giorgi, R. P. Weatherby, and P. W. Murphy, "Muscular strength, body composition and health responses to the use of testosterone enanthate: a double blind study," *Journal of Science and Medicine in Sport* 2 (1999): 341–355.

16. Ken Fitch, "Proscribed drugs at the Olympic Games: permitted use and misuse (doping) by athletes," *Clinical Medicine* (London), June 2012; Michele Verroken,

"Drug Use and Abuse in Sport," in David Mottram, ed., *Drugs in Sport (Fourth Edition)* (London: Routledge, 2005), 35.

17. Sigmund Loland, "Fairness and Justice in Sport," in Cesar Torres, ed., *The Bloomsbury Companion to the Philosophy of Sport* (London: Bloomsbury, 2014, 2015), 111.

18. Peter Morris, *A Game of Inches—The Game on the Field* (Chicago: Ivan R. Dee, 2006), 66–67.

19. Dave Nightingale, "Drugs, Alcohol Major Headache in Pro Leagues," *The Sporting News*, November 21, 1981, p. 13.

20. "Players Win Drug-Test Grievance," *New York Times*, July 31, 1986; Murray Chass, "Players Are Urged to Alter Drug Plan," *New York Times*, May 9, 1985; Jim Donaghy, "Drug Policy Under Fire," *St. Cloud (MN) Times*, July 5, 1992; Murray Chass, "New Call for Drug Program," *New York Times*, July 9, 1987; Mitchell Report 35–40.

21. Murray Chass, "Braves' Star Fails Drug Test, Clouding Hopes for Pennant: Nixon Falls," *New York Times*, September 17, 1991; Baseball Sets Drug Policy, *New York Times*, March 16, 1988; Mitchell Report, 40.

22. "Drug Policy of Major League Baseball, 1988," in Gary I. Wadler and Brian Hainline, *Drugs and the Athlete* (Philadelphia: F. A. Davis Company, 1989), 289–292; Mitchell Report, SR-15; "Drug Abuse Remains a Huge Problem for Baseball," *Great Falls Tribune*, July 21, 1988.

23. Rick Weinberg, "Dodgers Suspected Strawberry's Drug Use," *New York Times*, April 6, 1994.

24. "No Progress in Talks as Strike Approaches," *St. Cloud (MN) Times*, August 2, 1994.

25. Wadler and Hainline, *Drugs and the Athlete*.

26. Graham Womack, "Former MLB commissioner Fay Vincent talks PEDs, Buck O'Neil, gambling," sportingnews.com, January 12, 2016.

27. Jose Canseco, *Juiced: Wild Times, Rampant 'Roids, Smash Hits, and How Baseball Got Big* (New York: Regan Books, 2005), 11, 74, 80.

28. "Steroids? Canseco Denies Boswell Charge," *Des Moines Register*, September 30, 1988.

29. Canseco, *Juiced*, 135.

30. Bob Nightengale, "Steroids Become an Issue," *Los Angeles Times*, July 15, 1995.

31. Restoring Faith in America's Pastime: Evaluating Major League Baseball's Efforts to Eradicate Steroid Use: Hearing Before the H. Comm. on Gov't Reform, 109th Cong. 2, 10–11 (2005); Teri Thompson, Nathaniel Vinton, et. al., *American Icon: The Fall of Roger Clemens and the Rise of Steroids in America's Pastime* (New York: Alfred A. Knoff, 2009), 85–89; Teri Thompson, Christian Red, and Nathaniel Vinton, "Mark McGwire endorsement puts MLB commish Bud Selig at odds with FBI

steroid cop," *New York Daily News*, October 27, 2009; Chuck Modiano, "Modiano: How the Daily News I-Team exposed McGwire, Selig, white dopers and changed baseball history," *New York Daily News*, August 20, 2018; Greg Stejskal, "Column: FBI Director Mueller, Steroids and Getting Stranded on 3rd Base," ticklethewire.com.

32. Steve Wilstein, "'Andro OK in Baseball,' but Questions Still Abound," *Morris County (NJ) Daily Record*, August 23, 1998.

33. Restoring Faith in America's Pastime: Evaluating Major League Baseball's Efforts to Eradicate Steroid Use: Hearing Before the H. Comm. on Gov't Reform, 109th Cong. 277, 333 (2005); Bernie Miklasz, "La Russa Will Try to Ban AP from Cards' Clubhouse," *Indianapolis Star*, August 24, 1998; Jose Canseco, *Juiced*, 203.

34. Lawrence Rocca, "Baseball Defies Expectorations: Tobacco Use Is Banned from the Minor Leagues," *Washington Post*, June 16, 1993.

35. James C. McKinley, Jr., "Steroid Suspicions Abound in Major League Dugouts," *New York Times*, October 11, 2000.

36. Wilstein, "'Andro OK in Baseball.'"

37. James C. McKinley, Jr., "Steroid Suspicions Abound in Major League Dugouts," *New York Times*, October 11, 2000.

38. "To Cheat or Not to Cheat," *Sports Illustrated*, May 29, 2012.

39. Mike Berardino, "Is this Power Surge Really Better Baseball Through Chemicals," *St. Louis Post-Dispatch*, October 7, 2001.

40. Shaun Assael and Peter Keating, et. al., "Who Know," *ESPN the Magazine*, November 21, 2005, 73–74.

41. For a summary of potential side effects, see, NIDA. June 6, 2018. Prescription Stimulants DrugFacts. Retrieved from https://www.drugabuse.gov/publications/drugfacts/prescription-stimulants on September 5, 2021, and NIDA. August 12, 2018, Anabolic Steroids DrugFacts. Retrieved from https://www.drugabuse.gov/publications/drugfacts/anabolic-steroids on September 5, 2021; Steroid Use in Professional Baseball And Anti-Doping Issues In Amateur Sports, Hearing Before The Subcommittee On Consumer Affairs, Foreign Commerce And Tourism Of The Committee On Commerce, Science, And Transportation, United States Senate, One Hundred Seventh Congress Second Session, June 18, 2002.

42. "Steroid Use in Professional Baseball and Anti-Doping Issues in Amateur Sports," Hearing Before the Subcommittee. on Consumer Affairs, Foreign Commerce and Tourism of the Committee on Commerce, Science and Transportation, 107th Congress, Volume 7 (June 28, 2002).

43. Tom Verducci, "Totally Juiced," *Sports Illustrated*, June 3, 2002, p. 26.

44. "Steroid Use in Professional Baseball."

45. Ibid.

46. Jack Curry and Jere Longman, "Results of Steroid Testing Spur Baseball to Set Tougher Rules," *New York Times*, November 14, 2003; 104 of 1,198 players tested positive; eight positive tests were rejected, leaving 96 deemed positive tests

or 8 percent; Jon Pessah, *The Game: Inside the Secret World of Major League Baseball's Power Brokers* (New York: Little, Brown and Company, 2015), 396–397.

47. Mark Fainaru-Wada and Lance Williams, *Game of Shadows* (New York: Gotham Books, 2006, 2007), 58.

48. "McGwire mum on steroids in hearing," cnn.com, March 17, 2005.

49. George Vecsey, "Avoiding the Past, a Role Model Is History," *New York Times*, March 18, 2005.

50. Donald Fehr and Michael Weiner, Memorandum, September 7, 2007, reprinted in Mitchell Report.

51. "The recommendations below focus on three principal areas: investigations based upon non-testing evidence; player education; and further improvements in the testing program," Mitchell Report, SR-28; Joseph A. Reaves, "Players Union Able to Thwart Mitchell Probe," *Nashville Tennessean*, June 11, 2006.

52. Murray Chass, "Mitchell Report Revealed Little Original Work," *New York Times*, December 18, 2007.

53. Mike Fish, "A steroid life in baseball's fast lane," espn.com, January 23, 2009 (Updated January 28, 2009).

54. Jim Baumbach, "Tejada Guilty in Drug Case," *Newsday*, February 12, 2009; "Tejada Gets Probation for Lying to Congress," *New York Times*, March 27, 2009; Michael S. Schmidt, "Tumult Continues: Tejada Pleads Guilty to Lying," *New York Times*, February 12, 2009; Mitchell report, 201–204; "'02 AL MVP Tejada Guilty of Misleading Congress on Drugs," St. Cloud Times, February 12, 2009.

55. "MLB to test in-season for HGH," espn.com, January 10, 2013; Jerry Crasnick, "HGH and the new CBA," espn.com, November 22, 2011; "A-Rod's Drug Testing," *New York Times*, January 20, 2014.

56. Tom Verducci, "The numbers—and the truth—about baseball's PED problem and why it may never go away," *Sports Illustrated*, May 16, 2017.

57. Dominguez, *Baseball Cop*, 26.

58. Tom Verducci, "The numbers," *Sports Illustrated*, May 16, 2017.

59. WAR calculations by BaseballReference.com

60. Associated Press, "Schmidt might have used 'roids in late '90s," espn.com, August 5, 2005; Daniel R. Epstein, "Would you take PEDs? Choose your own adventure!," beyondtheboxscore.com, November 12, 2018.

61. Graham Womack, "An interview with Robert Creamer," baseballpastandpresent.com, January 17, 2012.

10. Grease and Glue

1. David Waldstein, "M.L.B. Says It Will Punish Doctoring of Baseballs" *New York Times*, June 15, 2021.

2. Bill James and Rob Neyer, *The Neyer/James Guide to Pitchers* (New York: Fireside, 2004).

3. Lawrence Ritter, *The Glory of Their Times* (New York: Macmillan, 1966), 55.

4. John J. Evers and Hugh S. Fullerton, *Touching Second: The Science of Baseball* (Chicago: Reilly & Britton Company, 1910), 113.

5. "Eastern League Umpires Have No More Authority Than A Ku Kluxer Would Have at a Banquet of the 'Hell Fighters' in Harlem," *Pittsburgh Courier*, September 12, 1925.

6. James Riley, *Biographical Encyclopedia of the Negro Baseball Leagues* (Carroll and Graf, 2002), 701.

7. *New York Age*, August 5, 1944; *New York Amsterdam News*, July 14, 1945.

8. Tyler Kepner, *K—A History of Baseball in Ten Pitches* (Doubleday, 2019), 229.

9. Emma Baccellieri, "Mud Maker: The Man Behind MLB's Essential Secret Sauce," si.com, August 7, 2019; "Baseball Rubbing Mud," Delaware River Basin Commission, June 11, 2021, https://www.state.nj.us/drbc/public/outreach/baseball-mud.html.

10. "Obituaries, Lena Blackburne, Former Player, Coach, Manager," *Sporting News*, March 16, 1968; Matt Breen, "South Jersey's mystery mud is the only foreign substance allowed by MLB to doctor baseballs," inquirer.com, June 18, 2021; Carolyn Beeler, "All MLB baseballs get treatment from South Jersey mud," why.org, October 7, 2011; Andrew Astleford, "Mud Plays Part in Game of Baseball," espn.com, April 7, 2010.

11. Baccellieri, "Mud Maker.

12. Lee Gutkind, *The Best Seat in Baseball, But You Have to Stand!* (New York: The Dial Press, 1975), 46.

13. "Hubbard Shifts Blame in Spitball Case to Sewell," *St. Joseph (MO) Gazette*, July 22, 1944.

14. Dick Young, "The Outlawed Spitball Was My Money Pitch," *Sports Illustrated*, July 4, 1955.

15. *The Sporting News*, July 6, 1955, p. 16. *The Sporting News*, July 13, 1955.

16. Roger Kahn, *The Boys of Summer* (Harper and Row, 1972), 291.

17. Ibid., 308.

18. Kepner, *K*, 234.

19. Milton Gross, "Are They Still Throwing the Spitter?," *SPORT*, October 1956.

20. Charley Feeney, "The Truth Is All Wet," *Pittsburgh Post-Gazette*, August 22, 1967.

21. "Schalk, in Tulsa Visit, Campaigns for 'Spitter.'" *The Sporting News*, November 4, 1937.

22. Dan Daniel, "Majors Split Over Spitter, Poll Shows," *The Sporting News*, December 14, 1949.

23. Herman Weiskopf, "The Infamous Spitter," *Sports Illustrated*, July 31, 1967.

24. Gutman, *It Ain't Cheatin'*, 22.

25. Charley Feeney, "The Truth Is All Wet," *Pittsburgh Post-Gazette*, August 22, 1967.

26. Jim Bouton with Leonard Shecter, ed., *Ball Four* (World, 1970), 212–214.

27. Whitey Ford with Phil Pepe, *Slick—My Life In and Around Baseball* (New York: William Morrow & Company, Inc., 1987); Whitey Ford with Joseph Durso, "Confessions of a Gunkball Artist," *New York Times*, April 3, 1977.

28. Gaylord Perry and Bob Sudyk, *Me and The Spitter* (New York: Dutton, 1974).

29. Gutman, *It Ain't Cheatin'*, 26.

30. Bob Sudyk, "Payoff Pitch Gaylord Perry, Master of the Illegal Spitball, Will Take His Place in the Hall of Fame Today," *Hartford Courant*, July 21, 1991.

31. Mark Armour, "Gaylord Perry," SABR's Baseball Biography Project, sabr.org.

32. Armour, "Gaylord Perry."

33. Tom Gorman as told to Jerome Holtzman, *Three and Two—The Autobiography of The Great Major League Umpire* (New York: Scribners, 1979), 70.

34. Doug Harvey and Peter Golenbock, *They Called My God—The Best Umpire Who Ever Lived* (New York: Gallery Books, 2014), 176.

35. Ken Kaiser with David Fisher, *Planet of the Umps—A Baseball Life From Behind the Plate* (New York: St. Martin's Press, 2014), 175-176.

36. Durwood Merrill with Jim Dent, *You're Out and You're Ugly Too! Confessions of an Umpire with Attitude* (New York: St. Martin's Press, 1998), 197-198.

37. Ibid., 197.

38. Kaiser, *Planet of the Umps*, 175–176.

39. Dave Phillips with Rob Rains, *Center Field on Fire—An Umpire's Life with Pine Tar Bats, Spitballs and Corked Personalities* (New York: Chicago: Triumph, 2004, 65–67.

40. Ron Fimrite, "The Pitch of the '80s," *Sports Illustrated*, June 9, 1986.

41. Mark Ruda, "Gura's Days Numbered; Is Candyman Coming?" *Arlington Heights (IL) Daily Herald*, June 5, 1985.

42. "Sandpaper found; Phils' Hurler Ejected," *Miami Herald*, August 11, 1987.

43. "Consensus: Sock It to Cheaters in Baseball," *The Sporting News*, August 24, 1987.

44. Ibid.

45. Scott McManis, "Mets Rally to Win After Howell Ejected," *Los Angeles Times*, October 9, 1988.

46. American League Championship Series, television broadcast, ABC, October 8, 1988.

47. Jonah Keri, "Whatever Happened to the Spitball?" Grantland.com, February 10, 2012.

48. Dan Connolly, "Orioles defend ejected Matusz, question rule, await discipline," *Baltimore Sun*, May 25, 2015.

49. Tom Verducci, "Trevor Bauer's Veiled Accusations of the Astros May Have Merit ... But They're Probably Personal," si.com, May 2, 2018.

50. Travis Sawchik, "Baseball's Top Staffs Have Come Around On The High-Spin Fastball," FiveThirtyEight.com, October 5, 2018.

51. Trevor Bauer (@BauerOutage), twitter.com, May 1, 2018.

52. Trevor Bauer (@BauerOutage), twitter.com, April 11, 2018.

53. Justin Bastian, "'There is a problem in baseball right now,'" bastian.mlblogs.com, May 2, 2018.

54. Hannah Keyser, "Baseball's sticky stuff controversy could be the best thing to happen to Spider Tack," yahoo.com, June 21, 2021.

55. Tom Verducci, "Sticky Cleanup: What Pitch-Doctoring Enforcement Means for MLB," si.com, June 14, 2021.

56. Mike Axisa, "MLB Trends: How substance crackdown has impacted spin rates," cbssports.com, June 30, 2021.

57. Robert Arthur, "The Sticky Stuff Crackdown Has Worn Off," Baseball-Prospectus.com, October 12, 2021; author research from baseballsavant.mlb.com.

INDEX

9 798985 263268